早期儿童数学
游戏、理念和活动

【英】爱丽丝·汉森◎著
Alice Hansen

陈　聪　汪博君◎译

Games, Ideas and Activities
for Early Years Mathematics

华东师范大学出版社
·上海·

Pearson

图书在版编目(CIP)数据

早期儿童数学游戏、理念和活动/(英)爱丽丝·汉森著;陈聪,汪博君译. —上海:华东师范大学出版社,2021
ISBN 978 - 7 - 5760 - 2214 - 8

Ⅰ.①早… Ⅱ.①爱…②陈…③汪… Ⅲ.①数学课—教学研究—学前教育 Ⅳ.①G613.4

中国版本图书馆 CIP 数据核字(2021)第 217401 号

Classroom Gems：Games，Ideas and Activities for Early Years Mathematics
by Alice Hansen
© Pearson Education Limited 2012

This Bilingual Edition of *Classroom Gems：Games，Ideas and Activities for Early Years Mathematics*，published by arrangement with Pearson Education Limited，copyright © East China Normal University Press Ltd.，2021

本书译自 Pearson Education Limited 2012 年出版的 *Classroom Gems：Games，Ideas and Activities for Early Years Mathematics* by Alice Hansen。

双语版 © 华东师范大学出版社有限公司,2021。

上海市版权局著作权合同登记 图字:09 - 2019 - 473 号

早期儿童数学游戏、理念和活动

著　　者　[英]爱丽丝·汉森
译　　者　陈　聪　汪博君
责任编辑　蒋　将
责任校对　宋红广　时东明
装帧设计　卢晓红

出版发行　华东师范大学出版社
社　　址　上海市中山北路 3663 号　邮编 200062
网　　址　www.ecnupress.com.cn
电　　话　021 - 60821666　行政传真 021 - 62572105
客服电话　021 - 62865537　门市(邮购)电话 021 - 62869887
地　　址　上海市中山北路 3663 号华东师范大学校内先锋路口
网　　店　http://hdsdcbs.tmall.com

印 刷 者　上海雅昌艺术印刷有限公司
开　　本　787×1092　16 开
印　　张　37
字　　数　803 千字
版　　次　2021 年 12 月第 1 版
印　　次　2021 年 12 月第 1 次
书　　号　ISBN 978 - 7 - 5760 - 2214 - 8
定　　价　112.00 元

出 版 人　王　焰

关于作者

　　爱丽丝·汉森博士毕业于英国坎布里亚大学圣马丁学院早期教育及小学启蒙教师教育专业。在读博之前，她一直在英国当地学校任教，也有海外任教经历。博士毕业后她没有选择留在高校，转而投身于教育咨询工作。目前，她在一家专门为幼儿及小学教育相关事宜提供咨询、研究和出版的公司担任董事。她曾和英国当地教育部、地方教育局等教育行政机构专业人员一同工作，主要研究在职数学教师的专业发展。

编写说明

    2021 年 3 月，新版《早期教育阶段实施框架》（Statutory Framework for the Early Years Foundation Stage，以下简称"新版 EYFS 框架"）首次推出，随后作为落地配套的指导性文件《发展很重要》（Development Matter）也是历经几稿后于 2021 年 7 月正式执行。 2021 年 9 月，新版 EYFS 框架在英国正式生效。是否新版本发布后，旧版本就失效了呢？新旧版本的关系是怎样的？

    英国早期教育这次对于 EYFS 框架的修订完全是基于 EYFS 在全球逐渐普及发展的需求，旨在让EYFS 教育体系在实践中能更多适用全球非英语体系国家的幼儿。因此，针对母语非英语的儿童，无论是新版 EYFS 框架还是新版《发展很重要》，最大的变化都是在支持英语作为第二语言的学习方面将提供更为详尽的指导。身体发展（Physical Development），个性、社会性与情感发展（Personal, Social and Emotional Development），交流与语言发展（Communication and Language），数学（Mathematics），读写能力 (Literacy) 等仍是新版 EYFS 框架的基础领域和核心领域，新旧版本在早期儿童学习发展领域上的底层逻辑是保持延续性的。特别是数学领域，新版的《发展很重要》还没有积累更多的实践经验。在这个层面上思考，反倒是一直在一线打磨数学领域教学策略的本书显得更为弥足珍贵。老师家长们可以更好地利用本书进行两个版本的新旧对比，并将新版的内容融合，将有助于探索幼儿数学学习的启蒙和发展。基于上述思考和认识，我们基于新版的改革趋势和理念重新审视了全书内容，并争取到了双语版的授权，希望读者们在汉英对照的语境中，原汁原味地收获 EYFS 的教育真谛。

导论

艾梅："我的房间是 4 号。"

阿克毛："我的房间是 12 号。"

杰克："我住在 73 号房。"

凯特："我在 106 号。"

艾梅："好啊，我的是 1 000 号！"

杰克："我的还是一百万呢！"

　　最近，我在一家托儿所听到了以上对话，四个三岁左右的小孩子一起站在地毯上，其中一个叫艾梅的小家伙第一个说了起来。令我惊讶的是别的小孩儿也自发地参与了进来，他们明白数字在不断增大，而且也知道艾梅和杰克最后所说的号码是多么滑稽。

　　孩子们几乎每天都会参与这种有关数学的游戏和对话，而刚刚那幕，仅仅是一个小小的缩影。幼儿似乎天生就拥有在游戏中不断运用数字和数学概念的能力，并且他们乐此不疲，觉得十分有趣。而作为教师或教育从业者，我们只需要为他们设计不同的活动、游戏和任务，在这些设计中自然地加入数学思维，同时为这些发生在孩子一日生活中与数学有关的活动创设情境或将其引入课堂。

　　本书主要面向早期发展阶段的幼儿，约四至五岁，书中包含了实操性的理念和多样的游戏及活动。同时，由于本书中所设定的情境丰富，涉及的领域广泛，很多内容对于较大年龄的幼儿也是适用的，比如六岁左右的孩子。你可能会发现本书中的一些主题，在该系列的另一些书中也有所提及。这是我们有意这样设计的，可以让老师们利用相同的主题在不同的领域中进行探索和学习。本书中的每个活动都包含了如下的几个部分：

标题

　　标题表明活动的主题（比如"海盗"）、所需材料（比如"骰子"）或是相关的数学概念（比如"数字"），这些内容都与该章中的活动、游戏和理念有关。

教学目标

　　教学目标对该活动的侧重点进行了概述。

所需材料

为读者呈现了一份所需材料的清单，其中有些材料是可选的，都在书中标注清楚。

准备环节

这部分内容说明了除搜集材料外还需要为活动的开展所做的其他准备。

具体步骤

这部分内容提供了每一步的操作指南，告诉老师们和小朋友们接下来该做什么。

小贴士

活动的组织、可用的材料、如何引导小朋友更好地参与其中、需要特别注意的数学领域概念，这些都会在小贴士中有所体现。

拓展①

这部分内容能引导读者去思考如何将该活动修改后用于别的主题，或如何加以改进用以收获更多的新理念。

该活动体现的数学思维

这部分对为什么该活动与数学领域有关进行了解释，同时也说明了这些思维是如何在孩子小学阶段甚至小朋友更高年级的数学学习中不断发展的。

本书中大部分的思维方式和教学理念对各种各样的主题都适用，因而请尽量在通读整本书的前提下寻求教学灵感，而非仅仅专注于所教授的某类主题。

本书在课程导学的部分，能为读者提供的不仅仅有解决问题的能力和推理计算的能力，更为孩子创造了广阔的空间，让他们得以对数学中的"奇思妙想"进行探索，比如那些能令孩子激动兴奋的"大数字"和"无穷"等概念。同时，本书中的一些想法，能帮助到幼年期间的孩子们为他们今后的数学能力发展打下基础。我们可以将这些活动、想法和游戏作为跳板，从而挖掘出那些在幼儿早期教育情境中能运用数学的机会。阅读本书后，希望读者能举一反三，从中收获一些新的想法。

---

① 此处原文为"Variations"，字面意思为"变量"，在科学活动中非常强调测验时的严谨性，因而有控制变量这一常规项。我们斟酌后统一译为"拓展"，强调呈现其他的可能玩法，以启发老师家长们。——译者注

目录

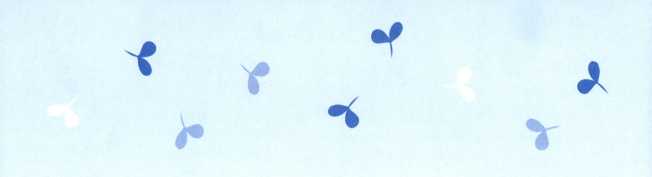

Contents

Appendices 561

第一章

让我们一起打扮吧！

引言

　　打扮是所有孩子都喜欢的活动。本章所设计的活动都在服装店场景设置下进行。当然，也可以准备一个装满衣服的手提箱，让孩子在这样的情景下进行讨论和试穿。请记住，一定要准备不同民族文化特色的衣服和首饰哦!

在服装店里

我们能配对成功吗？

通过找出相同颜色的服饰来练习配对的能力。

教学目标

- 准确识别不同的颜色。
- 能根据物品的颜色进行分类。

准备环节

- 收集相同颜色的男孩、女孩服装和配饰，比如衣服、鞋子、帽子或者包，以便幼儿可以在"服装店"里进行试穿。

具体步骤

（老师扮演店员，孩子们是顾客）

1）"服装店"正式营业，邀请一小部分孩子来"服装店"里逛逛。

2）给孩子们描述昨天"服装店"里顾客来购物的情形：一位顾客昨天买了一身绿色的服装和配饰，而你发现这样一身的搭配非常合适。

3）引导孩子在"服装店"里自己去挑选相同颜色的商品。

4）让孩子们讨论一下他们所选择商品的相同属性（如相同的颜色）和不同属性分别是什么。

小贴士

可以提前准备不同颜色（但是跟你挑选的服装配饰颜色一样）的卡片，让孩子提前挑选自己想要颜色的卡片，再根据该卡片的颜色去选择与之匹配的服装和配饰。这样做，可以避免不同的孩子选择相同的颜色。

拓展

- 如果我们没有足够大的空间来做这个"服装店"的角色扮演活动，我们可以选择其他的方案。比如，我们可以准备一些洋娃娃和泰迪熊要穿的衣物，为洋娃娃和泰迪熊搭配衣服；或者在不同颜色的纸上画不同的图案，让孩子们选择自己喜欢的图案进行粘贴搭配。

该活动体现的数学思维

能够识别物品的特有属性，并对他们进行分类。该数学思维可以帮助孩子们奠定处理数据的基础。颜色的配对有助于帮助孩子们进行同种属性物品——对应的练习。

试穿和整理衣服

在"服装店"试穿和整理衣服的时候，思考如何使用方位介词。

教学目标

- 会使用表示方位的词语。
- 会使用序数词。
- 会比较大小。

具体步骤

1）当孩子们在试穿衣服的时候，跟他们谈论一下他们在做什么，来加强对于方位介词的使用，如"在……上面"、"在……里面"、"在……之上"、"在……下面"、"穿过"。可以说："把帽子戴到你的头上，把胳膊穿过袖子，夹克衫穿在衬衫外面"。

2）在孩子们收拾衣物的时候，告诉他们放置衣物的地方，如"衣服放在抽屉里，裙子挂在衣架上，鞋子放在盒子里。"

3）当孩子们穿衣服的时候，跟他们谈论衣服的尺寸，如"这件上衣太大、太小，还是正好？"

4）告诉孩子们穿衣服的准确顺序，如"先穿袜子，再穿鞋子"。

小贴士　　　　一旦你建立这样的语言对话模式，就可以让孩子担任"服装店售货员"这一角色来运用这些语言。

该活动体现的数学思维

该活动训练孩子运用方位介词和描述尺寸大小，帮助他们建立描述形状和空间方位的意识，培养他们的几何思维（geometrical thinking）；使用序数词来帮助孩子思考做事情的顺序，也让孩子们思考数字的另一种表达方式；通过比较大小来帮助孩子们练习如何描述形状和尺寸。

多少钱?

创造给孩子买卖衣服的机会。

教学目标
- 学会描述货币的金额大小。
- 学会使用不等金额的硬币和纸币。

准备环节
- 在"服装店"里安装一个收银台。
- 和孩子们一起制作价格标签,并把价格标签放在对应的服饰上面。

具体步骤

1)请两位孩子担任该"服装店"的"店长",鼓励孩子们去读商品的价格,并向"顾客"收取所购商品对应的金额。

2)在交易过程中,"店长"收取现金并找零,也可以用信用卡来完成交易。

3)"店长"可以制作折扣优惠券来吸引顾客下次再来购买店内商品。

小贴士

在给"服装店"内商品定价格的时候,请跟你的同事商量确认好。因为有些老师会想要设置比较便宜的价格,以硬币购买为主,来帮助孩子精准地认识各类硬币的价值。还有些老师觉得定的价位要更切合实际,比如一般不可能通过 5 便士(即 0.5 欧元,约等于人民币 3.8 元不到。)购买一副手套。确保你们在定价的时候是达成一致意见的。

拓展
- 孩子们也可以使用计算器或者收银台来计算顾客购买商品的消费总额。

该活动体现的数学思维

对于孩子来说,学会识别和使用不等额的硬币是非常重要的。孩子们在理解硬币价值这一块很困难。因为不同价值的硬币尺寸也是不一样的(比如从金额上来讲,5 便士比 2 便士的价值更大,但是从硬币大小来看,2 便士的硬币却比 5 便士更大)。

一起做项链吧！

做项链的过程是一个谈论样式和顺序的有趣方式。

教学目标
- 会复制或者自己创建重复排列模式。
- 会使用序数词（如第一，第二，第三等）。

所需材料

1）串珠、纽扣、意大利面或者类似的线；　2）细绳或者毛线；　3）挑选珠子串成的项链或者手链（可以购买或者自己制作）来作为角色扮演的工具。

准备环节
- 把所准备的材料放入容器当中。对于年龄偏小的孩子，要提前帮助他们分好颜色。

具体步骤

1）选择两种不同的颜色的珠子，按照颜色交替出现的顺序做项链（ABAB 的形式，如红蓝红蓝），问孩子们他们观察到了什么？

2）让孩子们告诉你接下来是哪种颜色的珠子，或者接下来两粒或者三粒珠子的颜色分别是什么？他们是否可以做到？

3）开始制作另外一根项链，使用两种颜色的珠子按照以下形式排列（AAB 的形式，如红红蓝，红红蓝），问孩子们他们观察到了什么？

4）让孩子们告诉你接下来是哪种颜色的珠子，或者接下来两粒或者三粒珠子的颜色分别是什么？他们是否可以做到？

5）让孩子们制作自己的项链，看他们自己是否可以做一条有重复排列模式（规则）的项链。

小贴士
- 从使用两种不同颜色的珠子开始，年幼的孩子对于使用超过两到三种不同颜色的珠子会有一些困难。
- 制作一根长的项链过程是比较繁琐的，所以我们可以使用大的珠子串成项链，或者选择帮助泰迪熊制作项链，或者手链，这样会更容易一些。

拓展
- 用不同颜色的纸打印图案，让孩子们将图案剪下来给纸娃娃的衣服做装饰。

该活动体现的数学思维

　　数学充满了不同的模式，观察总结规律可以帮助我们解决不同的问题。通过观察现有排列的规律，来帮助孩子们想想接下来的形状或者颜色是什么。通过序数词（如第一、第二等）的描述，帮助他们精确地表达。

让我们设计衣服吧！

很多孩子喜欢装扮自己的娃娃或是自己。

教学目标

- 有使用布料的概念。
- 能预估长度。

所需材料

1）长度一致的布料（一定尽可能的宽）；2）丝带；3）剪刀；4）胶带；5）孩子们穿着不同服饰的照片（可选）。

准备环节

- 将准备好的材料呈现在孩子们面前。

具体步骤

1）鼓励孩子们去思考制作自己的衣服。

2）跟他们谈论要做什么样的衣服，并讨论这种材料是否适合做这种衣服。

3）跟孩子沟通他们需要多少布料来制作衣服。确定自己是否有充足的布料？布料是否足够宽，足够长？如何知道布料的尺寸？如何解决布料尺寸的问题？

4）和孩子们讨论，制作自己服装的步骤是什么？

5）确定和谁一起合作。

小贴士

- 孩子们或许会发现为自己的朋友制作一件衣服会更容易。
- 在孩子创作和展示的时候，建议拍照留下记录，同时为其他孩子提供灵感。

拓展

- 假设为新的超级英雄做一套制服，思考这套制服如何帮助超级英雄来使用他的超能力？

该活动体现的数学思维

通过估算这种方式，孩子们可以更有效地检查自己工作的精准度。孩子们通过不同长度单位（units of length）的描述（如孩子的身高）和标准测量工具的使用（如米尺），来提升他们对于长度单位的理解，并提高他们测量的准确性。

第二章

啊，我们喜欢在海边玩!

引言

　　在这个主题中，我们要为孩子们创造足够多的机会去接触不同纹理的材料。如果你想让孩子们大规模地探索这些，可以将学习或生活空间转换成为海滨环境，让孩子们可以身临其境地进行探索。

沙子与海水

利用这些材料来启发孩子们早期对容量的探索。

教学目标

• 学会填满、清空水桶，并能比较水桶的大小。

所需材料

1）大的防水布和浅水池（可移动的）；2）干的沙子；3）水盆；4）不同尺寸的水桶；5）挖沙和舀水的工具；6）漏斗和筛子。

准备环节

• 将装着沙子的防水布和浅水池放在地板上或者户外。
• 水盆里装上水（装满、半满、1/4 等）。

具体步骤

1）跟孩子们谈谈哪个桶装得多，哪个桶装得少？讨论我们如何去测量桶的容量？尝试将水从一个桶倒到另外一个桶，是否可以帮助去测量桶的容量？

2）如果是三个容器，孩子们是否可以按照容量大小排列？如何让他们确定自己排序是正确的？

3）在孩子们尝试的过程中用词语去描述桶里水或者沙子装了多少，比如装满了、空的、半满、接近满。比如，"我看见你在倒水/沙子装满这个桶，你还需要再多加点吗？""舀多少次可以把这个桶装满？这个桶装满要舀多少次？"

小贴士

• 使用食用色素将水染色，可以帮助孩子们更容易看清容器内的水位。
• 对于年幼的孩子来讲，容量守恒的理解比较难。我们在选择容器时，尽量选择尺寸和大小不一样的。有些容器看起来可以装很多因为这些容器看起来更高，但是实际装得更少，因为这些容器虽然很高但是很"瘦"。研究人员表示孩子们需要使用很多不同形状的容器来理解容量守恒这个概念。

该活动体现的数学思维

这项活动帮助提升孩子们提前了解容量的概念。同时，也鼓励他们去思考不同的空间如何被填满，以及理解不同形状的容器有可能具有相同或者不同的容量。

沙堡

使用一组容器来搭建沙堡。

教学目标

- 学习搭建沙堡。
- 学习装饰沙堡。

所需材料

1）大的防水布或浅水池（可移动的）；2）湿的沙子；3）不同尺寸的水桶；4）铲子或者其他挖沙的工具；5）贝壳、浮木和其他沙滩发现的物品；6）沙堡的照片（可选）。

准备环节

- 将装满湿沙子的防水布或者浅水池放在地上。
- 堆一个沙堡放在沙子上让孩子们去找。

具体步骤

1）问问孩子们以前是否有堆过沙堡，如果有，让他们展示一下是如何做的。鼓励他们谈论一下堆沙堡的步骤，在过程中加强方位/方向用语的使用（比如，把沙子装进篮子里，把沙子拍拍好，把桶倒过来）。

2）讨论如何把沙堡搭建超过一层，讨论不同层次的形状大小，第一次使用哪个篮子？为什么？

3）用贝壳、浮木、旗帜等装饰沙堡，并引导孩子们用相同的图案在沙堡外搭着围一圈。

小贴士　　　　在沙子中加入的水的总量是非常重要的。沙子如果太干或者太湿，都很难保持它所搭建的形状。在展示给孩子们之前，请老师家长们先尝试垒一下沙堡，确认是否可以搭建。

该活动体现的数学思维

堆沙堡需要很多解决问题的能力，特别是当沙堡第一次垒不起来的时候。孩子们需要思考为什么沙堡没有垒起来，并且思考下一次如何改进；不断地尝试和失败是一个有效解决问题的方式。

沙滩毛巾

让我们一起在沙滩上使用沙滩毛巾吧!

教学目标

- 根据通用标准进行分类。
- 比较尺寸大小。

所需材料

1)准备不同尺寸的沙滩毛巾(准备一条特别大的沙滩毛巾)。

准备环节

- 将不同尺寸的沙滩毛巾堆在一起。

具体步骤

1)让孩子们围着毛巾坐成一圈

2)告诉孩子们这堆毛巾是从"沙滩"上找到的,并且你想了解更多这些毛巾的特点。问孩子们想了解这些毛巾什么方面?

3)孩子们的反应会不一样,但是都是很积极的方面。但是,这个活动的目的是关注更多的数学思维,比如颜色、图案和大小。

4)选择一个特征(比如颜色),让孩子们依次上来选择一条毛巾,并按照这个特征进行分类。讨论每组特征对应下的毛巾数量。

5)找出最大的毛巾(孩子们可能在毛巾分类的时候找到这条毛巾)。看下多少孩子可以站在上面或者躺在上面。

6)问一下哪个孩子拿到的毛巾是最小的?你会发现会有一群孩子认为他们的毛巾是最小的。数一数有多少孩子可以站在或者躺在这条毛巾上。跟之前那条毛巾比较一下,学会用"更多"、"更少"等表示比较的词语来描述。

7)将这个活动重复使用在其他毛巾上,并让这些毛巾按照大小排列。讨论一下,这个与只按长度来排列有什么不一样。

小贴士

孩子对于面积(area)大小的形容是比较困难的。选择不同形状和面积的毛巾,其中有些看起来比较大因为它们更长,但是它们实际更小因为很窄。研究人员发现孩子们需要更多不同面积大小物体比对的经验来帮助他们理解描述面积大小。

拓展

- 孩子们可以比对不同面积和形状的纸，比如将纸盖在柜台、立方体或者其他物品上面。
- 孩子们可以将毛巾盖在地面上，且每条毛巾之间不重叠，不留下缝隙。

该活动体现的数学思维

这活动有助于帮助孩子们提早理解面积的概念。通过从不同的方向观察毛巾，讨论形状的大小，有利于发展对四边形概念的早期理解。

潮汐

潮汐是一种自然现象，它存在的时间和地球的年龄一样大。

教学目标

- 理解潮汐一天两次涨潮退潮。

所需材料

1）关于潮汐的图画书； 2）长的蓝色或白色雪纺（或者相似材质的布）。

准备环节

- 阅读关于潮汐的图画书。

具体步骤

1）讨论潮汐是如何涨潮和退潮的，从书中了解或者有去过沙滩的经验表述潮汐涨退对于各种生物的影响。

2）讨论潮汐一天两次涨潮退潮的时间。

3）让孩子们选择扮演书中潮汐涨潮退潮时的一种生物（或者其他的物品），而老师们用雪纺布料上下起伏表现海浪，而孩子们扮演退潮时留在岸上的生物。

4）让孩子们思考并讨论，他们扮演的这种生物在涨潮退潮时干什么。涨潮退潮对这些生物有什么影响？高潮和低潮时他们分别在干什么？为什么？

5）当潮汐保持高潮和低潮时会发生什么？

该活动体现的数学思维

潮汐是一种自然现象（一天之内，潮汐通常会有两次涨落，每次周期12小时25分钟，一日两次，共24小时50分钟，潮汐涨落的时间每天都要推后50分钟。）

对这种重复属性的理解，能帮助孩子们建立基本的数学思维。

（海边）岩石间的潮水潭

在潮水潭里找到不同的生物，总是能让小孩和成人都很兴奋。

教学目标

- 探讨潮水潭里面的生物特征。
- 根据这些生物特征进行分类。

所需材料

1）水盘；2）石头；3）沙子；4）塑料做的生物：如海参、虾、蟹、海胆、小章鱼和蜗牛；5）塑料做的海草：比如海王星项链、海白菜。

准备环节

- 用水盘创建一个潮水潭。
- 将塑料做的各种生物投放到这个"潮水潭"中。

具体步骤

1）鼓励孩子们去探索"潮水潭"；
2）当发现一个"生物"时，鼓励孩子们描述这些"生物"；
    孩子们可以给这些"生物"分类吗？比如他们身体上的图案，腿的数量或者水下陆地上行动的方式。

小贴士　　　　利用冰激凌外包装盒，让孩子们思考设计标签，用来给这些"生物"分类。每个冰激凌容器里装上水，也可以更好地帮助孩子们看清不同种类"生物"的特征。

拓展

- 作为拓展，孩子们可能通过以下两种标准来进行分类，比如在这个卡罗尔图（carroll diagram）（下图）中，孩子们该如何分类这些生物？
- 可以带孩子们去参观一个真的潮水潭。请记住潮水潭的环境对这些生物来讲是比较脆弱的，所以在带孩子们探索的时候要格外小心。

	6条腿	~~6条腿~~
游泳		
~~游泳~~		

该活动体现的数学思维

　　识别生物的特征需要孩子们去数数和观察。让孩子们提前接触并整理数据，根据种类/属性等对物体进行分类。

第三章

太　空

引言

　　在本章的活动中，你有可能想在房间里创造一个黑暗的区域，比如可以用厚厚的黑色聚乙烯薄膜（polythene sheeting）围起来。在这个全黑的环境下，孩子们可以使用手电筒探索发现不同物品。我们也可以用节日装扮常用的低能耗彩灯贴在这个区域的顶部，就像星星在天空中一样。

火箭发射!

教学目标

- 学会倒数。
- 学会遵循简单的指令。

所需材料

　　1）任务控制中心（可以在角色扮演的区域中任选用一个盒子作为操纵台）；　2）孩子们制作的火箭或者火箭玩具。

准备环节

- （角色分配）确定谁负责地面控制，谁是负责将火箭送去太空的宇航员。

具体步骤

1）从 3 或 5 或 10 依次开始火箭发射倒数。
2）让孩子们轮流扮演地面控制人员和宇航员。

拓展

- 改变倒数的起始数，问孩子们想从哪个数字开始倒数。
- 孩子们可以在很多不同的情景下开始进行倒数，比如在吃晚饭的时候，跑步比赛或者在玩玩偶盒时（有些玩偶会突然从盒子里跳出来）。

该活动体现的数学思维

　　孩子们要学会正数和倒数，然后他们学会按照步骤来做事。给到一个特定的时间节点（比如该活动中"发射"的指令），让孩子们学会按照指示来完成任务，并学会合理利用和珍惜时间。

制作火箭

选择三维图制作一个火箭。

教学目标

- 制作一个可以直立和飞行的火箭。
- 准备真实火箭的图片或者视频，或玩具火箭。

具体步骤

1）给孩子们展示一系列不同的火箭，讨论火箭的用途，以及什么样的特征帮助火箭达成目的。

2）询问孩子们打算选择制作什么形状的火箭。为什么选择这种形状（比如圆锥体的顶点可以帮助火箭在太空中旅行）。

小贴士　　建构准确的三维立体语言，比如圆锥体、圆柱体、长方体、正方体。

该活动体现的数学思维

　　制作火箭的过程，可以帮助孩子们了解不同的立体形状，同时也让他们思考不同形状的特征，以及帮助他们建立早期对于几何的理解。

无穷之旅

教学目标

- 思考我们跟物体间的距离是如何影响我们对物体大小的判断。
- 学会描述大小、距离/长度。

所需材料

1) 两个不同大小的球，例如一个足球和一个高尔夫球；
2) 需要一个大的场地，或者长形的空间。

准备环节

- 让一个成年人拿着大的那个球站得离孩子们足够远（这个球的实际大小取决于成年人距离孩子们有多远）。

具体步骤

1) 引导孩子们探讨火箭，以及火箭飞去哪里？孩子们希望火箭飞到哪里去？讨论火箭飞行离开地球的距离有多远（有可能当下的实际演练中，距离很近）。

2) 让孩子们告诉你远处的人拿着的球 A 是哪种球？大声告诉孩子们猜得不准确（如果孩子们猜对的话）。因为你在孩子这头拿着同样大小的球 B，但是看起来比远处的那个球 A 大。让孩子们讨论一下为什么？

3) 让远处的人慢慢走近，鼓励孩子们观察这个球 A 随着拿球的人靠近，发生了什么样的变化。将这个球 A 和你手里的球 B 进行比较。

4) 跟孩子们探讨同是球形的地球，一个巨大的球体漂浮在宇宙中。太阳比地球大很多很多倍，但是太阳看起来非常小，因为离我们的距离非常非常远。

该活动体现的数学思维

通过距离的远近来观察球的尺寸，孩子们可以有机会讨论距离对于物体大小感知的影响。距离是长度表达的另外一种方式，比如："从 A 点到 B 点的距离是多少？"与"A 点与 B 点之间的长度是多少？"意思是一样的。通过讨论太空内的距离来引导孩子们去理解无穷大的概念。

星星

教学目标

• 学会数星星的角。

所需材料

1）纸板；

2）装饰用的一闪一闪的灯，颜料或彩纸。

准备环节

• 裁剪含有不同星星的角的数量。

具体步骤

1）鼓励孩子们选择和装饰一些星星，在他们做的时候，让他们数一数星星有几个角？

2）相互谈论一下自己的星星有几个角。

3）把制作好的星星装饰贴在天花板上。

小贴士

我们需要帮助孩子记住从哪一个角开始数，以及哪个角是最后一个。通常孩子们喜欢重复数数，或者数到一个熟悉的数字才停止（比如10）。建议在刚开始数数的时候让孩子养成用手指去数数的习惯。

拓展

• 鼓励孩子们自己画出或者剪出带有他们想要数量角的形状。

该活动体现的数学思维

知道计数序列的最后一个数字，是孩子们计数能力发展的一部分。

星星的对称性

通过旋转和反射来探索对称。

教学目标

• 知道什么是对称。

所需材料

1）准备各种各样的星星，有些是对称的有些是不对称的；

2）大头针；

3）比这些星星还要大的纸板；

4）镜子；

5）纸和剪刀，让孩子们设计自己的星星。

准备环节

• 将只有一条对称线的星星对折。

• 将有两条对称线的星星对折再对折。

• 将一些旋转对称形（rotational symmetry）的星星放在纸板上，将大头针钉在星星的中心。

• 在这个星星周围用线画一圈，这样就可以看到星星旋转运行的轨迹。

具体步骤

1）让孩子们观察你所准备的星星。孩子们注意到这些星星折叠后有什么变化？当孩子们转动旋转对称形的星星时，又有什么变化？

2）让孩子们观察一下剩余的没有折叠或者钉住的星星，他们能找到对称的星星吗？这些星星可以折叠多少次？这些星星旋转多少圈才能回到起点？孩子们可以找到不对称的星星吗？

3）孩子们是否可以设计自己的星星？这些星星对称吗？它们是哪种对称形式？它们是镜像对称（即它们被折叠的时候每个点是重合的）或者是旋转对称（即它们围绕中心旋转）？

小贴士　　　　　孩子们有天生的对称意识，特别是一条垂直线上的反射对称。他们也喜欢用"对称"这个词。

拓展

• 孩子们在制作雪花的过程中也会发现对称这个特性（将一张圆形的纸对折好几次，再剪出不同的雪花）。

• 我们也可以去散散步，看看照片，会发现大自然中有很多对称的物体，比如叶子、花和水。

该活动体现的数学思维

对孩子们来说，学习对称很重要，可以帮助他们理解形状。

白天与黑夜

孩子们可以描述白天和黑夜很多的不同点。

教学目标

- 会讨论不同点。
- 思考白天黑夜不同时间的描述。

准备环节

- 带孩子来到户外。

具体步骤

1）让孩子们观察天空，现在他们可以看到什么？和昨天的一样吗？明天的天空会是什么样子的？

2）晚上的天空看起来是什么样子的？

3）晚上的天空有云吗？告诉孩子们云看不见是因为太黑了。其实云离我们更近，云是把星星藏在了后面。

4）讨论月亮的形状，有时候月亮是圆形的（circular），有时候是月牙形（crescent shape）。

5）孩子们讨论下白天和晚上分别在做什么事？

小贴士　　月亮在白天的时候也是存在的，认为月亮只在晚上出现是一种错误的观念。

该活动体现的数学思维

　　每 24 小时就会有白天黑夜的一次交替。这种交替是不断重复的模式，对人类生活有着重大的影响。对孩子们而言，把一天当做一个时间单位，比一周、一个月、一年当做时间单位来说更容易。思考月亮的形状在一个月里是如何变化的，同时也帮助孩子们思考时间是如何流逝的。

宇航员

用歌曲帮助孩子们思考如何倒数和理解减 1 的概念。

教学目标

- 学会倒数。
- 理解减 1 的概念。

所需材料

1） 硬纸板做的飞碟，并附有 5 个外星人的玩具；

2） 或者，带有 5 个宇航员的火箭，宇航员是可以被移走的。

具体步骤

1） 一起演唱歌曲《在飞碟中的五个外星人》。

2） 当唱到"一个外星人飞走了"，停止唱歌，并让一个孩子移走其中的一个外星人。然后让孩子们一起数剩下多少个外星人。告诉孩子们"之前是 5 个外星人，1 个飞走了，还剩下 4 个"。同时告诉孩子们术语"take away"（减少的意思）。

3） 把这首歌再唱一遍。再开始数剩下的外星人之前，让孩子们从"5"开始倒数直到数到飞碟中剩余的外星人数量。

4） 鼓励孩子们用他们的手指代替外星人。用 5 个手指开始倒数，把一个手指弯下来，代表 1 个外星人飞走了。"还剩下多少个手指呢，让我们一起数一数"。

小贴士　　　　如果你对这首歌不是特别熟悉，可以上网搜索。

拓展

- 你可以准备其他的包含倒数或者减数的歌曲。

该活动体现的数学思维

　　孩子们需要理解"减 1"的概念和倒数是一致的。他们也要开始增进对于减法的理解。使用手指代替其他对象，来帮助孩子理解抽象数学理念，比如手指就是歌曲中外星人的抽象体现。以后，孩子们会慢慢理解数字是抽象的，可以用来计数（比如 5 个宇航员，5 块积木，5 倍等等），还可以表示测量单位（比如 5 点、5 岁、5 米、5 度等）。

外星人

让我们一起数一数有多少外星人。

教学目标
- 学会数数。
- 会谈论模式。

所需材料

英文绘本《喜欢内裤的外星人》。

准备环节
- 读该绘本《喜欢内裤的外星人》。

具体步骤

1) 讨论每条内裤上的图案，哪一条是孩子们最喜欢的内裤？为什么？喜欢的内裤上有什么样的图案？

2) 讨论外星人的特征。书中的外星人有多少条腿？多少个手臂？多少只眼睛？是否有触角？是否有头发？等等。

3) 猜测有多少个外星人躲在了裤脚里？（绘本中有描述这一情节）。孩子们是怎么想的？大家互相讨论，表扬任何有逻辑的答案。

小贴士

鼓励孩子们找出外星人的特征并用他们的手指去数一数。这个会帮助孩子们去理解一对一的关联性（比如一双眼睛，两只手）。

该活动体现的数学思维

孩子们要理解任何东西都是可以被计数的。没有按顺序排列的物品对于孩子来说比较难用数字去计数。去猜测裤腿里躲着的外星人数量，有利于帮助孩子们去想象数量的多少。

设计一个外星人

这个活动能提供很多机会帮助你和孩子们更多地去讨论数字和数数。

教学目标

- 学会数数。
- 会识别属性。

所需材料

1）英文绘本《喜欢内裤的外星人》；

2）纸；

3）颜料、蜡笔、铅笔、其他多媒体资料等。

准备环节

- 阅读绘本《喜欢内裤的外星人》或者其他讲述外星人的书本，给孩子们观察。

具体步骤

1）让孩子们想象一下他们心目中的外星人长什么样子？他们有多少条腿？多少个手臂？多少只眼睛？嘴巴是什么样子的？是否有头发？他们的外星人特别的地方在哪里？

2）鼓励孩子们画出他们的外星人。在画的过程当中，跟孩子们谈论这些外星人的特点，鼓励他们用数字去描述这些特点（比如有 5 条腿，3 个手臂等等）。

3）对孩子们提问题，比如"你还要画多少只手臂"，或者根据你的观察描述"我看到你左右各画了 4 只眼睛，每一边的数量都是一样的"。

拓展

- 装扮成外星人。讨论这些外星人有多少条腿，多少个手臂，多少只眼睛等等。他们是怎么移动的？在哪里睡觉？表现成一个外星人的样子。谈论拥有更多的手臂可以帮助完成某些特定的工作，或者有更多的眼睛，可以帮助他们同时看到更多的东西。

该活动体现的数学思维

该活动鼓励孩子们去谈论数字，并且练习数数和加法。

第四章

钓　鱼

引言

　　试着把你的教室变成水下世界：让孩子们用浅蓝色的玻璃纸把窗户贴起来，再把鱼贴在上面，并把水下的其他生物挂在天花板上。蓝色、绿色和透明的纸贴在这些悬挂着的生物上面，点缀在其中，增加水下世界的感觉。

我钓到一条大鱼！

• 让孩子们练习身体技能，去钓一条"大鱼"！

教学目标

• 识别数字。
• 学会 9 以上的数字。

所需材料

1）将标有数字"0"至"9"的纸做成鱼的形状，涂上颜色，并塑封，在这个上面贴上回形针；

2）鱼竿：在杆子的一端挂上绳子，在绳子的一头系上吸铁石。

准备环节

• 准备一个"池塘"，并把这些塑封好的数字放在里面。

具体步骤

1）孩子们可以选择钓他们自己想要的数字。

2）说一下他们钓到了哪个数字。你可以数到这个数字吗？你知道哪个数字比你钓到的这个数字更小或者更大呢？

3）当所有的鱼（数字）都被钓完后，他们可以按照数字的大小排列吗？

4）鼓励孩子们将两个个位数放在一起变成另外一个数字，他们可以说说这个数字是多少吗？如果三个个位数放在一起呢？

小贴士

• 当这些代表数字的"鱼"放在一起的时候，它们变成了多个个位数，而不是一个数目。比如"6"是一个单独数字的时候，它是一个个位数。然而在"36"里面，"6"就变成了二位数当中的一个个位数。在幼儿早期的时候，区分个位数和数字是非常重要的。

• 你有可能想要更改这些数字的尺寸，比如大尺寸的"2"和小尺寸的"7"。这会引导孩子们去讨论在按照数字大小的排列同时，这些数字的大小，跟数字图片的尺寸大小不一样。

拓展

• 将渔夫的眼睛蒙住，其他的孩子可以给渔夫提供线索，让他来辨别钓到的这个数字鱼是多少，比如"这是一个偶数，比 6 大，是 4 的两倍"。

该活动体现的数学思维

　　正确理解数字的排列顺序，帮助孩子们对于数学数数方面更有信心，往后在加减乘除方面也可以用到这个技能，同时理解位数是组成数字的重要部分。给孩子们提供机会去讨论这些数字的属性，帮助他们去更好地理解数字。

去钓鱼!

这是一个传统的纸牌游戏。

教学目标

- 让孩子们熟悉数字。
- 提升解决问题和逻辑思维能力。

所需材料

准备塑封的白色 A5 尺寸卡片,上面有不同颜色的数字。卡片的数量取决于玩游戏的人数多少,比如 28 个孩子,你也许要准备:

蓝色	黄色	红色	绿色
10	10	10	10
11	11	11	11
12	12	12	12
13	13	13	13
14	14	14	14
15	15	15	15
16	16	16	16

准备环节

- 确保有足够大的空间玩这个游戏。
- 在这个空间中心划一条线,把孩子们分成两组。

具体步骤

1) 将卡片分发给孩子们,每人一张。

2) 选择七个孩子站成一组,另外七个孩子站成另外一组,面对面站好。

3) 其他的孩子坐到旁边,看着他们,并把自己的卡片藏好不被这两组的孩子们看到。

4) 面对面站着分好组的孩子们在组内互相讨论,并查看他们是否有相同数字的卡片,鼓励孩子们和他有相同数字的同伴站在一起。

5) 让第一组的孩子确认一个数字,他们要尽量去组成跟这个数字相同的四张卡片。他们问另外一组是否有这个数字。如果另外一个小组有这个数字,则有这个数字的孩子就要和第一组小组拥有相同数字的坐到一起。如果另外一个小组没有这个数字，则所有的孩子要一起说"去钓鱼吧"，则第一组的孩子们要从坐着的孩子中选一个加入到他们。

6）每个小组都轮流来说数字，当一个小组中的四张相同数字卡片被收集的时候，这四张卡片对应的孩子就要坐到这小组的后面。

7）最后获得最多相同数字卡片的小组获胜。

小贴士

- 这个游戏当中的数字你也可以把它替换成孩子们要提高的其他内容。
- 鼓励孩子们向人们解释，他们要哪个数字，并为什么要这个数字？

拓展

- 你可能希望将相同数字的卡片减少到三组，这样会加快游戏的进度，但是会减少讨论的机会。
- 拿到相同卡片的孩子们，还可以把卡片给老师来换取新的卡片，并重新加入到这个游戏当中。
- 坐在旁边的这些孩子们可以排队依次加入两个小组中，而不是让其他两组选择。

该活动体现的数学思维

这个游戏有助于提升孩子的逻辑思维。孩子们需要用数学的思维去讨论出来，他们需要问哪个数字。

钓鱼比赛

在这个钓鱼比赛中，谁得了第一名，第二名和第三名？

教学目标

- 会使用序数词（第一、第二、第三等等）。
- 理解速度。
- 理解距离。

所需材料

1）每个孩子发一条从 A4 纸剪下来的鱼；

2）准备 8 到 10 张报纸。

准备环节

- 孩子们可以将自己的鱼涂色或者将自己的名字写在上面来区分自己的鱼。
- 将报纸对折再对折折成 A4 大小的纸，纸的数量取决于你邀请多少个学生同一时间参加比赛。
- 最好是在一个大的空间里面举行这个比赛。

具体步骤

1）将孩子们和他们的鱼都排成一排，并站在起跑线后面。

2）当开始说"出发"的时候，孩子们要将报纸从上到下地扇动，这样他们的鱼就可以被扇出来的风吹着往前走。

3）孩子们要持续的扇动他们的鱼往前"游"，直到所有的鱼都过了终点线。

4）对剩余的孩子都按照以上的步骤走，直到所有的孩子都参加完比赛。

5）你可以为这些在预选赛中获得"第一""第二""第三"的孩子们举办半决赛和决赛。

6）为前三名的孩子颁发金银铜奖，你也可以为这些获胜者和他们的鱼拍照。

小贴士　　　　在比赛前给孩子们练习移动他们的鱼。

拓展

- 有些孩子们喜欢尝试不同尺寸或者不同材质的鱼做实验，在这个过程中，他们可以去发现哪种情况是最有效的。

该活动体现的数学思维

　　孩子们学会用序数词来描述谁是"第一"、"第二"和"第三",同时学会解决"哪种是最有效地移动报纸的方式"或者"哪种设计方案的鱼游得最快",帮助孩子们去思考因果关系。

五条小小鱼

让我们一起改编歌曲吧！

教学目标

- 学会倒数。
- 了解"减去"的定义。
- 学会一周中的每一天的叫法。

所需材料

1）歌词，详见下方；

2）鱼的服装或者是玩偶；

3）准备标有数字一到五和每一天名称的卡片。

准备环节

- 孩子们可以装扮成小鱼。

具体步骤

1）让孩子们一起唱歌（根据下面的歌词），曲调：5只小鸭。

歌词：

五条小鱼周一去游泳，

穿过河水，游得远远的，

鱼妈妈说："是时候回来啦！"

但是只有四条小鱼游了回来。

四条小鱼周二去游泳，三条小鱼周三去游泳，两条小鱼周四去游泳，一条小鱼周五去游泳，没有小鱼游回来。

（慢旋律）

伤心的鱼妈妈周六去游泳，

穿过河水，游得远远的。

鱼妈妈哭着说："不要离开！"

五条小鱼，周日游回家。

（欢呼）

2) 在每个段落之间，讨论一下多少条鱼离开了，用这样的句型造句"这里本来有 5 条鱼，1 条鱼离开了，所以 4 条鱼回来了"。给孩子们演示，5 条鱼中游走了 1 条只剩下 4 条鱼。

3) 在每个段落之间，讨论一下这周中接下来的一天是哪一天。

拓展

- 孩子们可以用手指布偶的鱼或者用手指来代表鱼的数量。

- 可以从 10 条鱼开始，然后再唱这首歌，一起讨论一下接下来的数字是什么。

该活动体现的数学思维

　　倒数和减去是两种早期的数学减法思维。选择一个代表性的物体，比如鱼的手指布偶，当孩子们用手指开始数数的时候，就可以将数字和这些物体所联系起来。

　　知道每一天的名称，并了解每天的顺序排练是一个指定的顺序，这对于孩子来说会记录时间和日期是一种非常重要的思考模式。

原来是渔网

增加或减少鱼的数量。

教学目标
- 学会如何往上数数。
- 学会数量的减少。

所需材料
1）小的鱼玩具，或者被塑封的鱼卡片；
2）每个孩子一个网（要提供可选择性的，有些孩子不喜欢，参照下面的小贴士）；
3）准备好不同的卡片，用袋子装好，参照下面；
4）黄色的卡片上写上：

抓到 1 条鱼	抓到 1 条鱼	抓到 1 条鱼	抓到 1 条鱼
抓到 2 条鱼	抓到 2 条鱼	抓到 2 条鱼	抓到 2 条鱼
抓到 3 条鱼	抓到 3 条鱼	抓到 3 条鱼	抓到 3 条鱼

5）红色的卡片上写上：

扔回去 1 条鱼	扔回去 1 条鱼	扔回去 1 条鱼	扔回去 1 条鱼
扔回去 2 条鱼	扔回去 2 条鱼	扔回去 2 条鱼	扔回去 2 条鱼
扔回去 3 条鱼	扔回去 3 条鱼	扔回去 3 条鱼	扔回去 3 条鱼

准备环节
- 把鱼放在"鱼塘"或者"海"里（这个"鱼塘"或者"海"是位于地面或桌子之上孩子能接触到的某个地方）。
- 有可能的话，给每个孩子都提供一个鱼网。

具体步骤

1) 孩子们依次从袋子当中取出一张卡片，他们根据卡片上的信息把鱼从"鱼塘"里取出来捞出来或者还回去，完成后把卡片还回袋子当中。

2) 第一个获取对应数字鱼的孩子获得胜利（比如15条或者20条）。

3) 如果孩子抽到一张红色的卡片，但是没有足够数量的鱼可以放回鱼塘中。他们可以选择跳过这一轮或者重新抽卡片。

小贴士 　孩子们需要更多的数数练习，他们可以将他们的鱼排成一列，而不是放在网里，这样更有利于他们数数。

拓展

- 使用更大的数字，使鱼的数量得到大幅度的增加。
- 袋子里可以只放黄色的卡片，只为让孩子们来数数。每个孩子都可以从 20 条鱼开始，当一个孩子的网空了以后，谁的网里面有最多的鱼就获得胜利。

该活动体现的数学思维

　这个游戏让孩子们有机会去数一数鱼的总数，在抓到（增加）和放走（减少）鱼的过程当中，对于总数的影响。

彩虹鱼

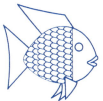

教学目标

- 学会识别数字符号。
- 学会精确地数数。

所需材料

书：《彩虹鱼》。

1) 每个学生一个鱼的模板（如右图）；

2) 计数器；

3) 骰子。

准备环节

- 为孩子们读故事《彩虹鱼》。
- 给每个孩子准备一个彩虹鱼卡片。
- 孩子们用计数器计算鱼的鳞片数。

具体步骤

1) 孩子们依次掷骰子，并根据骰子上显示的数字移去相同数字的鳞片（计数器上减去相同的数字）。

2) 孩子们必须掷出正确的数字才能完成。

3) 第一个把所有鱼鳞都去掉的孩子是胜利者。

小贴士　　　当孩子们把彩虹鱼的鱼鳞拿走的时候，让他们讨论一下，剩下的鱼鳞发生了什么样的变化？（比如数量减少了）

拓展

- 一对孩子可以共同分享一个彩虹鱼的模板，让他们一起数数，互相帮助。

该活动体现的数学思维

　　让孩子们使用骰子的时候可以看到确切数字的抽象表征。等有了经验以后，孩子们会明白每个数字的含义，而不用再数骰子的点数。

第五章

游 戏

引言

　　在你的教室里很可能有这样一块供小孩子做游戏的地方。这块地方是随时向所有孩子开放的吗？还是你会在不同的时间段提供游戏给孩子们玩?又或者两者兼有。游戏可以按照传统设计好的玩法来玩，这是肯定的。不过，你也许会想，有些游戏在一定程度上做一些调整，可以在大小不同的规模下进行。举例来说，孩子们能让他们的玩具在桌子上玩跳房子游戏；大型的蛇与阶梯游戏棋盘可以用粉笔画在室外区域；游戏中用到的骰子也可以选择不同大小尺寸的。

骰子游戏

通过使用骰子，孩子们也在学习另一种表示数字的方法。

数过来数过去

用骰子来决定向前或向后数几个方格。

教学目标

- 学会轮流。
- 练习数数。

所需材料

1）骰子；

2）一块"游戏棋盘"，在室内或户外都可以。

准备环节

- 如果条件允许，可以制作一个在户外玩的游戏棋盘。

具体步骤

孩子们轮流丢骰子，按照上面的数字让他们的棋子跳动相应的方格数。

小贴士　　　　确保每一个孩子都知道他们应该从棋子起跳的下一个格子开始数，而不用从所在的那一格开始数。这样做对孩子们是有好处的，在往前数的过程中，他们也接触到了加法。

拓展

- 如果想玩得规模大一点，孩子们也可以自己当"棋子"，在游戏棋盘上移动。想练习减法，就用两个骰子，按照得到的两个数的差是棋子移动所对应的格数。也可以选用一个常规骰子，另一个骰子上面显示"－"和"＋"的符号，或者"减"和"加"字样，又或者写有"向前"和"向后"的指令。

该活动体现的数学思维

　　在棋盘游戏中孩子们可以练习数数。棋子的使用给孩子们机会，让他们看到数字能用各种不同的方式来表示。在棋盘中数过来数过去，对于学习早期加减法的孩子们来说，是一个十分有利的教学场景。

蛇与阶梯

一种不同于传统棋盘游戏的三维构建玩法。

教学目标

- 练习数数。
- 理解大于或小于。
- 锻炼解决问题的能力。

所需材料

1) 剪成一条条的布料，用来代表蛇；
2) 硬纸板或纸张，剪成阶梯的形状；
3) 大大的数字方格，比如"1"至"50"；
4) 一个空白的骰子（按下面的指示进行准备）；
5) 一个常规骰子；
6) 棋子，每人一个；
7) 一套迷你数字卡片，数字和棋盘上的数字相同，仍是"1"至"50"。

准备环节

- 将数字方格摆摆好。
- 在空白骰子上的同一面画梯子和一条蛇，剩下的另外五面仍然保持空白。

具体步骤

1) 孩子们通过滚动两个骰子来开启棋盘游戏。
2) 如果留有空白面的骰子转到了空白面，孩子们仍按照常规的玩法，根据常规骰子上的数字来移动棋子。
3) 但如果他们转到了画有梯子和蛇的那一面，他们就要从一堆数字卡片中抽出一张。
4) 如果抽出的数字比他们当时所在方格的数字大，他们就要在所在方格与抽出的数字卡片对应的方格之间摆一节梯子。如果抽出的数字比他们所占方格的数字小，那么他们就要在两者之间摆一条蛇。
5) 在同一轮里，棋子如果遇到梯子或者蛇，都要顺着梯子或蛇到对应的数字。
6) 然后轮到下一个孩子滚动两个骰子，游戏继续。

取出制作蛇的一段布料，并允许孩子们将布料剪成想要的长度。鼓励孩子们思考蛇的弯曲度怎样影响裁剪好的布条最终的长度的。棋盘完成后，将它拍下来，照片打印在一张 A4 纸上，多打印几张叠成一叠。在课堂上或者下雨天的午餐时间，这些就是孩子们正好可以玩的棋盘游戏。

拓展

• 构思一番，这个游戏能被运用到一系列不同的情境中去，比如"杰克和仙豆"（在故事情境中阶梯变成仙豆，蛇变成巨人的靴子或一把斧子），"大老头约克公爵"（可以用不同深浅的绿色布料来表示上坡和下坡），又或者是有关天气主题（用阳光光束代替阶梯，雨滴流代替蛇）。

该活动体现的数学思维

• 孩子们在活动中数数，比较数字的大小，学习认识这些数字，并读出它们。

• 当他们谈论棋盘场上进展的时候，他们也是在推理和解决问题。

地面机器人游戏

地面机器人，如小蜜蜂、罗马牌、小仙子，对小孩子来说操作简单又好玩。

地面机器人比赛

谁的机器人会赢得比赛的胜利呢？

教学目标

- 通过往前数学习加法。
- 通过向后数学习减法。

所需材料

1）一到两个地面机器人；

2）两组数字卡片，卡片长度与机器人跨出一步的间隔相当；

3）两个骰子，一个红色，一个蓝色。

准备环节

- 将这些数字卡片排成两列，形成一个"数轨"，中间留一点空隙。如下图所示：

机器人	1	2	3	4	5	6	7	8	9	10

机器人	1	2	3	4	5	6	7	8	9	10

具体步骤

1) 将孩子们分成两队。

2) 各放一个机器人在数轨里数字"1"的旁边，注意不是压在数字"1"上面。

3) 两个团队轮流滚动两个骰子。红骰子表明机器人能向前移动几步（操作机器人前进相应的步数），蓝骰子表明机器人应该向后移动几步（然后操作机器人后退相应的步数）。

4) 最先抵达目的地的即为获胜团队。

小贴士

完成这个游戏需要一定的时间。为了加快游戏速度，可以让红骰子上的数字稍大一些。一旦孩子们已经可以熟练地操作机器人让它们跟着红蓝骰子上的数字向前向后，鼓励他们在脑子里想象机器人的移动轨迹，然后问他们怎样机器人才能用最短路径抵达目标数字。

拓展

- 尝试用不同的数字来玩，在数轨里选定一个不一样的数字作为开头和结尾。

该活动体现的数学思维

　　孩子们开始利用数轨直观地向前数、向后数。后续可以让机器人按照数轨（模向）和数列（纵向）的方式移动，从而同步进行加减法演算。

地面机器人目标

孩子们喜欢估算距离，然后操作机器人朝目标点进发。

教学目标

- 估算长度。
- 给出指令。
- 检验估算是否合理。

所需材料

1）封口胶带或者与之类似的物品； 2）两个地面机器人。

准备环节

- 用胶带在地上圈出一块目标区域。
- 将地面机器人摆在与上述目标区域有一定距离的地方。

具体步骤

1) 将孩子们分成两队，每一队负责一个机器人。
2) 鼓励孩子们在各自的团队里进行讨论，关于机器人距离目标区域中心有多少个跨步距离。
3) 每队派出一个代表，根据估算的距离来操作机器人走动相应的步数。
4) 距离目标区域正中心最近的团队获胜。

小贴士

　　你可以在目标区域中心竖一根小柱子，让机器人把它当成击倒的目标。探讨一下机器人距离正中目标还差几步或者多走了几步。

拓展

• 根据抵达区域的不同，可以相应给予不同的分数，距离目标越近，则分数越高。

• 使机器人背朝目标，所以孩子们必须想办法旋转机器人，他们会用到四分之一旋转，二分之一旋转，同时也是在运用对幅度的把控。

• 相较于唯一目标点，可以在地面周围布置出一个高尔夫球场，在球场内每一队必须操作他们的机器人抵达每一个目标点。用最少步数完成任务的团队获胜。

 该活动体现的数学思维

估算是一种重要的数学能力。通过估算机器人要走的距离长短，孩子们能在之后的实际操作中检验他们估算的合理性，并根据检验结果进一步调整他们的估算。

豆袋

豆袋，一个适合拿在手里并丢出去的东西。

教学目标

- 让数字形象化。
- 能理解"一共多少"表示的是加法。
- 能理解"还差多少"或"差"表示的是减法。

所需材料

1）5个用于投掷的小豆袋；

2）装豆袋用的袋子或小型容器；

3）桶或箱子一类的东西，活动中孩子们会把豆袋丢到里面。

准备环节

- 不作要求。

具体步骤

1) 展示给孩子们看老师手上有 5 个豆袋，和他们一起数一数。

2) 丢一些豆袋到桶里。问孩子们，"我丢掉了几个？"一起数一数来核对一下。

3) 多来几轮，鼓励孩子们也来丢豆袋。

小贴士　　　　有些豆袋也许会丢不进桶里。这时候问孩子们有几个豆袋进入了桶里，有几个没丢进。这是练习将三个数连加在一起的好机会——在桶里的豆袋数，掉在地上的豆袋数，还有手里尚未丢出去的豆袋数。

拓展

- 让孩子们闭上眼睛，听你或者其他孩子丢豆袋在桶里的声音。用不同数量的豆袋反复操练。
- 使用其他可以被丢在目标箱里的物品。
- 单纯玩丢豆袋的游戏，看有多少豆袋能被丢到桶里：将孩子们分拨成两组，每个成员轮流往桶里丢豆袋。最先达到预定分数的即为获胜小组。

该活动体现的数学思维

　　　　对孩子们来说，这是能让他们思考构成数字"5"的不同方式的一个机会。比如，可以是"1＋4"，"2＋2＋1"，等等。通过在桶里的豆袋将数字可视化，孩子们能更有效地理解这些简单的加法运算。

隐藏与计数

这个游戏和传统的金氏游戏类似。

教学目标

- 练习数数。
- 将一个特定数字可视化。

所需材料

1）任何可以被拿在手里数的物品；

2）一块茶巾或类似的可以用于盖住物品的东西，也可以是一个能将物品放在里面的袋子或箱子。

准备环节

- 不作要求。

具体步骤

1）数出 3 个物品。

2）将它们遮起来。

3）让所有人看到其中 1 个被拿走。

4）问孩子们："盖子底下还有几个？"

5）掀开盖子，核对一下。

6）用不同的数字反复操练。

小贴士　　　刚开始时先用小一点的数字，之后再增加需要用到的物品的数量。使用大一点的数字时，取走物品时先从小数目开始拿，或者拿走整体的一半。

拓展

- 孩子们能互相之间玩这个游戏。

该活动体现的数学思维

　　孩子们一边数数，一边将数字可视化。他们从拿走的行为中理解减法的概念。

分组游戏

这是一个消耗能量的体育活动，让孩子们通过分组这种有趣的方式，来进行锻炼。

教学目标

- 练习数数。
- 了解如何解决问题。

所需材料

开阔一点的空间。

准备环节

- 不作要求。

具体步骤

1) 喊出一个数字，要求孩子们自主组成小组，喊出的数字即为组员数。
2) 没有组成小组的孩子，在下一轮可以重新加入。

小贴士　　　　这个游戏鼓励团队协作。游戏组织者或老师可以尝试计时，鼓励孩子们提高效率，减少加入各自小组所用的时长。

拓展

- 这个游戏可以用竞赛的形式来玩，每一轮下来没有成功组成小组的孩子站到一旁，观看下一轮的游戏，（在场内）留到最后的孩子成为最终的赢家。

该活动体现的数学思维

整个活动过程中孩子们会练习到数数；他们还要一直判断自己所在的组人员是多了还是少了——这是两个重要的数学概念。

在你的自行车上！

孩子们喜欢沿着给定的路线骑他们的自行车，滑板车或三轮车。

教学目标

- 听从指令。
- 给出指令。

所需材料

1） 三轮车、滑板车或自行车；

2） 一块事先画好的区域，或者是用胶带贴出的道路，让孩子们在上面骑车；

3） 棒棒糖形状的写有"停"和"走"的指示牌。

准备环节

- 可以让孩子们和你一起设计并制作路线。

具体步骤

1) 孩子们扮演旅游者沿着路线走或者使用自有的行车工具（三轮车、滑板车等）

2) 一个孩子拿棒棒糖型指示牌，告诉旅游者是走还是停。

3) 可以这样问孩子："这儿是 T 字路口吗？现在你打算往哪条路走？"

小贴士

这个活动对你来说是一个机会，你可以和孩子们谈论很多行走路径，关于靠道路左边行驶啊，怎样经过路线上的一些物体，是从内部穿过，从上面经过，从底下经过，从两个建筑物体中间穿过，或者是沿着物体曲折地前行等等。

拓展

- 增加交通灯。问孩子们，"交通灯都有什么颜色？每一种颜色告诉我们要怎么做？"

该活动体现的数学思维

在这个活动中能被使用的数学词汇有很多。给出指令并听从指令，这能锻炼孩子们运用他们的推理能力。

捉迷藏

一个好玩的游戏，让朋友们通过指令找到被藏起来的物体。

教学目标
- 学会使用表示方位的语言。
- 学会估算距离。

所需材料
一组小物件。

准备环节
- 在房间里的各处或室外藏一些小物件，让它们只露出一点点。

具体步骤

1) 让孩子们在室内或室外空间四处寻找被藏起来的物件。事先和他们说明不可以把任何自己找到的物件的方位告诉其他人。

2) 一小段时间之后，让孩子们集合。鼓励他们每个人轮流描述某一个物件的方位，让大家能够找到它，绝对不可以用手指来指示！

小贴士
- 使用的小物件可以与当前学习的主题或话题联系起来。
- 鼓励孩子们使用表示方位的语言，比如"在……上面"，"在……下面"，"在……旁边"，"在……后面"，等等。

拓展
- 一部分人（可以是两个人一组）在其他孩子四处走动，以确定被藏的某个物件方位的时候，可以约定适时地说出"温暖"，"热"，"凉快多了"如此之类的暗语来帮助找的孩子明确自己距离目标物的远近。
- 一个孩子或多个孩子可以在其他孩子藏某个物件的时候离开房间，藏东西的孩子负责在之后给出指令。

该活动体现的数学思维

孩子们在活动中使用表示方位的语言，来形容在他们周围环境中某一具体物件的方位。这便是孩子们最初接触的几何学。如果操练上述拓展中的游戏，那么孩子们是在通过使用"热"，"暖"，"凉快"等一类词估算某一物件距离自己的距离。只用语句描述而不用手势，对于幼儿园的孩子而言是非常难的。

跳房子游戏

这是在传统跳房子游戏上进行改造的玩法，孩子们可以一个人玩也可以一组人一起玩。

教学目标

- 认读数字。
- 练习数数。

所需材料

1）在室外画出一个跳房子区域，或者用胶带在室内贴出一个；

2）一个可以丢的小物件，像是豆袋或小玩具。

准备环节

- 在没有室外空间的情况下，用胶带在地毯上或大厅的地面上贴出跳房子区域。

具体步骤

1）孩子们往跳房子区域丢豆袋。

2）他们有时单脚有时双脚地跳在跳房子里的数字上，豆袋落在的数字不跳。

小贴士

- 和孩子们谈论什么数字他们没有跳（因为豆袋在那上面）。讨论一下这个数字是在哪两个数字中间。可以这样问，"这个数前面是什么数？这个数后面又是什么数？"
- 谈论单脚跳和双脚跳，谈谈它们的不同：只用一只脚还是同时用两只。

拓展

- 用更传统的方式玩，按顺序往接连的数字上丢豆袋，一旦豆袋没有丢准方格就换下一个人玩。

该活动体现的数学思维

通过玩跳房子，孩子们一边认读数字，一边数数。

第六章

关于我的一切

前言

　　孩子们喜欢谈论自己和探索自己的身体。本章的活动涵盖很多的数学概念。将孩子们参加活动的瞬间拍摄下来，并用标签，标注出他们讨论数学技能的瞬间（比如数数的时候"我有 10 个手指头"，某某孩子说）。这些记录会让孩子们从中获得更多的数学概念，远远超过了该活动本身。

我的身体

我们可以用很多的数学概念来探索我们的身体。

教学目标

- 练习数数。
- 学会预估。

所需材料

不作要求。

准备环节

- 不作要求。

具体步骤

这是一个基于讨论的活动，根据以下问题进行提问：

1) "找一找你的身体，哪个部位的数量是"10"？"（比如脚趾、手指）。

2) "找一找你的身体，哪个部位的数量是"2"？"

（比如腿、手臂、眼睛、耳朵、脚、手、眉毛、鼻孔、膝盖、脚踝、腋窝。为什么这些部位都是两个呢？讨论一下身体的对称线。

3) "找一找你的身体，哪个部位的数量是"1"？"（比如鼻子、肚脐）

4) "为什么是 1 个呢？"（讨论身体的中间线或者对称线）

5) 数一数你有多少颗牙齿？大家都有相同数量的牙齿吗？为什么？你几岁了，牙齿数量跟你的年龄有关系吗？

6) 预估：你觉得你有多少根头发呢？

小贴士

- 在孩子们的周围做一个模板，让他们可以观察到自己的身体部位。

- 尽管最后一个是一个预估的活动，给到你一个参考信息即我们每个人平均有 100,000 根头发。尽管对于个人来讲，不同颜色头发的人所有拥有的头发数量会有差异。

拓展

- 不要及停留在数不连续的数字，要从不同的方式来使用数字，比如量一下孩子的身高。孩子们可以根据他们的身高来排队，或者把他们自己的身高跟他们的玩具或者房间里的其他事物比对。他们也可以量一下他们脚和手的大小以及腰围多少。

该活动体现的数学思维

　　年纪小的孩子不需要数两个物体。他们只要了解这些物体是一对的就可以了，就是因为他们很早就有了"一对的"概念。思考更大的数字，比如去预估自己他们头发的数量，会引发他们对于奇妙数字的兴趣，也促使他们能尽早地接触更大的数字。孩子们也有在思考对称性，这是一个直观的观念，最终他们还会学会比较的技能。

旅行

引导孩子们了解不同的交通工具，并思考他们的用途。

教学目标

- 用统计图表来呈现数据。
- 用统计图表来说明数据。

所需材料

用物体或者图片来代表不同的交通工具。

准备环节

- 不作要求。

具体步骤

1) 讨论一下："平时你是怎么去托儿所或者幼儿园的？"

2) 给每个孩子代表他们交通工具的一个物品或者图片。

3) 问孩子们："我们怎么知道有多少人使用车作为交通工具？"（通过观察现场的孩子手里的物品或者图片总结）。让所有孩子都混坐在地毯上，使这个问题回答的时候会有一些困难。然后询问孩子们如何让这个问题变得更简单一些。引导孩子们按照自己手中的不同物品和图片来分组。

4) 问孩子们"去托儿所或者幼儿园，哪一个交通工具是最受欢迎的？"或者说"更多的人喜欢用车还是走路？"讨论这些问题的时候，孩子们会发现虽然分组了，但是还比较难知道结果。引导孩子们站成一排排的队伍，可以比较出最长的队伍是哪一排。

5) 将代表交通工具的物品排成一排，或者将这些图片贴在墙上。

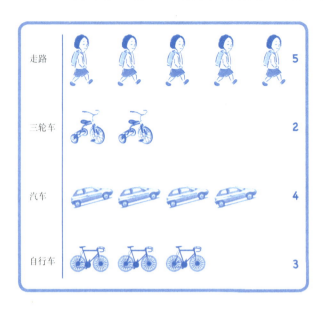

走路						5
三轮车						2
汽车						4
自行车						3

• 准备一部分的交通工具物品或者图片是不可能被用到的，比如飞机，然后讨论一下为什么没有孩子用这类交通工具？

• 对于比较聪明的孩子，可以"哄骗"他们说，墙上图片数量比较少的那一组实际上是更多的学生选择使用这种交通工具。让孩子们来讨论为什么我的观点是不正确的，并且鼓励学生用数据纠正我的看法。让孩子们讨论为什么图片或者物品拥有相同大小这一点很重要，而且还要确保这些物品之间存在对等的距离。

拓展

• 用统计图表还可以呈现不同的主题，比如鞋子的种类、鞋子的尺寸、生日月份、眼睛的颜色、兄弟姐妹的数量、最喜欢的书本种类等等。

• 如果使用块图，给孩子们不同颜色的方块来替代给孩子们物品或者图片。例如，他们根据回答的问题搭建成一个高高的塔（一个方块代表一个种类的物品）。跟让孩子们将不同颜色的卡片按照不同种类物品贴在墙上一样。

该活动体现的数学思维

这种数据处理的方法帮助孩子们在图形和实际数据之间建立连接。通过图片的形式来帮助他们更好的理解数据。一些无效的举例（例如文中举例的飞机）也是给孩子们一个很好的机会，去理解为什么有些组是没有数据的。

我的一天

此次活动给到孩子们一个机会去思考如何把他们日常的生活按照时间顺序来排列。

教学目标

- 将事件按时间顺序排列。
- 使用跟时间相关的词语。

所需材料

1）描述孩子们日常生活的照片。（比如：起床、刷牙、吃早饭、吃午饭、喝茶、洗澡、喂养宠物、睡觉、往返托儿所/幼儿园、拜访爷爷奶奶、玩，等等）；

2）给孩子们空白的卡片来画他们自己额外的常规事项；

3）用胶水把这些照片按照时间顺序粘贴起来。

准备环节

- 塑封这些照片，如果你希望再次使用的话。

具体步骤

1) 跟孩子们谈论一下，他们一天里面会做些什么。

2) 准备跟这些事件相关的图片，且并不要按顺序摆放。

3) 让孩子们按时间排列这些图片，并问他们问题，例如"你早上做的第一件事情是什么？""然后你做什么？""睡前你做的最后一件事情是什么？""这两件事情之间你会做什么？"

4) 鼓励孩子们谈论他们的一天，并尽可能多地使用跟时间相关的词语，比如早上、下午、傍晚、晚上、中午、黎明、黄昏、白天和黑夜。

小贴士　　　　准备更多的卡片，有可能有些活动在一天当中会重复出现。有些孩子的日常生活安排顺序会出乎我们的意料，而给我们带来不少的惊喜。

拓展

- 给这些日常生活确定具体的时间，比如午饭的时间是中午 12 点，睡觉的时间是晚上 7 点。

该活动体现的数学思维

　　了解日常生活的排序和它们的具体时间安排，可以帮助孩子们更有秩序地安排生活。事情的先后顺序安排是一项非常重要的技能，可以帮助解决问题。

第七章

家 与 房 子

引言

　　这一章的很多游戏在室内和室外都能玩。为了很好地进行这些活动，你可以在角色扮演区域设立一个房产中介，还可以去附近走一走探索一下不同的房屋类型。制作兽穴和房屋模型的规模可大可小，所能使用的制作材料也多种多样。

别人的家

孩子们会发现，了解别人家房子的建造方式是十分有趣的。

教学目标

- 谈论形状。

所需材料

非传统英式的房屋图片（比如圆顶冰屋，圆锥帐篷，泥屋，高跷房屋，树屋以及船屋等）。

准备环节

- 不作要求。

具体步骤

1) 讨论一下附近区域看到的房子都是什么样子的，它们又是怎样被建造的。谈一谈长方形的门、窗和墙。讨论建筑本身，比如它的三角屋顶，它是用什么材料建造的，如矩形棱柱砖。

2) 向孩子们说明接下来你要展示给他们一些其他类型房子的图片。里面有他们认识的吗？鼓励他们讨论对于其他类型的房子他们知道多少。

3) 向孩子们展示图片，讨论一下这些房子是怎样建造以维持稳固的。在这些住房里识别出不同的形状。

小贴士

- 灵活调整以上步骤中的第一步，使它尽可能适用于你所在的地区。
- 在表达二维和三维形状的语言时要示范准确，比如，一个屋顶可以是三角形的，但它本身不是三角形。有了大人的正确示范，再通过仔细的讨论，大部分孩子都能很快地使用恰当的语言。
- 探索一番为什么特定的形状被用在不同的建筑物上。比如，圆顶冰屋是圆顶状的，因为拱形是很牢固的形状。而且圆顶不需要其他结构（比如房梁或是柱子）的支撑。另外，一个圆顶有着最小的可能表面积，它为房子提供了最好的保护性。

拓展

- 让孩子们设计自己的房子并制作房子的模型。讨论一下打算让房子坐落在哪里，打算用什么材料，什么形状来使房子适用于特定的用途。

该活动体现的数学思维

　　在这个活动中孩子们是在探索关于形状是如何在建筑物上运用的，从而使建筑物达到稳固的目的。

一栋奇怪的房子

在这个荒谬的设计活动中尽情发挥你的创造力。

教学目标

- 使用和形状相关的语言。
- 思考不同形状的特性。

所需材料

1）可供选择的不同形状彩纸；

2）A4 纸；

3）胶水。

准备环节

- 你也许会制作出属于你自己的奇怪的房子，展示给孩子们看。

具体步骤

1）和孩子们谈论他们的房子，以及为什么一个物体的形状通常会成为它的特性（比如，为什么门是长方形的?……）。屋子里的物品也纳入讨论（比如，为什么桌子是平的?……）。

2）鼓励孩子们去想象一个奇特的世界，在那里有各种不能使用的房子。比如，一座坐落在山顶的摇摇欲坠的球形房子，一张四方底座的、金字塔形状、睡起来不舒服的床，或是一辆用三棱柱当轮子的滑板车。

3）给孩子们提供一个日常物品作为练习对象，或是让他们自己想一个。（比如，一辆车，一栋房子，一辆自行车，一张桌子，一台电视，一张沙发等）

4）鼓励孩子们和朋友谈一谈他们的作品。他们是怎么做才让作品变得尽可能奇特的？然后在小组内分享答案。

5）将作品的形状摆到一张 A4 纸上，摆好后用胶水粘住。

6）完成后再一次和大家分享。

• 确保孩子们对谈论形状有持续的热情。他们也许会谈到制作的物体所用的材料，但这个活动围绕的重点仍然是可能会用到的形状。

• 你可以将孩子们的设计收集起来，连成一个故事，讲述"形状小姐"或"形状先生"在一个奇特世界度过一天的生活。

拓展

• 用废弃模型代替卡纸形状，制作奇特的物品。

该活动体现的数学思维

孩子们在创造无比奇特的物品时，他们也是在运用自身拥有的关于形状特性的知识。通过自己动手设计某个不能实现用途的物品，他们能进行创造性思考，思考形状的特性，以及为什么我们选用特定的形状来实现特定的功能。

制作兽穴

孩子们超爱制作兽穴，和朋友们、大人在里面玩!

教学目标

- 练习解决问题。
- 学会测量。

所需材料

1）制作兽穴所需要的材料，室内的或室外的；
2）茶杯，水果或饼干，水（或是一套用于角色扮演的茶具和茶品）。

准备环节

- 看看室内或室外，是否有足够大的空间来进行这个活动。

具体步骤

1) 从提供的可利用资源里挑选材料，让孩子们独自制作一个兽穴或者帮他们一起做。
2) 兽穴建好后，给孩子们喝下午茶或给他们一块点心，和他们一起在兽穴里享用。鼓励孩子们在倒水、分点心的时候要分配平均。

小贴士

在兽穴的建造过程中，和孩子们讨论他们的设计以及为什么他们选择这样的方式建造他们的兽穴。帮助他们认识自己所用空间的布局，示范恰当地表达方位的语言，比如"在……下面"，"在……旁边"，"在……上方"，"在……中间"，以及最简单的几何语言像"遮盖，占"，"大的"，"角落"，"顶部"和"边"。在倒水的时候，谈论"快满的"，"满的"，"空的"，"半满的"和"半空的"这些状态用语。

拓展

- 利用已有场所比如温迪屋（Wendy House，供孩子玩耍的游戏室）或室外的草地，和孩子们一起享用下午茶。

该活动体现的数学思维

当孩子们创造他们的兽穴的时候，他们也是在解决与建造相关的问题。举例来说，他们需要考量用什么材料最好，他们用数学的语言彼此交流。而往杯子里倒水的过程，则让孩子们有机会建立与容量相关的概念。之后的食物分享环节涉及等份切分的学习。

正好在我们街头

沿街并排的城市房屋布局，给我们提供很多机会进行有关数字的数学讨论。

教学目标

- 识认数字。
- 学习数字模式。

所需材料

1）一排排房子正门的照片或者图画，每一扇门上都标有清晰的门牌号；

2）画好的一条街道或一块地图，可以在上面摆好房屋模型（可选做）。

准备环节

- 如果是街道场景，一定要在孩子们开始这个活动之前就将其拿出来。确定房屋模型都被牢牢地粘住了，否则孩子们在将其他房子安到正确的地方时可能会不小心碰掉。

具体步骤

1）看房子的照片或图画，我们能在上面看到什么？（门牌号）

2）提问："想一想谁可能住在隔壁呢？哪两座房子相邻，你是怎么知道的？"

3）鼓励孩子们在路的两边，按正确的顺序放置房屋模型。

小贴士

- 这个活动可以关联邮递员和通信等相关主题。可以让孩子们扮演邮局职员，将邮件分类，然后以最快的方式投递到相应的街区房屋里。

- 鼓励孩子们注意开头的数字，沿街看过去时从中指认出看到的任何一种数字模式（比如街道的某一边都是以2、4、6、8和0结尾的数字），还谈一谈奇数和偶数。

拓展

- 一些死胡同里有按数字排序的房子。对于年龄偏小的或认知水平还比较低的孩子，可以鼓励他们沿着从大路叉开来的死胡同摆列房子。

- 你可以提供各种不同的房屋类型，让孩子们在接受挑战中加深对数字的理解。举例来说，可能会出现一家工厂或仓库的门牌号是24—28，因为它在就是路的同一边且有三户的大小。

该活动体现的数学思维

　　这个活动鼓励孩子们注意数字模式。其中一个模式会用到数数，游戏中孩子们边走在街上，边数数。另一模式是学着看街道两旁门牌号的奇偶数。能够识别不同数字的模式，为孩子们之后学习涉及更复杂的数字模式打下基础。这个活动也能帮助他们明白数字是有目的的（如识别一所房子），以及房子的顺序是怎么确定又是怎么排列的，如何使来访的人都能比较容易地找到特定的房子。

我的家

给孩子们一个机会，让他们加深对自己家的理解。

教学目标

- 识认数字并排序。
- 锻炼推理能力。

所需材料

不作要求。

准备环节

- 鼓励孩子们的家长和他们谈论自家的门牌号，朋友家的门牌号，以及邻居们的门牌号，作为正式活动前的一个准备。

具体步骤

1) 提问："你住的房子门牌号是多少？""谁住在你隔壁？"以及"他们家的门牌号是多少？"

2) 提问："你家有几个房间？""在一天中的什么时候，会使用这些房间？"，"如果你饿了，你会去哪里？""你经常在哪里坐下来吃饭？"以及"当你感到累了，你会去哪？"

小贴士

有一些孩子可能不知道自己家的门牌号，那么你可以在活动开始之前查看一下孩子的记录表，帮助他们完成有关门牌号的问题。大多数孩子很可能会不知道他们邻居的门牌号。当孩子们发现邻居家的门牌号或许并不是他们家门牌号前面或后面的数字时，他们可能会大吃一惊！

拓展

- 和孩子们谈论更多一点关于他们生活中的门牌号。"23a"可能会是什么意思？在一排公寓房里的"1/33"又代表什么呢？有哪家没有门牌号吗？或许这些房子会有一个名字，像是"玫瑰小舍"，人们用它来标示自家的房子。

该活动体现的数学思维

在这个活动中孩子们在讨论他们日常环境中很熟悉的数字。他们也能谈论家中每一个特定房间的作用，以及为什么选择这间房间的原因。

墙面装饰已完毕!

这是一次观察家中墙面上重复图案的机会!

教学目标

- 识别重复图案。

所需材料

1）墙纸样品；

2）墙纸边框样品。

准备环节

- 你或许会想准备一组带有重复图案的墙纸或边框样品，孩子们可将其中重复的图案剪下来，粘贴在卡纸板上（或者塑封起来）。这样的话，孩子们就可以在墙纸样品中来回使用。

具体步骤

1）谈一谈人们都是怎样装饰家中墙面的。一些孩子家中会有绘制的墙面，或是墙面上有标题字样（尤其是浴室的墙面），而另一些用的则是墙纸。

2）展示其中一个你收集的墙纸或墙纸边框。让孩子们将他们看到的形容出来，引导他们识别出：墙纸是由重复的图案构成的。

3）孩子们能看明白图案是怎样重复的吗？它沿着纸面滑动了吗（平移）？它被转动了吗（旋转）？又或者被快速翻转了（反射）？如果你准备了一组重复图案墙纸的样品，用它来帮助孩子们描述他们所看到的图案。

4）给孩子们分组，两人一组或更多人一个小组，给他们其他的墙纸样品，鼓励他们弄明白墙纸图案是怎样构成的。

小贴士　墙纸和边框样品可能从装饰店免费获取，选取对孩子们有吸引力的墙纸。由几何形状组成的墙纸比由热门卡通形象组成的墙纸能让孩子们更多地使用数学语言去描述。

拓展

- 当活动的主题是庆祝会或赠送礼物时，选用不同类型的包装纸来替代墙纸。

该活动体现的数学思维

　　孩子们学会在活动中探索几何图形，并用变化几何的初级语言进行描述。他们也开始意识到重复的图案没有尽头，可以一直重复下去。

成为室内设计师

这是一个有趣好玩的后续活动。

教学目标
- 复制重复图案并让图案继续呈现。
- 创造一个重复的图案。

所需材料
1）10 cm × 50 cm 左右的纸条；
2）切成不同形状的海绵或土豆，用于印画；
3）画笔颜料（最多三种颜色）；
4）迷你白板和马克笔，或者便条纸和蜡笔。

准备环节
- 进行"墙面已装饰完毕"活动，为这个活动作准备。

具体步骤

1) 展示给孩子们看一块墙纸，讨论重复图案。
2) 向孩子们（如果你喜欢可以让两个人一组）说明，他们将要设计的图案。
3) 展示海绵或土豆，讨论可以用的形状。
4) 告诉他们能用的颜料是哪几种。
5) 鼓励他们和搭档谈论他们将用什么形状（限制到两到三种，鉴于他们的认知能力）和什么颜色。
6) 让孩子们在迷你白板上或便条纸上记录下他们的想法。
7) 孩子们在小组间分享他们的图案是如何重复的，用到的形状和颜色都要考虑在内。如果有孩子旋转了他们的图案，也要讨论。
8) 一旦图案设计定稿，发给他们大纸条、海绵和颜料，让孩子们创造属于自己的墙纸。
9) 所有的孩子都完成后，问孩子们以下问题："第三个形状是什么形状？""什么时候那个形状又出现了？""再一次出现呢？""第十五个形状会是什么形状？"（确保你选择的序数对应的图案在纸上找不到，所以孩子们需要将之后的图案在头脑里可视化）："这个红方块的前面/后面是什么形状？""你怎么知道下一个形状是黄颜色的？""你的图案中用到的最基本的图案组是什么？"

小贴士

- 在印画的过程中，一边和孩子们谈论他们正在使用的形状，以及他们的图案是如何重复的。
- 在展览的墙纸边框上，让孩子们写下他们是如何制作重复的图案的。
- 可以让孩子们看一段你从一档室内设计节目中截取下来的片段，里面用到了墙纸。
- 对于小一点的孩子，你只是给他们一个图案，让他们接下去。将用到的形状限定在两到三个，颜色一到两种。

拓展

- 孩子们可以自己打印纸张，用来包一本特别的书，制作一件特别的 T 恤或者当作独特的缎带等。

该活动体现的数学思维

孩子们设计制作了自己重复的几何图案。通过向他们提问下一个出现的形状是什么，孩子们能够讨论图案。说明三角形出现在第几个位置时，孩子们将图案和序数词联系在一起（比如第二个，第四个，第六个等等）。另外，在纸上看不到的地方，他们在头脑中将图案可视化。

洋娃娃的房间

在创造的小小世界里进行游戏，总是激发孩子们的想象力。

教学目标

- 使用表示方位的语言。
- 学习如何规划事情的先后顺序。

所需材料

洋娃娃的房子，配套物品齐全。

准备环节

- 不作要求。

具体步骤

在小组的孩子玩洋娃娃的房子的时候，鼓励他们谈论：

1) 洋娃娃在做什么？比如，上楼梯，上床睡觉。

2) 洋娃娃度过了怎样的一天？"这一天洋娃娃都做了什么？"孩子们能按顺序讲出这些事情吗？

3) 为什么洋娃娃在一个特定的房间？提问："现在是洋娃娃的午餐时间吗？""在午饭之前他们要做什么准备？""你能帮助洋娃娃准备好上床睡觉吗？"

小贴士

这个精心组织的游戏活动，要由你示范准确的词汇表达，并且抓住恰当的时机，推动孩子们进一步探索其他的数学概念。

拓展

- 我们要创设更多能吸引孩子的情境如一个农场，超能英雄的基地，或者创设其他的"小小世界"，让孩子们在不同的情境中可以探索学习相同的数学理念。

该活动体现的数学思维

通过小小世界这个游戏，孩子们再现现实生活中的或想象中的事件。通过这一自然的行为，你能够向孩子们示范数学词汇并鼓励他们使用。在这个活动中，使用从表示方位的语言发展到几何概念，规划事件时要考虑与时间相关的概念，将任务和房间联系在一起有利于提升孩子们的解决问题和推理的技能。

第八章

泰迪熊们的野餐

引言

    让孩子们来计划和实施泰迪熊的野餐，是给孩子们一个机会一起合作完成一个项目。你可以从幼儿园里挑选出年长的孩子组成一个小组，为幼儿园所有的孩子去计划和实施野餐计划；也可以让整个班级来安排一天的活动，让孩子的朋友和家长们一起参与。还可以安排摆一些小吃摊，收取少许费用，作为非常有趣的筹集资金的方式。

哪一条毯子是最佳选择?

教学目标

- 锻炼解决问题的能力。
- 学习面积的概念。

所需材料

不同大小的毯子: 一部分是非常小的,如果可以,准备一条或两条非常大的毯子。

准备环节

- 把这些毯子混在一起,然后放进一个非常巨大的盒子里。

具体步骤

1) 和孩子们说明,带毯子去野餐来说是非常重要的,因为我们可以坐在毯子上野餐。

2) 给孩子们看大箱子,并说明没有人能搬动这么大的箱子去野餐,可能盒子里有太多的毯子了。

3) 问孩子们,如果想帮忙准备野餐,可以帮忙挑选一些合适的毯子。

4) 给孩子们一些帮助和提示,让他们知道挑选毯子的标准是什么;或者让孩子自己去探索盒子里的内容,自己找出合适毯子的标准。

5) 在挑选结束后,让孩子们说明挑选这些毯子的原因。

小贴士

- 鼓励孩子思考,每一条毯子上可以座的人数。思考为什么一些毯子(例如那些很长但是很窄的毯子)比那些看起来大的毯子能坐下的人要少。

- 对于孩子们选择这些毯子的原因,保持乐观的心态。当你想说选毯子时应该根据它的实用性,一些孩子却觉得毯子的外观更重要。

拓展

- 一些主题需要孩子们思考一个模型的面积,也需要孩子们学会如何分类。例如,孩子们需要决定用哪张桌子在红鼻子日(Red Nose Day)的午餐时间做促销,或者使用哪张纸来打包大小不同的盒子。

该活动体现的数学思维

用这种方式来探索面积,帮助孩子们思考面积守恒定律。让孩子们理解这样一个概念,形状的面积实际大小和看到形状时在大脑中的映像是有所不同的,这个概念会帮助孩子理解许多生活的实际经验。

什么时候去野餐？

思考什么时间去野餐，会帮助孩子们使用时间词汇去描述时间。

教学目标

• 学习在模拟时钟上画整点。

所需材料

1）钟盘；

2）空白纸或邀请函模板。

准备环节

• 如果需要，准备好邀请函模板。

泰迪熊的邀请函

致：＿＿＿＿＿＿＿＿

地点：户外

日期：6月4日，星期五

时间：＿＿＿＿＿＿

具体步骤

1) 向孩子说明，他们将要邀请他们的一只泰迪熊去参加野餐。

2) 谈论野餐举行的时间（二点整），并给孩子们看模拟钟上的二点整。

3) 鼓励孩子们创造自己的邀请函（或者填写邀请函模板）并在邀请函上画出模拟钟
的二点整图表，让他们的泰迪熊知道二点整是几点。

小贴士

• 所需要的邀请函的数量，取决于孩子们的自信心和写的热情。一些孩
子可能更喜欢画一幅泰迪熊的画。

• 有一些孩子没有泰迪熊，鼓励孩子带上自己选择的玩具，并说明这个
玩具不一定要是泰迪熊。

拓展

• 当孩子们邀请别人来和她们聊天时，要使用时间相关的邀请函，或在将要举行校园开放
日，让孩子们写时间相关的通告。

• 谈论时间的持续性可以帮助孩子意识到时间的流逝。

该活动体现的数学思维

感知时间有两种方式：度过时间和描述时间。在模拟钟上读时间是非常复杂和令人困惑的。例如，模拟钟上显示十二点差十分，但当分针指向八，不代表是十二点差八分钟。每小时的数字都可以从时针上看出来，但是读分钟只能从刻痕中数出来。过了十五分钟也可以说过了一刻钟，但是分针是指在数字 3 上。

筹备和实施野餐计划

野餐的日子来了，让我们一起准备吧！

制作三明治馅料

一项收集数据的任务，确保孩子们在野餐时可以吃上自己喜欢的三明治馅料。

教学目标

- 练习数数。
- 学习处理数据。

所需材料

1）提供三明治馅料的大图片；

2）便签。

准备环节

- 如果你想，可以塑封三明治馅料的图片，在三明治制作的时候可以再使用。
- 在便签条上写上孩子的名字，一个孩子一张便签条。

具体步骤

1) 向孩子们说明，在野餐的那天，他们将制作自己的三明治，这样每个人都可以拿到他们自己喜欢吃的三明治，现在要知道我们需要买多少馅料。

2) 给孩子们看可选择的馅料图片，讨论时要可以清楚地看到图片，让孩子们为他们的三明治选择最喜欢的馅料。

3) 发给孩子们写了他们名字的便签条。

4) 问其中一部分孩子他们最喜欢的馅料，给他们馅料的图片，让他们站在一个指定的区域。一直重复，直到所有的馅料图片都发出去了。

5) 让剩下的孩子们坐在有他们最喜欢的馅料图片的孩子旁边。

6) 拿着馅料图片的孩子，会接过和他坐一起的孩子们带有名字的便签，并把它们贴在图片上。

7) 让各组依次归还图片，并把在白板上整理信息。然后讨论哪种馅料是最受欢迎，哪种是最不受欢迎的，并讨论原因。

8) 提醒孩子，他们在制作自己的三明治时会使用他们已确定好的馅料。

小贴士　　　　鼓励孩子去检查便签条的数量，是不是和他们小组的人数数量一致。

拓展

• 孩子可以自己在便签上写出自己的名字。该项活动在"旅行"这一活动中使用，也可使用象形图、块状图代替。

该活动体现的数学思维

　　孩子们对三明治馅料进行了分类，并且计算出了每种馅料需要的数量。这种处理信息的方式，帮助孩子达成了一项的具体的目标，并且减少了浪费。

如何制作三明治

在野餐的那天，孩子们可以制作自己的三明治了。

教学目标

• 遵循制作步骤。
• 估计数量。

所需材料

1）在食谱卡上写上制作步骤（可标有数字、图解说明）；

2）面包；

3）黄油或酱；

4）馅料；

5）黄油刀；

6）砧板和盘子；

7）馅料图片，上面贴有写着孩子的名字的便签条（来自上个活动）。

准备环节

• 在每个桌子上，准备好器具，面包，黄油和一种馅料以及它的制作步骤。

具体步骤

1) 向孩子们展示怎么根据食谱卡片上的制作步骤来制作三明治：

    1） 平铺好面包；

    2） 在面包上涂好黄油；

    3） 涂抹上果酱（或者是放在桌子上的其他馅料）；

    4） 放上另一片面包片；

    5） 把三明治放在盘子上。

2) 提醒孩子们，放在桌子上的馅料是和坐在这张桌子上的其他同学一起使用的，在使用馅料的时候要注意适量。

3) 确认好每个孩子应该在哪张桌子上完成三明治的制作。

4) 每组依次去洗手。

5) 孩子们开始制作自己的三明治。

6) 让孩子们把三明治放在盘子上，也从馅料图片上拿下写有自己名字的便签条放在盘子上。

小贴士

• 对于有些需要一点其他人帮助的孩子来说，越多的大人出现，意味着越多的帮助可以给到这些孩子。

• 当孩子们跟随标数字的制作步骤制作时，鼓励他们使用第一，第二……等等。

拓展

• 制作吐司时，使用不同的酱来涂抹。

• 为熊爸爸，熊妈妈，熊宝宝的拜访制作粥时，添加不同的麦片。

 该活动体现的数学思维

跟随制作步骤制作，例如菜谱的制作步骤，会帮助孩子们思考序数词（第一，第二，第三……）。孩子们制作三明治时能估计所需的黄油和馅料的使用量。

形状美观的三明治

孩子们喜欢吃那些制作成奇形怪状的三明治。

教学目标

- 练习节约使用面积。
- 说出不同形状的名字。

所需材料

1) 前一个活动中制作的三明治；
2) 准备一些可选择的饼干切割模具。

准备环节

- 如果现在这个活动不是前面那个活动（如何制作三明治）继续的话，那么就制作一些额外的三明治，或面包片吐司，让孩子们去切。

具体步骤

1) 讨论孩子们平常是怎么切三明治的。在白板上画图展示，或用现有的三明治做展示，讨论它的形状（直角三角形，正方形，长方形）。

2) 告诉孩子们今天要使用不同形状的切割模具来制作。

3) 展示给孩子们供他们使用的饼干切割模具，讨论他们要制作的形状。

4) 展示如何安全地使用切割模具（例如，检查锋利的一端贴着面包，放平手掌然后往下推）和最有效率的方式（例如确保摆放切割模具是经过仔细计划的，要避免浪费，并在拿走切割模具前要检查，切割模具是否完全切割了三明治）。

5) 展示一块面包被切割模具在中间切割后，剩余的面包没有办法切出其他形状，或者只能切出小小的形状。

小贴士　　　不要丢弃一些不常见，对孩子来讲名称比较难的形状。例如，下面的形状是一个十二边形，因为他有十二条边。孩子们非常喜欢去学习说出新形状的名字。

• 当孩子们在制作饼干时，该活动同样适用。揉出饼干面团后，在烘烤前切割出不同的形状。

 该活动体现的数学思维

　　孩子们要使用面积守恒定律的知识去判断，把饼干模具放在哪个位置上，可以切出最完美的面包，不会浪费面包。同时，孩子们在切面包的过程中会发现，切割模具的大小和实际切出的面包大小会不一样。

可以打包啦!

终于，可以打包三明治带去野餐啦!

教学目标
• 估算表面积。

所需材料
1) 三明治;
2) 防油纸或普通纸张，用来打包三明治;
3) 小的包包，用来放三明治，方便带去野餐。

准备环节
• 把防油纸切成不同的形状，其中一些形状不能用来打包三明治，因为这些形状太小或太大，太大的形状用来打包三明治是浪费纸张。

具体步骤
1) 把一些被剪裁过的纸放在每张桌子的中央。
2) 鼓励孩子们轮流去挑选备用纸张，选择一张用来打包自己的三明治。
3) 等待中的孩子可以讨论正在挑选的孩子挑选的纸张，讨论纸张是否太大、是否太小，尺寸是否合适。
4) 当孩子们把三明治放到包包里的时候，确保三明治上写着孩子们名字的便利贴还在，每个人一个。

小贴士 可以鼓励孩子们自己去剪裁形状。

拓展

• 将不同尺寸的包装纸和盒子，不同大小的杯子和瓶装水，不同大小的糖衣和饼干进行匹配。

该活动体现的数学思维

估算一个物品的表面积是比较棘手的。这个活动让孩子们练习使用视觉线索去估算。他们练习得越多，他们的估算就会变得越准确。

第九章

双　脚

引言

　　本章节的活动可以作为第 6 章 "关于我的一切" 活动的一部分进行策划和组织，或者是单独进行。除了对于孩子们自己脚的思考，孩子们也还能够探索其他动物的脚并且思考为什么那些脚具有某些特定的特征。在一些文化中，向他人露出脚可能是一种侮辱，所以在实施这些活动之前，请注意了解你班级中的孩子是否有这种情况。

我的脚

孩子们喜欢和其他孩子比较他们的脚。

教学目标

- 比较长度。
- 了解排序。

所需材料

1）空白纸质表格（或者是带有 2cm 大小方格的纸，可自行选择）；
2）蜡笔或者是水彩笔；
3）剪刀。

准备环节

- 如果可以的话让孩子们脱掉鞋靴等，或者如果他们自己想穿着鞋子也可以。

具体步骤

1) 让每一个孩子站在白纸上并且你（或是他们的朋友）围绕着他们的脚画一圈。
2) 孩子们可以剪出他们脚的图案或者把图案留在表格上。
3) 鼓励孩子们用其他方式将他们的脚排序，比如从最长到最短。

小贴士　　当有人围着孩子们的脚画圈的时候，他们可能会觉得有点痒，所以对此富有一些同理心。如果你用带有两厘米大小的方格纸，孩子们可以通过数方块来对比他们脚所占的区域。越小的方块越难准确地计算。

拓展

- 围绕着手或者整个身体画。

该活动体现的数学思维

　　孩子们能够将他们的脚与他人的脚对比。通过活动孩子们知道如果同学 A 的脚比同学 B 的脚要短，同时同学 B 的脚比同学 C 的脚短，由此产生了间接的比较，同学 A 的脚一定比同学 C 的脚要短。这种说法是由皮亚杰提出来的——传递性。它构建了数学中的逻辑推理。

鞋子的尺码

让我们一起来看看我们的鞋码吧!

教学目标

• 在丈量的情景中使用数字。

所需材料

来自知名鞋店的量鞋器一个(可自行选择)。

准备环节

• 不作要求。

具体步骤

1) 让孩子们脱下鞋子,并辨认他们鞋子上的鞋码。

2) 将这些鞋子按鞋码大小排序,提问:"谁穿最大码的鞋?""谁穿中等码的鞋?" "我们有什么办法能知道呢?"(如果有鞋号鼓励孩子们从鞋的数字计算找到中等 大小的鞋子)

3) 讨论鞋码的含义——这意味着最长还是最宽还是说二者皆是呢?提问:"什么是 鞋码?"

小贴士　　　　比如说英式鞋码是字母数字格式米标注的,包含了关于宽度的含义,那 么讨论可能会进行到宽度。

拓展

• 可以讨论一下中国鞋码与英国鞋码的不同之处,老师讲解一下国际鞋码对照表,对于相 同长度各国的鞋码都是多少,让孩子了解其间关系。

该活动体现的数学思维

　　　讨论关于鞋码给了孩子们在另一个环境里讨论数字的机会。当有统一标 准时,鞋码是一个孩子们通常情况很少使用的测量方法。

鞋子的种类

为"角色扮演"的店铺进行鞋子分类

教学目标

• 整理和分类。

所需材料

1）鞋店角色扮演区域；

2）挑选鞋子；

3）鞋盒；

4）在角色扮演区域放置搁板，用于鞋子的展示和存放。

准备环节

• 如果角色扮演区域已提前设置好，则无任何必要准备。

具体步骤

1) 向孩子们解释活动场景：店里刚进了一批新的鞋子，但是和之前的鞋子混在一起了。孩子们能够将它们分类并且将他们按照不同的鞋子类别做标签贴在搁板上吗？

2) 分类进行中和结束后，和孩子们讨论关于他们所做出的决定。可这样提问引导孩子："你将鞋子安排进了哪个组？这里面有哪些鞋子是不适合这个组的吗？你将用它做些什么？你是准备将这些类别的鞋子如何安排在存放区域呢？你正在做什么标签？"

3) 鼓励一些顾客来到店里去评论鞋店里鞋子的摆放。询问："你觉得售货员摆放的鞋子的分类怎么样？如果是你会做出不一样的分类吗？为什么？"

4) 允许孩子们提出他们自己鞋子分类的方法。分类可以包括颜色、实际穿法、季节、采用的材料、喜好和尺码。

拓展

• 任何的物品都是能被分类的，取决于所关注的话题或者是主题。举个例子，当看着《杰克与魔豆》孩子们可能会将种子进行分类，或者是当学习食物的时候孩子们可能会根据食物的类型来分类。

该活动体现的数学思维

　　将物品按照不同的属性进行分类是资源管理中非常重要的一步，对物品进行编号，有助于之后解决更难的计算问题。

试穿鞋子

角色扮演：在商店挑选你的鞋子并且今天就买下它们!

教学目标

- 会使用关于尺码的术语。
- 会识别写下来的金额。
- 会识别硬币和纸币。

所需材料

1）挑选孩子们的鞋子（让所有的孩子都带上他们自己写了名字的鞋子）；

2）来自鞋店的量鞋器（可自行选择）；

3）鞋子的价格标签；

4）用于放置新购买物品的包；

5）玩具纸币；

6）存放钱的抽屉。

准备环节

- 角色扮演区域将会于活动前提前设置好，用价格标签展示孩子们认为鞋子应收取的费用。

具体步骤

1) 鼓励孩子们进入角色扮演的区域。一些孩子是售货员，而另外一些是顾客。

2) 孩子们有的扮演在商店中服务他人的售货员，有的扮演顾客，通过试穿一些鞋子，听一些推荐和关于鞋码的反馈来体验服务。

3) 只要发现了一双合适的鞋子，孩子即可购买那一双鞋。

小贴士　　　　鼓励孩子去运用词汇，比如：鞋码，大，紧，小，宽。

拓展

• 这种类型的活动可以在另外的商店角色扮演区域展开，比如试穿衣服、帽子、或者手套。

该活动体现的数学思维

孩子们在运用数学语言对鞋子的形状和尺码进行说明，将其和他们的脚进行对比。尽管在这个阶段，交换的货币金额是不太现实的，但是孩子们在对他们来说很有意义的情景中运用了数字。

盒子

将鞋子放进和码数及颜色标签匹配的盒子中。

教学目标

- 学习分类。
- 练习逻辑思维。

所需材料

1）挑选一系列多种颜色和款式的鞋子图片（小贴士参考以下标准）。

	第一双	第二双	第三双	第四双	第五双	第六双	第七双	第八双
尺码	成人	成人	成人	成人	儿童	儿童	儿童	儿童
颜色	蓝色	红色 	绿色	黄色	蓝色	红色	绿色	黄色
绑鞋方式	魔术贴	魔术贴	鞋带	鞋带	魔术贴	魔术贴	鞋带	鞋带
适穿季节	夏天	冬天	夏天	冬天	夏天	冬天	夏天	冬天

2）根据鞋子贴上标签的鞋盒（这些"盒子"可能在塑料封皮上贴上标签或者是类似）。
标签样本：

ADULT			

准备环节

- 整理鞋卡（查看在之前"所需材料"板块的小贴士表格）。

具体步骤

1）展示带有标签的鞋盒；

2）鼓励孩子们：a）挑选一个盒子并找到符合鞋子标签上的标准的鞋子；或者b）选择任意一双鞋并且找到他们属于哪一个鞋盒。

小贴士

- 你不必用所有你设计出的标准将盒子贴上标签。
- 如果你正在设计你自己的标准，有逻辑性地去计划鞋子尤其你想要在下一个板块（查看下方"猜猜是谁？"）再次使用同样的鞋卡。

拓展

- 孩子们可能会想要设计符合盒子上标签标准的他们自己的鞋子。将标签塑封后，它们可以作为游戏的一部分被其他的孩子们使用。
- 任何的情景都可以使用，比如说，（虚构的）昆虫可以通过尺寸，背部的图案花色，眼睛的数量，腿的长度等等。设计树，可以通过高度、颜色、叶子的形状等等来思考；设计恐龙可以通过长度、高度和体重，饮食需求等等角度。最重要的是所制定的标准都是要有一定的逻辑性的。

该活动体现的数学思维

孩子们运用逻辑推理去解决问题，他们会判断这个鞋是适用或是不适用于这个标准。

猜猜是谁？

找到这一组中少了哪一双鞋？

教学目标

- 练习逻辑思考。

所需材料

1）上一个活动"盒子"的鞋卡；
2）箱子上面的标签（可自行选择）。

准备环节

- 如果卡片已经做好了，则不用准备更多。

具体步骤

1) 将所有鞋卡正面放置于桌上，保证团队里的人都知道鞋子的属性特质。
2) 两个孩子离开队伍同时剩下的孩子们拿走一张卡片，将剩余的卡片重新排列顺序，这样就不会立马看出牌是从哪里拿的。

3) 当孩子们回来时，他们需要辨认缺失的鞋子的属性（这时鞋盒上的标签上描述的属性就有提示的作用）。

4) 只要鞋子被找到，游戏就从新的一组小朋友重新开始。

小贴士

• 玩这个游戏只能是在孩子们已经玩过"盒子"游戏（上一次活动）一段时间之后。他们需要对于鞋子和他们的属性特点非常熟悉，这个游戏才能顺利完成。

• 你可以先从少量的鞋子开始玩这个游戏。（换言之，如果只使用少量的孩子的鞋子，会使这个游戏变得简单）

拓展

• 同上一个活动"盒子"中的拓展。

该活动体现的数学思维

为了去解决谜题，孩子们必须使用逻辑思考来找到哪一个属性消失了。逻辑思考是解决问题的先决条件，之后才能深入数学的研究。

成双的鞋子

在数鞋子的场景下，教会孩子一次数两只鞋。

教学目标

- 练习一次数两只鞋。
- 运用"一双"来指两只。

所需材料

1）带有数字"1"，"3"，"5"，"7"，"9"，"11"，"13"，"15"，"17"和"19"的卡片并且只用一个颜色，比如：黑色；

2）带有数字"2"，"4"，"6"，"8"，"10"，"12"，"14"，"16"，"18"和"20"的卡片并且只用第二个颜色，比如：红色；

3）准备十双鞋。

准备环节

- 成对地将鞋子排列整齐。

具体步骤

1) 询问孩子们关于鞋子他们发现了什么（具体的回答比如"他们是两只"）。

2) 让孩子们数鞋子的数量（1，2，3，4等等）。

3) 已经数过的鞋子上放置一个数字的卡片。

4) 鼓励孩子们去思考数鞋子的另外一种方式（如两只两只地数）。

5) 一次数两只，让孩子们观察偶数数字卡片，询问孩子们"你们发现了什么？"

6) 重复两只两只地数，当孩子们发现每双鞋的第二只和偶数数字相关联时，开始拿走奇数数字卡片。

7) 在移走奇数数字卡片的过程中，鼓励孩子们思考数字奇偶数属性，并尝试记住不同数字的属性，如1是奇数，2是偶数。

小贴士

- 鼓励孩子去使用术语"一双"来指两只鞋子。
- 孩子们会在认知（自然规律下的）和符号（数字化）中产生连接，因为你将所有鞋子和号码牌放置在一起。
- 孩子们会看到什么样的规律？

拓展

- 延伸并询问，"我有三双鞋，那么我总共有多少只鞋呢？"
- 可以通过数孩子们举起手或者是手的图片，展示五根手指，练习一次数五个。一次数十个可以通过用两只手来实现。一次数三个可以通过用三轮车的图片来实现（数车轮子），并且一次数四个可以通过数动物来实现。（数他们的四条腿）

 该活动体现的数学思维

一次数两个是学习理解二次表格的先决条件。

你看过鞋底吗？

用不同的鞋底创作鞋印图片。

教学目标

- 辨认并讨论其对称性和花色。

所需材料

1) 各式各样的带有有趣和多种花色鞋底的旧靴子和鞋子；

2) 各种颜料和大且浅的托盘将颜料倒入；

3) 用于印花的大的纸张或者硬纸板；

4) 围裙；

5) 旧报纸；

6) 用来清洗鞋底的洗脸盆；

7) 用于弄干洗过鞋底的旧毛巾。

准备环节

- 用报纸或者塑料覆盖地板，从而保持地板的干净。

- 将大纸张固定于地板上。

- 将颜料放于大且浅的托盘中（足够大到能放置靴子的鞋底并浸满颜料）。

具体步骤

1) 和孩子们讨论他们能看见和感受到的鞋底的花色图案。他们能发现不同种类的鞋子会具有不同种类的鞋底吗？（比如说一只靴子与拖鞋相比可能会有更薄的鞋底和更深的鞋槽，而拖鞋底会更窄和更平整光滑）

2) 让孩子们用不同的颜色和鞋子去创造一幅图画。告诉他们，不同的鞋印可以创造出不同的图案，并让孩子们用不同的颜色和鞋印去作为他们图画中的元素。

3) 展示给孩子们如何能够用鞋底进行印花，辨别出涂有相同颜色颜料的鞋底分别在图画的哪边，并且展示给他们如果他们想要改变颜色应该如何清理鞋底的印花。

4) 孩子们可以先设计他们的图画，或者他们可以边想边创造！

小贴士

- 这个活动最好成对地展开或者是分小组围在一张大纸周围。

- 在孩子们着手设计和印制作品时，鼓励他们谈论每个鞋底的图案和纹理。

• 鼓励孩子们去识别平行线、曲线、圆圈、波浪纹和其他的几何图案，例如还有薄的、厚的、长的、短的等等。

拓展

• 根据不同的主题或话题，可以用其他物品来展示不同的纹理。

该活动体现的数学思维

孩子们运用几何语言去形容他们在鞋底所观察到的图案。

第十章

歌　谣

引言

　　儿童喜欢唱歌，这个章节内的歌曲都是与学习数学概念相关的，比如数数和倒着数数，两个两个地数，以及形状和方位语言的探讨。故事和童谣可以拓展孩子们的数学思维，你还会发现故事和童谣的有些内容也是相通的。给孩子一个带有麦克风或耳机的音乐播放器，不停地播放，这能激励他们一起跟唱，甚至能在他人面前进行表演。

1, 2, 3, 4, 5

准备鱼用来数数以及学习左和右。

教学目标
- 练习数到十。
- 分辨左和右。

所需材料
背景音乐（随意）。

准备环节
- 如果你对曲调还不确定，用第一行歌词去网络上搜索歌曲。

具体步骤
1) 一起唱整首歌，边数边用手指展示数字。
2) 唱到最后一句时用右手小手指展示。

歌词
1、2、3、4、5，
有一次我抓到一条鱼，
6、7、8、9、10，
然后我又把它放了
"你为什么把它放了？"
因为它咬了我的手指
"它咬了哪一只手指？"
（它咬了）右手小手指。

小贴士　　确保孩子们是用右手来展示"右手的小手指"。

拓展
- 其他数数的歌曲，例如《老年人》和《海盗之歌》等。

109

该活动体现的数学思维

　　孩子们在活动中练习到数数以及分辨他们的右手小指头。数数能发展成为加法。另外，区别左右对后期发布指令以及听从指令非常重要。

一头大象出来玩儿

大象能帮助我们记住如何数数。

教学目标

- 练习数数。
- 学会使用"＋1"。

所需材料

背景音乐（随意）。

准备环节

- 如果你对曲调还不确定，用第一行歌词去网络上搜索歌曲。

具体步骤

1) 让学生围坐成一个圈。

2) 指定一个孩子来当大象，在圈子中间玩，跳舞，就像在一张蜘蛛网上一样。

3) 唱歌（歌词如下）。

歌词

有一天，一头大象到一张蜘蛛网上玩，他/她觉得特别有趣，所以他/她叫了另一只大象一起玩。

4) 当歌唱到一头大象叫了另一头大象，第一个孩子叫另一个孩子到中间来。

5) 空间允许，尽可能的玩下去。

小贴士

每头大象加入之后都要暂停歌曲，并且数一下现在有多少头大象了。

拓展

- 歌曲进行时，让孩子把大象的照片放在绳子做的蜘蛛网上。你可以写下或展示出数字，来代表蜘蛛网上大象数量。

- 画一张与众不同的卡片来展示更多被叫出来玩的大象，歌词会变成这样，例如：

有一天，六头大象到一张蜘蛛网上玩
他/她们觉得特别有趣所以他/她叫了另外三头大象一起玩。

• 计算出现在蜘蛛网上一共有多少头大象。

该活动体现的数学思维

再叫一头大象代表"＋1"。了解数字"＋1"帮助孩子们更好地理解数数和正向数数的概念，这就是早期的加法。

十个绿色的瓶子

用这个过去特别喜欢的游戏来练习倒着数数。

教学目标

- 练习倒着数数。
- 理解"一次拿走一个"。

所需材料

1）10个绿色的瓶子；

2）背景音乐（随意）。

准备环节

- 如果你对曲调还不确定，用第一行歌词去网络上搜索歌曲。
- 把瓶子放成一排。

具体步骤

1) 开始唱歌（见下面的歌词），当歌唱到一只瓶子不小心掉下，拿走一个瓶子或照片。

2) 一直唱到所有的瓶子都没了。

歌词

十个绿色的瓶子挂在墙上

十个绿色的瓶子挂在墙上

如果一个绿色瓶子不小心掉下

就有九个绿色的瓶子挂在墙上

九个绿色的瓶子挂在墙上

九个绿色的瓶子挂在墙上

如果一个绿色瓶子不小心掉下

就有八个绿色的瓶子挂在墙上

八个绿色的瓶子挂在墙上

八个绿色的瓶子挂在墙上

如果一个……

就有一个绿色的瓶子挂在墙上

一个绿色的瓶子挂在墙上

一个绿色的瓶子挂在墙上
如果一个绿色瓶子不小心掉下
就没有绿色的瓶子挂在墙上

小贴士　　　　　　每次拿走标注最大数字的那个瓶子，这样能展示正确的剩下瓶子的数量。数一下瓶子检查一下。

拓展

• 与这个主题相关的其他东西也能用来代替绿色的瓶子。

• 可选择其他能鼓励孩子们去倒着数的歌曲包括（可通过第一句歌词来搜索）：《五个葡萄干面包》（在烘焙店里……），《五只有斑点的小青蛙》（坐在一个长斑点的木头上……），《五只小鸭子》（有一天去游泳……），《床上的十只小熊》（小熊说"翻身吧"，"翻身吧"……）和《飞碟上的五个小人》（有一天绕着地球飞行……）

该活动体现的数学思维

倒着数数是早期接触减法和理解"减一"的一种方式。

"没有瓶子了"可以帮助孩子们理解倒着数数是可以数到"0"的，即使我们从"1"开始数也可以数到"0"。

十根胖胖的香肠

活动中两个两个倒着数

教学目标

• 学会减 2。

所需材料

背景音乐（随意）。

准备环节

• 如果你对曲调还不确定，用第一行歌词去网络上搜索歌曲。

具体步骤

1) 选十个孩子志愿来当平底锅中煎得嘶嘶响的香肠，让他们站在前面。

2) 开始唱歌（歌词如下）。当歌唱到一根香肠"pop"，第一个孩子原地坐下，唱到另一个香肠"bang"，第二个孩子也坐下。

> **歌词**
> 十根胖胖的香肠在平底锅中嘶嘶作响
> 十根胖胖的香肠在平底锅中嘶嘶作响
> 如果一根 pop，另一根 bang
> 将有八根胖胖的香肠在平底锅中嘶嘶作响
> 八根胖胖的香肠在平底锅中嘶嘶作响……

唱到所有孩子都坐下为止。

小贴士

• 在开始之前确定好香肠"pop"和"bang"的顺序，一旦歌曲开始保持良好的势头。

• 段与段之间给一些时间让孩子们算出盘子上还剩下多少香肠。

• 练习两个两个倒着数。

拓展

• 平底锅中嘶嘶作响的香肠可以变成任一流行的话题，比如天空中飘着的十个气球。

该活动体现的数学思维

　　倒着数数是早期接触减法的一种方式，这首歌可以帮助孩子们理解"减二"的概念。

　　"没有香肠了"可以帮助孩子们理解倒着数数是可以数到"0"的，即使从"1"开始数也可以数到"0"。

我是一个圆

用众所周知的《两只老虎》旋律来唱歌词！

教学目标

- 探索圆的有关性质。

所需材料

圆的或者球形的东西来滚（随意）。

准备环节

- 如果你对曲调还不确定，用歌词"你在睡觉吗，你在睡觉吗，约翰哥哥"去网络上搜索歌曲。

具体步骤

1) 一起唱歌（歌词如下）。
2) 鼓励孩子们能用他们的手指在空中画圆圈，或者用某个圆形的东西滚给小伙伴或在房间里滚。

> **歌词**
> 我是一个圆圈，我是一个圆圈
> 大又圆，大又圆
> 我能滚向你，我能滚向你
> 贴着地面，贴着地面

小贴士　　　如果使用球形的东西，尽可能地选各种类型的东西。

拓展

- 在后面的段落中，用其他东西比如轮子或者球体来代替圆圈。

该活动体现的数学思维

孩子需要知道形状是有相关属性的。通过唱一个圆圈是圆的，他们可以学到圆圈的曲边。通过唱一个球体是圆的，他们可以学到球体的曲面。假设孩子们带了很多不同的东西，要帮助他们去拓展形状的相关属性，而不是仅限于一、两个例子。

渐渐成形的农场

用《麦克唐纳德老人》来帮助我们学习形状。

教学目标

• 用相关属性来描述和识别平面图形。

所需材料

1）一副牌，其中一面画了一种形状；

2）一个足够装得下这些牌的束口袋。

准备环节

• 打乱卡片装在束口袋里。

• 如果你对曲调还不确定，在网上用"麦克唐纳德老人有一个农场"去搜索歌曲名。

具体步骤

1) 选一个孩子从袋子拿出一张卡片，当歌词到口述部分的时候，将它说出来（歌词如下）。

2) 一起唱歌。

歌词

在这个袋子里我有一种形状，让我想想是啥形状？

你愿意帮我找到这个形状是什么吗？

（口述）他有____个角和____条边。

（唱）所以，你知道这个形状是什么了吗？如果你知道就告诉我吧。

3) 给了线索的孩子用"是"或"否"来回答孩子们的猜测。

小贴士

• 用不同的方向和颜色来画卡片上的形状，以此让孩子们知道形状不仅限于它的原始形状。（例如：只有直角三角形才是三角形）。

• 画图形的同时也在卡片上写下形状的名字。

拓展

• 用立体图形的图片让孩子来描述或在袋子里放一个立体图形让孩子们来感受并说出它的性质（角、顶点和面的数量）

该活动体现的数学思维

　　孩子们需要知道形状有很多属性。在唱歌中，孩子们能用到平面几何的词汇，比如角和边。如果玩立体的版本，它们可以用到顶点（锥形的最高点），顶点数和面。

表示方位的语言

很多歌曲可以帮助我们学习使用方位语言。

教学目标

- 使用精确的方位语言。

所需材料

背景音乐（随意）。

准备环节

- 如果你对曲调还不确定，用第一行歌词去网络上搜索歌曲。

具体步骤

1) 用方位语言唱一系列歌曲，包括：

> 伟大的老约克公爵
>
> 他有一万人
>
> 他率领他们到了山顶的
>
> 又让他们走下来
>
> 他们一会儿在上面
>
> 他们一会儿在下面
>
> 当他们在半山腰的时候
>
> 他们不在上面也不在下面
>
>
> 蛋头先生墙上坐
>
> 蛋头先生跌下墙
>
> 所有国王的马儿和士兵
>
> 都没办法把他拼回去
>
>
> 杰克和吉尔上山
>
> 去打水
>
> 杰克一跤摔破头
>
> 吉尔跟着也摔倒
>
> 杰克爬起来

撒腿跑回家
跑到床上包住头
用的是醋和牛皮纸

绕着玫瑰圈起舞
满口袋的花香四溢
阿嚏！阿嚏！
我们都倒下了

2) 歌词唱到方位语言的时候，可以让孩子演出来。

小贴士　　　　记住这些方位语言，你可以跟孩子们一起唱，来重点强调这些词。

拓展

• 看这些经典童谣的视频，或让孩子们用手偶演出来。

该活动体现的数学思维
　　　用方位语言来帮助孩子们建立图形感和空间感，以及他们的几何思维。

第十一章

数学漫步

引言

　　我们学习数学是为了帮助我们理解这个世界，当我们需要探索更远的领域的时候，我们需要数学这一门有趣的学科带着孩子们一起探索。本章是一个开始，在这个的领域里，你会发现不同的数学概念，可以引导孩子们一起探索。如果可以，你也可以选取本章介绍的活动在室内跟你的孩子们一起玩。

越小越好

教学目标

- 用语言描述物品大小。

所需材料

可以供一个孩子或一组孩子使用的小容器。

准备环节

- 室外寻找一条可供孩子收集物品的路线，事先检查路线是否有安全隐患，该路线上是否有足够的物品可以供孩子收集。

具体步骤

1) 给孩子们合适的容器，询问他们："想一想什么样的物体可以小到放进你盒子里？"让孩子们一起讨论分享。

2) 在返回的路上鼓励孩子们寻找五个可以装进盒子里的物品。

3) 在返回路途中，让孩子们互相比较讨论谁收集到的物品是一样的，哪些物品是不一样的。

小贴士　　　确保事先与孩子们讨论过关于健康和安全的问题，以及尊重邻居和生物的必要性。

拓展

- 为成人组提供一个盒子，以便沿途可以引发更多的讨论。

该活动体现的数学思维

　　孩子们视觉上看到的物品可能比盒子要小，所以孩子们把物品放进盒子里的过程是一个持续尝试和纠错的过程。他们在这个体验中会发现事物中的相同和不同之处，他们也会使用例如太大了或是刚刚好这样的词来探索和描述周围的环境。

探索高度

这次散步是鼓励孩子去思考比他们更高或是更矮的物品。

教学目标

- 预测高度。
- 比较不同标准的物品。

所需材料

数码相机。

准备环节

- 事先检查活动路线是否有安全隐患，在该路线上是否有足够的物品可以供孩子拍照记录。

具体步骤

1) 跟孩子们解释你们将一起去寻找比他们高或是矮的物品。
2) 事先预想可能会在沿途看见的物品，将他们记录在板上或是清单上。
3) 在步行途中，让孩子们站在比他们高或是矮的物品旁边并拍照记录下来。
4) 结束后将这些数码照片在交互式白板上展示出来，并让孩子们讨论哪个更高或是更矮。

小贴士　　　　确保事先与孩子们讨论过关于健康和安全的问题，以及尊重邻居和生物的必要性。

拓展

- 打印一些散步过程中拍摄的照片，在另一个活动中鼓励孩子们将更高的和更矮的物品进行分组。鼓励他们去讨论这些物品会以后是会保持这些高度还是会有其他的改变，并分析原因。

该活动体现的数学思维

　　孩子们会使用他们的预测能力，并通过照片的方式直接将他们和相邻的物品进行比较。

发现不同的形状

去发现不同点。

教学目标

- 观察周围环境中不同的形状。

所需材料

将一系列小卡片装进小挂袋里便于孩子们可以挂在脖子上，或者是装进一个便于携带的信封里（一套或是一组卡片装进一个信封里）。

准备环节

- 事先检查活动路线是否有安全隐患，在该路线上是否有足够的满足标准的物品。

具体步骤

1) 在出发前，告诉孩子们查看他们自己包（小挂袋或信封）里卡片上的形状。确保孩子们可以说出相应的形状（例如：球，长方体，圆柱体）。
2) 拍摄孩子们看到的物体。
3) 返回后在白板上展示照片并讨论。

小贴士　　　　确保事先与孩子们讨论过关于健康和安全的问题，以及尊重邻居和生物的必要性。

拓展

- 打印照片并在墙上展示出来，在每日所见的物品旁边将其相应的名称展示出来。
- 准备的挂袋或是信封装的卡片可以包括二维的形状，例如三角形，圆形，长方形，但是要确定孩子知道只是物体的表面被拍摄下来，并不表示该物体是二维的，我们要讨论的是整个立体三维的形状。

该活动体现的数学思维

　　孩子们用他们的视觉去想象和观察周围环境中三维的形状。他们可以用精确的术语去讨论他们的发现，以此来提高数学交流技能。

形状捕捉

每天探索一种形状

教学目标

- 观察环境中被人们使用的形状。

所需材料

不需要。

准备环节

- 事先检查活动路线是否有安全隐患，在路途中能否发现符合标准的物品。

具体步骤

1) 在出发之前告知孩子今天要讨论的是什么形状，比如： 圆形。

2) 在步行途中询问孩子看到了什么样的圆形。

3) 识别这些圆形是否只是一些物体的表面，比如车轮，圆棱镜或是球体。

4) 孩子在返回之后要画出自己看到的形状，然后展示一下今日所学的形状。

 小贴士

- 确保事先已经和孩子们讨论过关于健康和安全的问题，并且不要影响邻居和周边环境。

- 可以每周一个形状甚至是每月一个形状

- 确保给孩子通过不同的方式来展示形状，从而可以扩展他们观察形状，并可以在真实环境中使用。

拓展

- 鼓励孩子将展示的物品带去幼儿园，这样在家和幼儿园都能开展这些活动。

该活动体现的数学思维

孩子们在用他们的视觉去想象和观察周围环境中的三维形状。他们可以用准确的单词去讨论自己的发现，这样可以提高他们的数学交流能力。

色彩

通过取景器观察自然中的美景。

教学目标

- 鉴别颜色。
- 分类颜色。

所需材料

把一张卡片中间挖洞，并涂色；每个孩子三张卡片。

准备环节

- 在打完孔之后可以将卡片过塑以便卡片可以更结实并可以重复使用。
- 事先检查活动路线是否有安全隐患，在路途中能否发现符合标准的物品。

具体步骤

1) 让孩子在沿途发现和自己已有颜色一样的物品。
2) 讨论物品的颜色并拍摄照片。

小贴士

- 通过小洞观察可以帮助孩子鉴定颜色。
- 确保事先与孩子们讨论过关于健康和安全的问题，以及尊重邻居和生物的必要性。

拓展

- 拍摄好的照片可以打印出来贴在墙上，也可以做一个彩虹，或者让孩子们用颜色来给物品分组。

该活动体现的数学思维

尽管形状更多情况下被认为是艺术或者是设计而非数学，但数学中（配比的概念）可以用来调配颜色。每一个物体可以根据特定的颜色来分类。颜色也可以用在科学（园艺学）上。当孩子在看到棱镜在不同角度反射出不同颜色的光时，也可以让孩子们将数学和科学联系在一起。

感受不同质感

在散步时候给孩子提供机会去感受和触碰物品。

教学目标
- 根据不同的质感给物品分类。

所需材料

描述不同质感的词汇卡片或一张词汇列表（可选择）。

准备环节
- 事先检查活动路线是否有安全隐患，在路途中能否发现符合标准的物品。

具体步骤

1) 发现不同质感的物品：光滑，粗糙，冷，柔软，海绵，干燥，等等。
2) 收集起来或是拍照。
3) 返回学校/教室的时候，将物品按照不同质感分类。
4) 展示。

小贴士　　　　　　确保事先与孩子们讨论过关于健康和安全的问题，以及尊重邻居和生物的必要性。

拓展
- 让孩子带来一些有特定质感的物品。

该活动体现的数学思维

孩子们可以根据物品的不同质感进行识别和分类。

第十二章

海　盗

引言

  "海盗"总是孩子们很喜欢的话题。本章的课堂活动中，我们通过"海盗"这样一个主题，将数学思维运用于一些日常开展的活动里。例如，我们在室内或室外都可以让孩子们制作或阅读地图，规模可大可小，取决于有多大的空间可以利用到。你可以将整个教室都变成一个珍宝岛，进行角色扮演，模拟场景，或者在地毯上做一个临时的岛也是可以的。

逼真的珍宝岛

谁能找到宝藏?

教学目标

• 会指路且能听懂他人关于方位的指示。

所需材料

1) 一些能将场景变成珍宝岛的物品(比如: 一些铁环,彩纸,"珍宝");

2) 指示东西南北的标签。

准备环节

• 和孩子们一起做一个珍宝岛。

具体步骤

1) 小朋友坐在珍宝岛上面或围坐在岛四周;

2) 选择其中一个小朋友离开;

3) 剩下的小朋友把珍宝(比如金币)藏在岛上一些物品的下面;

4) 刚刚被叫走的小朋友会根据方位指示去寻找所藏的宝藏。

小贴士　　　　每一次的引导,都要求孩子们尽量使用表示方位的词,比如: 东、南、西、北。

拓展

• 我们可以不用指南针指示方向,而是用距珍宝岛上特定地点所需的步数来表示。

该活动体现的数学思维

该活动能让孩子们先弄清楚周边的空间,之后再用坐标表示。

藏宝图

用 X 标注地点!

教学目标

• 学会如何指路。

所需材料

1）空白地图模板（可选择的）；

2）白纸；

3）铅笔和彩笔。

准备环节

• 可在上一个活动"逼真的珍宝岛"的基础上完成该活动。

• 我们可以在很多有关海盗的书里面找到大量的珍宝图，比如彼得·哈里斯和德博拉·奥尔赖特合著的《夜盗》或是罗素·庞特和克里斯蒂安·福克斯所写的《海盗的故事》。

具体步骤

1）鼓励小朋友去画他们自己的宝藏图，可以是他们熟悉的一座岛屿，也可以是他们自己假想的岛；

2）用×来标注地点——宝藏所在的地方；

3）问孩子们一些问题，比如："在地图上还有什么别的东西呢？"以及"怎么从这个小海湾去藏宝地？"

4）鼓励孩子们说一说他们自己的地图，将图例放在地图上并说明所使用的标识。

小贴士　　　　你可以事先把地图放在凉茶里蘸一下，捞出来拧一拧，这样看起来比较有年代感。

拓展

• 一些别的主题或话题也可以用来制作地图，比如，孩子们也许会愿意用画地图的方式来展示从家到托儿所/学校、公园、亲戚家或当地商店的路线。

该活动体现的数学思维

孩子们都是才刚开始将三维世界转化为二维指示图，并用标识和图例来说明它们的。之后他们会学习其他的标识，也会对地图有更深的了解。孩子们也会说明如何往返于特定的位置，还要能听懂他人关于方位的指示，这需要他们有清晰的逻辑思维能力。

瓶子里的信息

发送藏宝图。

教学目标

- 让小朋友练习如何估算。
- 学会检验结果。

所需材料

一些不同形状大小的干塑料瓶，确保每个小朋友手中不止有一个。

准备环节

- 保证每个小朋友都有足够的塑料瓶。

具体步骤

1) 让孩子们讨论藏宝图一般来说怎样放在瓶中才能避免被海水弄湿。

2) 询问孩子们讨论的结果（比如：将藏宝图卷起来放入瓶中）。

3) 分组后，让他们选择适合各自藏宝图的瓶子。

4) 将藏宝图卷起来，并且尝试着放入瓶中。

5) 如果需要的话，他们可以更换瓶子。

小贴士　　　　在让小朋友检验所选的瓶子是否合适之前，需要先给他们说明为何要选择特定的瓶子。

拓展

- 鼓励孩子们两两合作，这样能更高效地进行估算。

该活动体现的数学思维

孩子们需要想象藏宝图在瓶子里的位置，需要将地图卷起来后的长度与瓶子本身的高度作对比，同时也得根据瓶颈的大小知道该把地图卷多紧。这些都会涉及表面积守恒的相关知识。

小金库

啊哈，我的伙伴们！寻宝之旅是如此的传奇！

教学目标

- 学会如何解决问题。
- 学会分享。

所需材料

1) 一个小金库（可以是一个用金色彩纸包装好并带有盖子的盒子）；

2) 珍宝（一些巧克力金的硬币或一些人造珠宝首饰）；

3) 天平（让孩子们学会用称重的方式进行分享）。

准备环节

- 确保盒子里的珍宝可以平均分配给各个小组中的孩子们。

具体步骤

1) 探索盒子里有什么东西；

2) 问孩子们："里面有多少珍宝？"

3) 问孩子们："我们怎么才能将珍宝平均分配？还有别的方法吗？还有其他的方式吗？"让孩子们讨论分配珍宝的方式，直到"海盗团体"达成一致。

4) 询问孩子们，他们在分配珍宝的过程中是如何得知珍宝的分配是平均的呢。

小贴士　　　对于某些珍宝（比如：巧克力做的硬币），小朋友可以用数一数或称一称的方式来分配。有时候，他们也许需要互相交换手中的珍宝（比如：一条项链可以换两个手镯）。

拓展

- 也可以使用一些别的东西，只要和当下的主题或话题有关就可以。

该活动体现的数学思维

　　孩子们在平均分配的过程中可以增进他们对除法的理解。与此同时，因为珍宝种类繁多，所以对孩子们来说这个任务还是有一定难度的，在活动过程中，他们需要不断运用逻辑思维去解决问题，谈判协商。

一个海盗的调查

这个难解的调查会让你的海盗团绞尽脑汁!

教学目标

- 锻炼逻辑思维和推理能力。
- 学会沟通。
- 锻炼解决问题的能力和调查的能力。

所需材料

1) 需要三套海盗帽、眼罩和弯刀（每一套的颜色都和其余两套不同）;

2) 一些蜡笔、彩色铅笔或水彩笔（三套需要是相同的颜色）;

3) 记录单（可选，要视下方的准备环节而定）。

准备环节

- 鼓励孩子们使用记录单，复印成套的帽子、眼罩和弯刀，可用 A4 纸并印上 8 套。样式
参考:

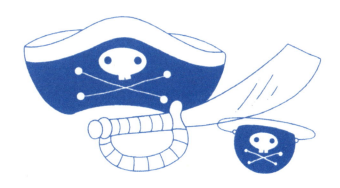

具体步骤

1) 请一个小朋友自愿充当不知如何选择装备的海盗。

2) 向剩余的海盗展示箱子，让他们从里面拿出一顶帽子、一个眼罩和一把弯刀，然后佩戴在身上。

3) 随后，把箱子中剩下的东西拿给大家看，让他们从中选择一个、两个或三个物品来替换他们目前身上佩戴的东西。这样重复多次，直到你认为孩子们都明白了那个海盗可以有很多种搭配方式。

4) 询问孩子们:"对于那个不知怎么选装备的海盗来说，他可以有几种不同的搭配方式?"

5) 两人一组的去探讨这个问题。

6) 学会运用记录单（可以用三种不同的颜色给上面的东西上色），这样能帮助孩子们跟踪讨论进程。

7) 最后，对得出的结果进行讨论，有必要的话，可以让那个有困扰的海盗再把装备穿一遍。

小贴士

• 一旦孩子们觉得他们弄清楚了所有的可能性，可以鼓励他们用缜密的逻辑（系统地）再确认一遍。一个可行的方法就是最开始保持所有物品的颜色相同，然后一次只改变其中一个物品的颜色，然后再改变两个物品的颜色，最后改变三个。

• 对于年龄比较小的孩子们，我们最开始可以先试试只用两套（颜色）。

拓展

• 此活动可以被用于很多主题或话题。比如，与冬天有关的主题中，小朋友可以用三套不同的帽子、围巾和手套来做活动。

该活动体现的数学思维

本调查游戏鼓励孩子们用系统的方式解决问题，确保覆盖所有的可能性。这是孩子们有待养成的一种重要的调研方法。

啊嗨，那里!

建造属于你自己的海盗船。

教学目标

- 理解估算。
- 学会用直接比较来检验估算结果。

所需材料

1）角色扮演的地方或施工的地方；

2）制作海盗船的材料；

3）带有海盗船的图片或书籍。

准备环节

- 为孩子们提供一些建造海盗船的地方。

具体步骤

1) 如果允许的话，让孩子们选择是在角色扮演的地方大家一起建造海盗船还是在施工的地方单独或两人一组来造船。

2) 让孩子们讨论建造一艘海盗船需要哪些东西（比如：旗杆、厚木板、桅杆瞭望台），大家的灵感可以来自图片和书籍。

3) 在建造的过程中，可以问一些问题，比如"我们需要多少厚木板（贴在墙上的纸条）？"或"那里应该用什么形状？"

小贴士　　　　尽可能多地提供各式的海盗船图片，这样孩子们就可以从中找出共同点，并运用于自身海盗船的建造上，同时也避免了千篇一律。

拓展

- 此活动中，角色扮演和建造的地方都可以用于修建其他任何与当下主题或话题相关的建筑。

该活动体现的数学思维

孩子们需要选择所使用的材料，估算所需材料的量，使用这些材料并且检验自己的估算是否合理。如果有必要的话，他们会尝试选另外的材料。这种用"试错法"解决问题的思维会贯穿数学学习的始终。

海盗旗

制作并让海盗旗迎风飘扬。

教学目标

- 认识反射对称。

所需材料

1）A4 纸——全黑和全白的都需要；

2）白色的彩铅；

3）一些剪刀；

4）胶水。

准备环节

- 如果需要的话，要做一个半张海盗旗的模板（如下图）。

具体步骤

将黑色的 A4 纸发给孩子们，让他们将其对折。

让孩子们用白色的铅笔画半边海盗旗，如果需要的话，可以用事先准备的模板。

1) 将头盖骨和十字骨从对折的纸上面剪下来，再剪出眼睛和鼻子，使其脱落。

2) 展开手中的黑色纸面。

3) 把黑色的纸粘在白纸上面。

4) 让海盗旗在海盗船上迎风飘扬或在房间里展示它们。

小贴士

- 让孩子们讨论为什么海盗旗的左右两边看上去是一样的，这与将纸对折又有什么关系。

- 这个活动对孩子们来说有一定的困难，要确保他们身边有足够多的成年人能帮他们一把。

拓展

• 在不同的主题中，我们可以让孩子们剪出不同的对称图形，并将这些图形贴在用以对比的背景上。比如，剪雪花就非常受欢迎，孩子们可以用蓝色的纸剪出雪花，然后贴在白纸上，反之亦然。

 该活动体现的数学思维

　　让孩子们学习一些关于对称性的知识是非常重要的，因为这会帮助他们更好地定义图形。

于我而言，海盗的一生

设计一件海盗的上装

教学目标

• 学会画并持续画出一个循环的图案。

所需材料

1） 一个空白的 T 恤模板（如下图）；

2） 彩铅、蜡笔、颜料或用以裁剪和粘贴的彩纸条。

准备环节

• 选择一些带有海盗上装的图片。

具体步骤

1) 仔细翻看搜集的图片，讨论海盗的上装。问孩子们："你们注意到了什么？"老师需要帮助孩子们意识到海盗上装通常都会出现两种不同颜色交替绘制的条纹。

2) 问孩子们他们是否愿意设计自己的海盗衬衫。

3) 得到肯定回答后，为他们提供一个空白的 T 恤模板以及所需的媒介。

4) 当孩子们在绘图并上色的时候，给他们讲讲衬衫上的循环图案。比如，"接下来你们要用什么颜色呢？为什么是那种颜色？第五个条纹应该是什么颜色呀？你是怎么知道的呢？"

小贴士　　　　一旦孩子们选择了他们所要使用的颜色（通常来说有两种），我们需要将别的颜色拿开，这样他们就不会使用那些原本没打算用于绘制循环图案的颜色了。

拓展

• 有些小朋友也许喜欢设计那种不止有条纹的 T 恤。

• 在小朋友设计好自己的 T 恤后，他们可以用布彩颜料在自己带的旧 T 恤上作画，之后若是遇到海盗扮演日，或需要在海盗船里进行角色扮演之时，就可以直接拿来穿了。

该活动体现的数学思维

数学中处处皆是图案，观察这些图案能帮助孩子们解决问题。能说出接下来是什么，会锻炼孩子们对于形状或颜色以及图案的想象力。运用有序的语言（比如：第一，第二……）能让他们更精确的表达。

第十三章

大　小

引言

　　全方位地学习尺寸与度量之前，我们需要让孩子们先了解物品的大小。每当孩子们找到或做出特别大或特别小的物品，他们都会非常兴奋。我们可以将头顶上方投影仪的光，投射在墙面上一张很大的纸上，这样可以形成很大的影像，孩子们也可以这样做出自己的图片。

排序！排序！

将一些物品按照从小到大的顺序排序。

教学目标
• 按照大小进行排序。

所需材料
一些物品，可以是校区里的任意物品，也可以是与特定主题有关的物件。

准备环节
• 没有固定的要求。

具体步骤

1) 将准备的物品放在桌子上，然后让小朋友去看看都有哪些东西。

2) 让孩子们讨论他们看到了什么，说一说这些物品都有什么特性，看看他们对这些东西了解多少。

3) 问孩子们："桌上最大的东西是哪一个？你是怎么知道的？那最小的又是哪个？为什么这么认为？"

4) 将刚刚孩子们认为最大的和最小的物品拿出来，分别放置在桌子的两端，让孩子们将剩余的物品从小到大放在中间，排成一列。

5) 当孩子们在排序的时候，问问他们是如何做决定的，比如："你是怎么知道这个比那个大的呢？"

小贴士　　　　我们要慎重选择那些代表"大"物件的东西，如果一个玩具大象比一个玩具老鼠更小的话，会令人困扰的！

拓展

• 大小到底意味着什么呢？我们还可以让孩子们按照别的方式来排序，比如：高度、宽度、重量或容积等，随后给孩子们一些材料，让他们检验下自己所估计的是否准确。

该活动体现的数学思维

　　此活动给了孩子们比较不同物品的机会，孩子们会从中学会间接比较，比如，当物品A比物品B小，物品B又比物品C小，那么物品A一定比物品C小。这种特性被皮亚杰命名为传递性，这是数学中许多逻辑论证的依凭。

把东西变大

用放大镜或显微镜能创造许多可能。

教学目标

- 学会利用放大。
- 寻找图样。

所需材料

1）一些小物件，可以是任意搜集的，也可以是与特定主题有关的；

2）一些放大镜；

3）显微镜（可选）。

准备环节

- 将搜集来的物品陈列好。

具体步骤

1）先让小朋友讨论所搜集的物品，问他们："你喜欢哪一个东西啊？为什么喜欢它呢？"

2）用放大镜看这些物品，让孩子们说一说，当他们透过放大镜来看这些东西的时候，有什么不一样的效果吗。

3）问孩子们："你们能看见什么？"让他们描述透过放大镜所看到的物品上的纹案。

小贴士

在之前做过的"材料质地"的活动中，我们曾让孩子们用放大镜观察过物品，他们会发现不同质地的物品表面是有差异的。

拓展

- 用一个影印机或扫描仪来把这些东西变大。

该活动体现的数学思维

此活动能让孩子们对自然形成的纹案有所了解，早在很久以前，数学家们就对此很感兴趣，直到今天，依然有大批数学家和科学家在研究天然纹案。

调查小动物

学习一些户外环境的小知识。

教学目标

- 练习解决问题的能力。
- 寻找纹案。

所需材料

1）寻找一处有丰富昆虫或野生动物的室外场所；

2）进行昆虫观察所需的材料（透明的容器和放大镜）；

3）有关此户外场所中的野生动物的书籍或图片；

4）从宏观层面用以拍照的数码照相机（可选）；

5）用以绘制昆虫草图的纸张和铅笔。

准备环节

- 到户外去调查你可能会发现的生物，需要的话，我们可以把一些潮湿的木头平放在地面的背阴处，这样会引出一些生物，比如木虱之类的。

具体步骤

1）告诉孩子们他们将要去野外探索。

2）将孩子们所需的装备分配好，并让他们讨论这些东西的用途。

3）告诉孩子们要对生命有所敬畏。

4）外出途中，每次只能在容器中放入一只昆虫来放大观察。

5）孩子们观察昆虫的时候要很仔细，数一数它们有多少条腿，找到它们身体的三部分（头部、胸部和腹部）。

6）找一个成年人在活动中拍照，或让孩子们画一些昆虫的素描。

7）记录发现昆虫的地点以及所对应的栖息地的环境。

小贴士

- 我们可以参考下由厄斯伯恩出版社出版，艾玛·赫尔布罗与泰瑞·高尔合著的《需要认识的一千零一种昆虫》。
- 当观察结束后，需要确保生物都被小心地放回它们自己的栖息之处哟。

拓展

- 你们可以去更远的地方，走进鸟类保护区或蝴蝶屋之类的地方。

该活动体现的数学思维

　　昆虫身上有很多花纹，这体现了自然中的数学之美。比如，蝴蝶和瓢虫身上就有能体现对称性的纹路。昆虫总是有六条腿的：三条在身体左边，三条在右边，与此相似的是蜘蛛左右两边各有四条腿，一共有八条。

为野生动物提供一个家园

让更多的野生动物回归大自然的怀抱。

教学目标

- 练习测量。
- 学会分类。

所需材料

为野生动物提供住所、创造家园所需要的材料。

准备环节

　　• 调查并研究那些与你所选的室外环境相匹配的野生动物的家，将大家手头上所有需要的材料整合起来，一同为野生动物创造一个家园。如果可能的话，让孩子们学会做决策。

具体步骤

1) 和孩子们一起来建造庇护所或家园，过程中，孩子们会进行测量、修剪、粘贴以及捶打等活动。

2) 一旦建造好了，我们需要观察野生动物是如何使用它的。（比如：鸟儿在饮食供应站是如何表现的）

3) 可能的话，拍一些动物表现的照片，做好记录。

4) 将成果展示出来。

小贴士　　　　　　美国野生动物保护联盟面向所有的学校和托儿所，发布过一份很实用的清单（可网络搜索），这份清单会告诉我们如何建造一个野生生物栖息地。

拓展

　　• 我们还可以在家园或庇护所内安装照相机，这样就可以用学校或托儿所的电脑进行远程拍摄并观察野生动物在其中的表现了。

该活动体现的数学思维

　　为野生动物制作家园或庇护所的活动会锻炼孩子们的测量能力，当他们了解了更多有关长度的知识后，他们能测量得更准确。一旦在原地建好了家园或庇护所后，在观察野生动物的过程中，孩子们会进行一定的数据处理，也会观察到动物行为中的一些固有模式。

制作一些大的东西

教学目标

- 讨论大，更大和最大！

所需材料

废弃的模型材料，包括对孩子们来说比较大的一些东西。

准备环节

- 确保你准备了足够多的材料能让孩子们开展此次活动。

具体步骤

1) 问孩子们："你所知道的最大的东西是什么？"用这种方式可以开始讨论非常大的物件。

2) 问孩子们，他们是否愿意尽可能地做出一件最大的东西。

3) 找一个空地，室内或内外皆可，让孩子们可以在此处着手建造。

4) 问孩子们："它现在足够大了吗？我们怎么让它变得更大啊？你可以做出的最大的东西是有多大啊？"

5) 在保障安全的前提下，尽可能地做出更大的东西。

小贴士

- 更大的概念和物体的很多物理性质有关，所以你要提供足够多的经验给到孩子们，比如他们需要考虑高度、宽度以及重量。

- 由于做好了的物品随后很快会被拆除，所以孩子们做好了之后，我们要拍照记录，除非你有很大的地方来陈列这些东西。孩子们也会非常享受拆除它们的过程，你可以抓住这个机会，给他们说说小，更小和最小的之间的关系。

拓展

- 不用废弃材料，看看孩子们是否能用建筑材料来制作出最高的塔。孩子们可以使用"混凝纸"① 来让成品更加稳固。

---

① 混凝纸，又名制型纸，指加进胶水等经浆状处理的纸，可以用来做成纸型。——译者注。

该活动体现的数学思维

  用这种方式探索大小能让孩子们对形状和空间有更深的理解，他们甚至会明白什么是无穷，知道空间是无穷无尽的。

第十四章

杰克与魔豆

引言

　　《杰克与魔豆》作为一个一直以来备受人们喜爱的故事，为孩子们提供了很多数学活动。本章中有些活动可能要花费较长的时间才能完成，比如种子的萌芽活动，但有些活动我们可以很快完成。孩子们在完成某些活动的过程中需要对高度和距离进行构想，他们要对脑海中的图像进行处理和加工，从而让他们在整个小学阶段甚至是今后的学习生活中，形成良好的数学思维。

种豆

观察杰克所种豆子的成长情况。

教学目标

- 学会进行测量。
- 练习排序。

所需材料

1) 菜豆种子（任何能向上生长的类型都可以）；
2) 用作种植的一些透明容器（透明的酸奶瓶可以被再回收用作此途）；
3) 一些棉绒或混合肥料；
4) 数码相机（可选）。

准备环节

- 在托儿所或教室里找一处易于观察瓶中豆子生长情况的地方。

具体步骤

1) 将能向上生长的菜豆种子种植在透明容器里，如果你想要孩子们观察菜豆根部的生长情况，你们需要让种子紧贴容器壁。
2) 保持菜豆种子水分充足。
3) 每天都需要观察植物的生长情况，可能的话，你们可以拍照记录种子每日的长势。
4) 拿出拍摄的照片，向大家呈现种子的生长情况。
5) 所拍的照片要按照合适的顺序排序。

小贴士　　豌豆与向日葵也是生长很快的植物，我们也可以用它们来观察。

拓展

- 在植物生长的过程中，可以让孩子们测量豆芽的长度，并将精确到厘米的测量结果记录在表格中。
- 我们也可以用照片来记录一些别的变化，比如一天中阴影的位置。

该活动体现的数学思维

　　我们可以用拍照或别的方式（比如：测量）来记录那些随着时间的推移所产生的变化，明白这一点，能让孩子们学会如何对科学现象进行记录，同时也能让他们对数据处理有更深的理解。

让我们为它弹奏竖琴吧

制作一个竖琴，为能下金蛋的鹅弹奏竖琴，让她下一些金蛋。

教学目标

• 学习关于长度和音高的知识。

所需材料

1) 橡皮筋;

2) 木材;

3) 钉子;

4) 锤子。

准备环节

• 没有固定要求。

具体步骤

1) 沿着基准线，用锤子将一排钉子钉入木料中，然后在每颗钉子上方用锤敲击，一一对应地钉入钉子，需保证每次钉的钉子与下方基准线处的钉子之间的距离是逐渐增大的（具体细节见下面的图示）。

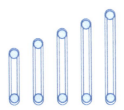

2) 将每一根橡皮筋纵向固定在基准钉与上方对应的钉子上。

3) 弹一弹这个"竖琴"，听听声音是如何随着橡皮筋的长度变化而变的。

4) 讨论下为什么声音会有所改变。

小贴士　　　　　橡皮筋拉伸得越长，音调越高。

拓展

• 除了可以用木材和钉子，我们还可以将橡皮筋用于各种各样、不同大小的塑料容器上。

该活动体现的数学思维

　　音高和谐波与数学中的分数有着紧密的联系，这是对此概念的初步探索方式。

金蛋

帮助杰克和巨人记录金蛋的数量变化。

教学目标

- 练习加法。
- 练习减法。

所需材料

1) 一些金蛋（可以把鸡蛋煮熟后进行喷涂，也可以是用金色纸包装的复活节彩蛋或塑料的玩具蛋）；

2) 一个篮子。

准备环节

- 可能的话，让孩子们重读《杰克与魔豆》的故事，然后围绕鹅下金蛋与杰克偷金蛋的行为进行讨论。

具体步骤

1) 数三枚蛋放入篮子里，告诉孩子们鹅为巨人下了三枚金蛋。

2) 告诉孩子们杰克拿走了两枚金蛋，然后将两枚蛋从篮子里拿出来。

3) 问孩子们："现在巨人的篮子里还剩多少枚金蛋呢？"然后，让他们解释是如何思考得出这个结果的，并确认结果是否正确。

4) 继续这个活动，在篮子里放入一些金蛋，然后拿走一些。

小贴士

- 让孩子们自己说鹅在篮子里下了多少枚金蛋，杰克又偷走了多少枚。这会帮助你评估孩子们在此情境中对数字的理解。
- 所使用的金蛋数量取决于孩子们自身对数字的掌握程度。

拓展

- 除了用篮子，你也可以用鸡蛋的纸板箱来装蛋，这会帮助孩子们在他们更熟悉的语境里对数字的增减进行思考。

该活动体现的数学思维

　　该活动中，孩子们需要对金蛋的增减进行计算，他们需要思考篮子里金蛋的数量，这能锻炼他们的心算能力。

复述《杰克与魔豆》的故事

对发生的事件进行排序。

教学目标

- 学会按照一定的顺序描述发生的事件。
- 学会对给定的事件进行排序。

所需材料

1) 《杰克与魔豆》的故事；

2) 给孩子们一个空白的范本，让他们将故事里发生的主要事件画下来或写下来，或是给他们书中主要事件的图，让他们排序；

3) 可以给孩子们一些提示，比如序号卡或与时间有关的词，作为他们记忆的辅助工具（可选）。

准备环节

- 没有固定的要求。

具体步骤

1) 阅读（或重读）《杰克与魔豆》的故事。

2) 一起讨论故事最开始发生了什么。然后问孩子们："接下来发生了什么呢？"让孩子们讨论，并继续提问直到把整个故事都复述下来。

3) 让孩子们两两一组，互相将故事复述给对方听。让他们学会使用表示顺序的词，比如：首先、第二、第三、接下来、然后以及最后。合适的话，可以将这些能够辅助记忆的词给他们看。

4) 两两复述结束后，将准备好的范本或故事的图片给孩子们，让他们用正确的顺序重组故事。

小贴士　　　若孩子们年龄较小，可以让他们看着书上的图来复述故事。

拓展

- 除了上面提及的重组故事外，我们还可以分小组，让他们进行角色扮演，将故事演出来。

• 除了这个故事外，你们也可以选择别的故事，复述的过程中，孩子们需要尽量去使用表示时间和顺序的语言。

该活动体现的数学思维

　　一些数学任务要求孩子们用特定的顺序一步一步地来寻求解决问题的方法，这个活动能让孩子们思考如何排序，让他们学会使用表示顺序的语言，比如：首先、第二、第三以及一些和时间有关的词汇，比如：接下来、然后和最后。

在豆茎上攀爬

教学目标

• 学会对长度和距离进行思考。

所需材料

没有固定要求。

准备环节

• 可能的话，重读故事《杰克与魔豆》，让孩子们对杰克是如何沿着豆茎爬上爬下的进行讨论。

具体步骤

1) 让孩子们假装自己是杰克，现在要沿着豆茎攀爬了。

2) 对妈妈挥手说拜拜，开始攀爬想象中的豆茎。在开始爬的时候，看向妈妈身后的房子，问："它有多大啊？"（答：很大）。

3) 过一会儿后，问一问有没有人已经觉得累了。向孩子们展示你已经累了，比如：你可以用一只手臂擦擦额头，然后迅速抓住豆茎，以免掉下去。向孩子们说明你的手臂很疼，你的腿也酸了。

4) 和孩子们说，你们是如何沿着豆茎爬了很长一段距离的，你们已经接近巨人的房子了。

5) 问孩子们："这是什么声音？"向他们解释你听到了巨人的声音，你们需要赶紧回家。向下看去，问他们："你们能看见自己的房子吗？从这里看上去它有多大啊？"（它非常得小，小到几乎都要看不见了！）

6) 你又沿着豆茎向下爬，再次往下看去，问孩子们："你们现在能看见什么？""你们的房子现在有多大？"（鼓励他们想出一个和目前所看到的房子大小差不多的东西，比如一只老鼠。）

7) 你沿着假想的豆茎向下爬着，继续让孩子们往下看，并让他们说自己的房子现在看起来有多大。根据孩子们的回答，你需要告诉他们现在距离地面大概有多远。对孩子们之间不同的回答进行比较，告诉他们这个小朋友肯定比另一个小朋友往下爬得快。

165

小贴士　　　　　如果活动的参与者中还有别的成年人，在开始往下爬的时候，他们可以适时地大喊："嘿嘿喝哈！"来鼓舞士气。

拓展

• 当你们上下攀爬的时候，也可以朝上看看是否能瞧见巨人的城堡。

该活动体现的数学思维

　　孩子们在豆茎上进行假想的上下攀爬的时候，他们需要学会对远景进行探索。他们要使距离具象化，并判断距离对远处物体的影响。艺术家们绘制图中远景的时候经常会使用到数学，运动场上的喷绘广告中也会使用到与视角相关的数学知识，这会让这些广告拥有巧妙的设计，从而看起来更立体鲜活。

杰克的一小步，
房外的一大步！

调查巨人的脚印，对巨人加深了解。

教学目标

- 练习如何使大小具象化。
- 练习测量。

所需材料

1) 泥巴、沙子或一些别的能用来做巨人脚印的东西；
2) 来自巨人的信；
3) 如果需要的话，准备带有脚印的模板。

准备环节

- 在孩子们到来之前，用合适的材料在室外做一个巨人的脚印，脚印需要尽可能的大。
- 还需要一些别的成年人，告诉他们需扮演的角色。

具体步骤

1) 你和孩子们正一起做事的时候，找个理由让其他成年人在事先安排好的某个固定时间到外面去。
2) 等他们回来后，他们要表现得非常激动，因为他们看到巨人在外面留下了一个泥泞的脚印，认为巨人正在托儿所或学校附近寻找杰克呢！
3) 和孩子们一同出去看看巨人留下的证据。和孩子们讨论下脚印："这个脚印有多长啊？"可能的话最好测量一下。"这个脚印有多宽啊？所以你们觉得巨人的脚实际上有多大？告诉我他的脚趾可能有多长？"
4) 如果这是他的脚印，让孩子们去想一想巨人大概有多高。小朋友可以找托儿所或学校内的建筑作为参照物，想象一下巨人的高度。

小贴士

- 如果你觉得你自己没信心能很好地勾勒出脚印，你可以用投影仪，将一只鞋子的投影投射在一张很大的卡片上，用它作为你的模板。
- 如果你认为，有些孩子因为觉得一个巨人要走进教学楼里而紧张，不愿意参加这个活动，我们可以使用备用方案——你或者别的成年人发现了一封来自巨人的信，内容如下：

亲爱的孩子们：

我正在寻找杰克，因为我知道是他偷了我的金蛋。恐怕我刚刚在你们的操场留下了一个相当泥泞的脚印，你们的扫把对我来说太小了，我根本用不了，所以我不得不将脚印留在那儿了。

我知道杰克没有和你们在一起，所以我不会再去打扰你们中的任何一人了。我对我的突然拜访感到抱歉，我也想让你们知道我真的是个友好而礼貌的家伙，并不像故事中所说的那样。

在此致以亲切的问候！

巨人叔叔

拓展

• 我们可以在地毯里面用粉笔画一画，保留脚印的部分，使巨人的脚能刚好将其填满。

• 孩子们可以给巨人叔叔回信，说说他们都调查了什么，告诉他他们已经知道了他的身高、脚趾大小以及脚部的长度等信息。

该活动体现的数学思维

用脚的大小得出巨人的身高，这是孩子们对比率与比例概念的初步探索。

第十五章

高　塔

引言

　　本章节与长度和高度紧密相关。如果附近有一座很高的建筑，建筑内有许多台阶直通顶层，你可以带着孩子们爬一爬，数一数你们爬了多少阶台阶。世间有各种各样的高塔，有些在孩子们的成长环境之中，有些则距离他们比较遥远，让他们讨论并思考这些高塔，能让他们对建筑物有更深的理解，这会为他们今后学习几何学打下基础。

高塔比赛

谁的塔更高?

教学目标

• 学习如何间接比较长短。

所需材料

1) 施工设备;

2) 纸胶带;

3) 没有标记的木棍。

准备环节

• 用纸胶带锁定一个空间,孩子们必须在里面修建他们自己的高塔,要确保高塔之间有足够远的距离。

具体步骤

1) 对孩子们宣布,我们要进行一个比赛,孩子们需要用施工工地中的材料修建高塔,看看谁的塔更高。

2) 将孩子们分好组,要带他们到纸胶带围成的地方,告诉他们要在里面修建高塔。

3) 给他们一个限定的时间,让他们开始行动。

4) 在修建高塔的过程中,告诉他们如何修塔,怎样设计才能建得高,或能建成最高的塔。

5) 高塔快修好的时候,让他们讨论哪座塔最高,问他们在不移动塔的前提下,如何才能确定呢。

6) 孩子们需要使用没有标记的棍子,将棍子依次放在每个高塔旁边,在棍子上标记出每座塔的高度,以此来找出最高的塔。

7) 赢的那组,你可以奖励他们一份小礼物。

小贴士　　　　此活动需要大量材料,你可以从别的教室借来一些,同时,你需要想个方式做下标记,这样活动结束后才能将这些借来的东西顺利还回去。

拓展

• 你们也可以每次只让一组修建高塔，修好之后用木棍标出塔的高度。看下一组的孩子们能不能打破这个记录，如此持续进行下去，直到所有的小组都参加了一轮。

• 除此之外，也可以让每个小组都参与修建，大家一同修建一座高塔。

该活动体现的数学思维

在此活动中，孩子们需要对长度的概念进行探索，还要明白一些相关术语的含义，比如：更长。他们要使用木棍进行间接比较从而找出哪座塔最高。这种情况下我们通常会用到间接比较，如果孩子们知道塔 A 比塔 B 高，塔 B 比塔 C 高，那么塔 A 一定比塔 C 高。这便是皮亚杰所称的"传递性"，数学中的许多逻辑论证都要靠它进行下去。

建造一个高塔

将上个活动的竞争性降低后的版本。

教学目标

- 练习对长度的直接比较。

所需材料

1) 各种形状的木块；

2) 准备一些世界闻名的高塔的照片，比如：巴黎的埃菲尔铁塔，迈阿密的自由之塔，德里的古特伯高塔，迪拜的酋长塔。

准备环节

- 研究这些来自世界各地、闻名海外的高塔的照片。

具体步骤

1) 让某个小组合力去修建高塔，看看他们能否建得比组内小朋友的身高还高。

2) 在他们修建高塔的过程中，告诉他们要如何设计，怎样才能确保塔不会倒。让他们想想要用什么样的形状才能尽可能地让高塔稳固，给他们高塔的照片，让他们画出在这些图片上都看到了什么。

小贴士

如果塔的底部粗一些，顶部细一些，这样的塔，会更稳固。

拓展

- 可以使用各种各样的建筑材料。

- 除了修建高塔外，也可以修别的。

该活动体现的数学思维

该活动中，孩子们需要利用他们所掌握的有关形状和空间的知识，建造出比自己还高的塔。整个过程当中，他们会反复试错，学会从错误中吸取教训，这对他们今后养成良好的数学素养也是尤为重要的。

画一个塔

教学目标

- 探索长度与高度之间的关系。

所需材料

1) 又长又窄的纸;
2) 铅笔数支。

准备环节

- 为了让孩子们"建造一个高塔",你搜集了各种高塔的图片,将这些图片展示给孩子们看,让他们思考塔都是什么样的。

具体步骤

1) 给孩子们很多不同长度的纸条,让他们从中选择。
2) 让孩子们在纸条上画出他们自己的高塔,和他们一起讨论塔有多长,多宽。
3) 孩子们画完之后,在墙上将这些塔的图画都展示出来。一起讨论这些塔的高度,然后给它们排序。将这些塔平放在桌子上,这时,它们看起来有什么不同吗?它们是真的变了吗,还是看上去与之前一样?

小贴士　　　　允许孩子们选择不同的维度来进行此活动。比如,他们是想在地板上画,还是想画在钉于墙上的纸上呢?鼓励他们在不同的方向举起所画的纸。

拓展

- 该活动不限于画塔,孩子们可以画人、长颈鹿、花草树木或各种图形,他们也可以在长纸条上写下数字。

该活动体现的数学思维

　　对于年龄较小的孩子们,他们可能很难理解,将物体从水平面变成垂直面其实物体本身并没有发生改变,反之亦然。让孩子们将自己的画作或纸张任意摆弄,这能使他们对长度守恒的概念有一定的理解。

对于塔的思考

我们为什么需要高塔？

教学目标

- 让孩子们理解高层建筑的用途。

所需材料

一些高塔的照片，可以是在当地拍摄的，也可以是到远处拍摄的。

准备环节

- 孩子们手中已经有很多正在使用的图片了，我们再在附近拍一些高塔的图，将这些图片放在一起。

具体步骤

1) 和孩子们讲一讲他们周围那些熟悉的高塔，在准备好的照片库中找出他们正在讨论的高塔，让剩下的孩子们也能更好地参与进来。

2) 向他们展示其他的高塔，问：“这些高塔都是用来做什么的呢？”

3) 在讨论过单个的塔后，让孩子们试着说出一些高塔的共通之处。例如，这些高塔作为居住场所或办公大楼，只用占据有限的地面空间就可以让很多人在里面居住或工作。有些高塔（比如：架线塔）是用来让某些物体（比如：电缆）能安全地远离人群和地面的；还有些别的塔（比如：移动通信基站或航空控制塔），是用来将一些东西（比如：信号或控制器）永久地送入高空的。

小贴士　　　　此活动能让孩子们思考高塔都有哪些不同的用途，这会推翻他们对于高塔用途的固有印象（比如：在《长发公主》里的魔塔形象）。

拓展

- 还可以让孩子们说一说历史上的塔，比如灯塔和电视信号发射塔。

该活动体现的数学思维

　　此活动，不仅能让孩子们了解一些数学事实，也使他们明白数学概念是如何运用于现实生活中的。让数学的学习更有意义，同时也向他们展示了数学在生活中是如何发挥作用的。

要很高

你可以有多高？

教学目标

- 让自己变得很高、更高、最高。

所需材料

不作要求。

准备环节

- 不作要求。

具体步骤

1) 问孩子们："你们能像一座塔那样伸高么？做给我看。"
2) 让孩子们模仿他们知道的高个动物（比如：长颈鹿、大羊驼或大象），在房间里走动。
3) 问孩子们："为什么这些动物需要长得很高呢？"

小贴士

这些动物比我们高，但是他们的移动方式是不同的。还有些生物长有翅膀，因而可以飞到空中捕食，同时也可以更好地保护自己。

拓展

- 孩子们可以通过模仿动物移动的方式去探索别的内容，比如速度或敏捷性。

该活动体现的数学思维

此活动中，孩子们对高度进行了探索，同时，明白了一些与测量、形状和空间有关的概念，这为他们今后形成更复杂的几何学思维打下了基础。

把她关在塔里面

用动画电影来探索并想象螺旋形和高度。

教学目标

- 将高度和形状联系在一起。

所需材料

一个剪辑好了的动画电影,电影里面有一个漂亮姑娘(也可以是公主或类似的人物)被关在一座高塔里。

准备环节

- 不作要求。

具体步骤

1) 放映准备好的动画电影。

2) 讨论:"你觉得这个女孩因为什么被关在塔里了?"(由于一些无法理解的原因。)

3) "怎样才能进到位于塔顶的房间里呢?"(通过一个旋转阶梯。)

4) "为什么要修旋转阶梯呢?"(因为如果楼梯不是旋转着上升的话就太陡了。)

5) "还有别的路线能让女孩逃走么?"

小贴士　　　　　　向孩子们展示别的影像剪辑,用来和刚刚放映的作对比。

拓展

- 想出的逃跑路线要尽量有新意,哪些逃跑路线是最有创意的呢?为什么?

该活动体现的数学思维

孩子们需要在一座圆锥状的塔里想象出一个螺旋形。从数学角度来讲,如果塔不是越向上越窄而是圆柱体,学术上来说它的楼梯就是一个螺旋,但是我们也别太吹毛求疵了!该活动,让孩子们明白了一些与测量、形状和空间有关的概念,这为他们今后形成更复杂的几何学思维打下了基础。

第十六章

咖 啡 馆

引言

　　本章的活动要在较大的空间内才能开展，比如学校大厅、室外空地或在角色扮演的场所设置出一个咖啡馆。该活动可以让所有的孩子们一起参加，让他们扮演不同的角色，比如服务员、厨师或顾客。或者，孩子们可以轮流扮演不同的角色。在活动之前，你可以先带他们去参观当地的咖啡馆，然后在学校或托儿所里，让他们布置出自己的咖啡馆。他们也可以邀请爸爸妈妈或其他班级的孩子们来参加咖啡馆的活动哟。

那些桌子

将房间变成一个咖啡馆。

教学目标

- 练习——对应关系。
- 两个两个或五个五个地数数。

所需材料

1) 教室里的桌子；
2) 标注桌子所需的编号；
3) 一些椅子。

准备环节

- 将桌子排成咖啡馆内的模样，可能的话可以找一些孩子们来帮忙。和孩子们讨论他们想要将桌子排成什么样子。

具体步骤

1) 将桌子排好，一个桌子坐两个人或五个人——这样孩子们就可以两个两个或五个五个地数人头数，算出咖啡馆里有多少人。
2) 在每个桌子上面放上桌号，这样点餐和下单会更方便（见下方的活动）。
3) 每套餐桌上应该放些什么呢？勺子、一些餐具垫、餐巾？一旦做好决定，让他们在自己要坐的位置上摆好盘碟。

小贴士 带孩子们去当地的咖啡馆，让他们看看馆内的桌子都是如何摆放的，也可以让他们观察咖啡馆内都发生了什么。

拓展

- 你们可以在玩偶之家、餐厅或家中能进行角色扮演的地方摆放桌椅，也可以于午餐时间在饭厅或吃饭的地方进行活动。

该活动体现的数学思维

　　让孩子们掌握一一对应关系是非常重要的，这需要他们找出两个或多个物体之间的联系。例如，在本活动中，他们需要知道每个小朋友要有一把叉子、一把刀、一个勺子以及一个平底玻璃杯。在今后的数学学习中，除了一一对应关系外，他们还会继续学习别的关系。我们可以用这些数学关系解决问题，进行数据分析，学习代数以及处理一些别的任务。

服务员，我想要点餐，谢谢！

在咖啡馆点餐。

教学目标

- 识别并理解价目表中的数字。

所需材料

1）咖啡馆的菜单；
2）钱币（可以是玩具钱币也可以是真的钱币）。

准备环节

- 事先可以让孩子们制作菜单。
- 给孩子们一些钱币，让他们在咖啡馆内使用。

具体步骤

将孩子们分成两两一组，给他们看菜单和上面所列食物的价格，他们要相互讨论要点什么，然后讨论食物的价格以及他们要花多少钱。

小贴士

你需要和孩子们先讨论下菜单，如果他们并不知道如何制作菜单，可以用一些食物的图片来帮助他们更好的理解，也可以向他们展示所需硬币的数量以及这些数字所表示的价值。

拓展

- 日常生活中的很多情景下，我们都会进行点餐和付款，角色扮演的场所为孩子们提供了一个完美的机会，让他们能对此进行练习。这些场所可以是卖炸鱼和薯条的店、中餐外卖店、印度餐厅、面包店、法式蛋糕店、馅儿饼店或肉店。

该活动体现的数学思维

孩子们需要识别并说出不同硬币的面额，当我们真正进入无现金交易的社会时，任何物品都是用银行卡或别的方式进行支付的，因而，让孩子们尽快明白金钱的价值是非常重要的。

请问您现在要点餐吗?

继续在咖啡店中进行此活动。

教学目标
- 学会写数字。

所需材料
1) 一些铅笔和笔记本;
2) 为每个服务员(男服务员和女服务员)准备角色扮演所需的服饰。

准备环节
- 如果之前的两个活动都进行了的话,此活动没有别的要求。

具体步骤
1) 给服务员们说清楚他们要做些什么,其中包括:
a. 记录桌子的编号
b. 点餐
c. 把账单留给客人
d. 收钱
2) 在成人的帮助下,派服务员们到客人跟前去。

小贴士　　　　如果你将菜单上的每样食物都标上了编号,服务员们就只用写下对应的数字,而不用把食物的名字都记下来了。

拓展
- 你们之前所列出的任何地方都可以进行点餐,诸如下面这些角色扮演所需的场景: 卖炸鱼和薯条的店、中餐外卖店、印度餐厅、面包店、法式蛋糕店、馅儿饼店或肉店。
- 在这些地方,你们还可以通过电话来点餐。这样,当顾客走进餐馆的时候,他们所点的食物已经准备好了,正等着被打包带走呢。

该活动体现的数学思维

此活动中,孩子们需要使用数学来记录信息。例如,他们需要记录餐桌号以及菜单上的食物名称或其对应的数字。在日常生活中,学会运用数学知识来解决问题是非常重要的一种能力,孩子们的这种能力今后还有待提高。

混合饮料

做出美味的果汁饮料，在咖啡店里喝。

教学目标

- 练习数数。
- 使用比率。
- 学习有关容积的知识。

所需材料

1) 新鲜的水果浓缩液；
2) 有柄有嘴的壶；
3) 一些杯子或平底玻璃杯；
4) 饮用水。

准备环节

- 翻出孩子们的病例，看看他们有无过敏史，确保所有的孩子们都可以参与该活动。

具体步骤

1) 需要制作饮料，呈送给顾客。
2) 让大家一起读一读果汁饮料上的标签。"每一份浓缩液中添加六份水"是什么意思呢？
3) 让他们进行讨论："这个壶能装多少？"让孩子们数一数这个壶能装多少杯水。先从第一份浓缩液开始，将它加入壶中，然后再加入六份"饮用水"。随后，让他们讨论是否还有足够的空间再装七份液体，如果够的话，继续向壶中倒入液体，直到加满为止。

小贴士　　　　请仔细思考：在该活动中，我们是用什么来算作"一份"的。我们不仅仅可以用杯子，其他的干净容器也是可以的哟。试着找一些小容积的容器，以便孩子们能多次反复地进行操作。

拓展

- 根据菜谱，可以制作水果鸡尾酒。以"鲜橙柠檬风味"为例，需要五份橙汁、一份柠檬汁以及三份柠檬水。

我要那个玻璃杯

玻璃杯的大小有一定的迷惑性哟。

教学目标

- 明白容积守恒。
- 检验结果的精确度。

所需材料

准备一些平底玻璃杯（大概六个），杯中液体的量需有所不同。

准备环节

- 与剩下的杯子相比，你们需要确保有两三个平底玻璃杯中装的液体比看上去的少。

具体步骤

1) 告诉孩子们，他们可以选择任何一个杯子来喝自己喜欢的饮料。

2) 让他们讨论要选哪个，并说出选择的原因。

3) 我们需要注意，有哪些孩子们选择了那个能装得最多的杯子。问他们："你们是怎么知道那个杯子是能装得最多的啊？我们又如何才能验证呢？"（在这一步不要去验证。）

4) 让孩子们将杯子的容积从大到小，进行排序，看看他们是否能够完成。

5) 在他们讨论的过程中，需要的话，让他们进行思考。例如，如果他们在排序的过程中只是注意到了杯子的高度，我们可以指出那个高的杯子非常细，但是另一个矮的杯子却很粗。

6) 当他们完成排序后，问问他们要如何验证自己的排序是否正确。

7) 让孩子们用自己的方式来验证，如果其中有什么错误的话，让他们自己讨论错误的原因。

小贴士　　　　有的小朋友选择杯子的时候，会选择他们觉得好看的而不是根据大小来选的，这样选择也是可以的。但是，该活动中我们要注意的是谁选了最大容积的杯子，看看这个小朋友有什么回应。

拓展

• 我们还可以用瓶子来研究容积守恒。不同大小和重量的包裹也可以用来让孩子们研究重量守恒，比如一些很小但非常重的包裹和一两个较大但很轻的包裹。

该活动体现的数学思维

容积守恒的概念对于孩子们来说理解起来有一定的难度，因为我们会被物体所呈现的视觉效果所影响，与物体的容积相比，我们通常只会注意到物体的高度。在活动中，孩子们会有很多机会来探索物体的容积，这些体验能让他们对容积守恒有更深的理解。

装饰饼干

你想在自己的饼干上弄什么样的图案呢?

教学目标

• 制作图案并让它循环出现。

所需材料

1) 饼干数片;

2) 白色糖衣;

3) 糖霜笔;

4) 糖果;

5) 巧克力碎屑。

准备环节

• 孩子们可以事先自己做好饼干或从商店里购买一些饼干。

具体步骤

1) 将饼干上涂满白色糖衣。

2) 用糖果、巧克力碎屑或糖霜笔来设计图案。

小贴士　　　　　　需要准备各种形状的饼干,比起长方形的饼干,圆形的可以让孩子们在上面用更多的对称线设计出对称图案。

拓展

• 可以根据所需的主题将饼干冰镇，也可以自己做饼干，这样孩子们装饰的时候就能有更多的形状可以选择，比如星形。

 该活动体现的数学思维

数学学习的过程中，我们经常会遇见不同数量和形状的图案。学会看图能帮助孩子们解决问题。能够说出接下来是什么，会帮他们使形状、颜色和图案具象化。运用有序的语言（比如：第一、第二等）会让他们说话更准确。

展示你的饼干

在附赠式有奖销售中，我们如何"炫耀"这些饼干？

教学目标

• 了解图案。

所需材料

1) 蛋糕盘——一种选择；

2) 数码相机（可选）。

准备环节

• 没有固定要求。

具体步骤

1) 问孩子们，要卖得多，该如何陈列这些饼干呢。

2) 他们可以将饼干放在一个分层的蛋糕台上，如果这样的话，陈列需要有逻辑性么？（每一层可以放置不同数量的饼干，或将相似的饼干放在一起，也可以把不同的饼干交替放置……）

3) 孩子们可以给饼干拍照，然后展示这些照片。

 小贴士　　　请让孩子们自行决定，他们的创意可能会使你惊讶哟。

拓展

• 还可以把这些饼干挂在圣诞树上。

该活动体现的数学思维

　　该活动中，孩子们需要在饼干上设计出自己的图案，他们需要运用一定的逻辑思维才能完成此任务。在他们的数学学习过程中，设计图案与逻辑思维都是很重要的能力，都将有助于他们完成今后的数学任务。

第十七章

有趣的数字

引言

　　本章的教学活动中，孩子们会学习有关数字的知识。他们会在各种各样的情景下研究数字，会看到用不同方式表示的数字。我们也会让孩子们对一些较大的数字进行思考，他们看到或读出这些数字（比如：100 或 1 000）的时候，会很激动的！

空中的指尖数字

写出数字，只需要你的食指。

教学目标
- 读出并写出数字。

所需材料

不作要求。

准备环节
- 不作要求。

具体步骤

让孩子们用他们的食指在空中写出数字，注意动作幅度要大哟。

小贴士　　　　孩子们喜欢写与他们自身有关的数字，比如他们的年龄、明年几岁、他们的房间号码，等等。

拓展
- 孩子们可以拿着绑有丝带的短棍子，然后用棍子的尖端在空中写数字。

该活动体现的数学思维

小朋友能学习如何写数字符号。

在你指尖的其他数字

该活动会使用许多不同的材料，在指尖创造出数字。

教学目标
- 读出并写出数字。

所需材料

1) 颜料；

2) 剃须泡沫；

3) 沙子；

4) 托盘。

准备环节

- 将每样材料倒入他们自己的托盘内，颜料只需非常薄的一层。

具体步骤

1) 用剃须泡沫、颜料或沙子来写数字。

2) 让孩子们跟着你写。

3) 让他们写某些特定的数字或问他们想写什么数字。

4) 用手将剃须泡沫复原，或是晃动装有颜料或沙子的托盘，让一切回到初始，重新开始写数字。

小贴士

- 剃须泡沫给孩子们提供了一种稍有不同的书写材质，让他们可以好好探索。

- 除了让孩子们写数字外，还要问他们有关这些数字，他们都知道些什么。比如，它是你的年龄吗？妈妈的年龄吗？接下来你准备写什么数字？再接下来呢？

拓展

- 胶水、闪光剂或聚乙烯醇以及毛线或细绳都可以给孩子们提供不同的书写材质哟。

- 还可以尝试对着镜面呼气，然后用手指在镜子上凝结的水汽中写数字。

该活动体现的数学思维

小朋友能学习如何写数字符号。

彩泥中的数字游戏

做很多条小蛇，然后将它们都变成数字吧。

教学目标

• 读出并写出数字。

所需材料

彩泥。

准备环节

• 允许的话，自己制作彩泥。如果你还没找到制作方法，这有一个你可以借鉴：

纯面粉 250g，盐 50g，水 140ml，食用油 1—2 大勺，还可以准备几滴食用色素。

在一个大碗里将面粉和盐搅和在一起，然后加入水和食用油。揉面直至面团变得光滑而且不黏手（需要的话，可以再加点儿面粉和水）。加入食用色素，继续揉面直到颜色混合均匀。随后，将其放入一个塑料袋中，置于冰箱冷冻。

具体步骤

1) 让孩子们用手滚揉彩泥，把其做成"蛇"状（又长又瘦，像香肠一样的形状）。

2) 用"蛇"状的彩泥制作出他们熟悉的数字。

3) 以组为单位，看看每个小组能不能将一到十的数字都做出来。

4) 已经做出来的数字能否被用来做他们知道的别的数字呢？

5) 他们目前所知道的最大的数字是多少？

小贴士　　　可以指定一个他们正在学的数字，让他们用彩泥将同一个数字做成大小不一的版本，这会让他们记住这个数字长什么样子，因为在制作的过程中会反复重复。

拓展

• 孩子们可以用彩泥字母做出他们的名字。

 该活动体现的数学思维

孩子们会学习认读和构造数字。

条状物品所做的数字

让我们开始粘贴吧！

教学目标

• 读出并写出数字。

所需材料

1) 胶棒或工艺胶；

2) 细绳或毛线；

3) 卡或厚的纸张。

准备环节

• 不作要求。

具体步骤

1) 让孩子们用胶水"画出"一个数字。

2) 把毛线或细绳放在胶水所画的数字上面。

3) 展示给他人看。

小贴士　　　　在任务完成的过程中，和孩子们说说他们所画的数字，比如："这个数字是怎么做出来的啊？你会在哪儿看到这个数字呢？你数数的时候，发现这个数字是在几和几之间的啊？你可以告诉我一个比它更大的数字吗？你可以告诉我一个比它更小的数字吗？"

拓展

• 用胶水画出数字后，孩子们也可以在上方撒上闪光剂。

该活动体现的数学思维

　　孩子们会学习认读和构造数字，同时，他们还要和同龄人以及成年人分享对于这些数字的看法。

做出大数字

用整个身体来做出数字。

教学目标

• 读出并写出数字。

所需材料

1）较大的空地，比如大厅；

2）一些写有"1"至"10"的 A4 纸，数张。

准备环节

• 不作要求。

具体步骤

1）让一个小组的小朋友躺在地上，让他们的同龄人将他们摆弄成一个数字的形状。

2）重复做出多个数字。讲一讲哪些数字的长相是比较像的，并说一说为什么。

小贴士　　　　　对着地上做动作的孩子们拍照，这样他们之后也可以看到自己做的数字的成品。

拓展

• 让他们做出较大的数字，或让每个组的孩子们自己决定并做出数字，这样每次就会有更多的学生参与进来。

该活动体现的数学思维

此活动能让孩子们识别数字是何处相似、何处不同，这能帮助他们说出大家所犯的共同错误，比如：将 5 和 s 写反，把 2 和 5 弄混等。

我会用计算器

让孩子们去玩，去探索。

教学目标

- 读出并写出数字。

所需材料

一些计算器

准备环节

- 不作要求。

具体步骤

1) 给孩子们提供计算器，让他们看看自己能按出什么数字。

2) 如果他们不能读出自己按出的数字，读给他们听。

3) 让他们两两之间进行挑战，看看能否读出对方所按的数字。

小贴士　　　　如果你读出了计算器上那些他们从未听过的数字，他们会非常开心的。比如：23 000 000，464 000，176。

拓展

- 给孩子们一定的时间，让他们自由使用计算器，期间不用给他们引导。给定的时间到点后，让他们互相分享自己都发现了什么。

该活动体现的数学思维

该活动中，孩子们所探索的那些数字，会比他们平时幼儿园或日常活动中接触到的大很多。除此之外，还会引入小数和负数，会让孩子们非常兴奋，他们会想要对这些新的数字有更多的了解。

我们所用的数字

我们一直都在使用数字——大家一起来探索吧!

教学目标

- 认读数字。
- 使用和应用数字。

所需材料

一些照片或图片,上面有日常生活中常见的数字(可参考"具体步骤"的内容)

准备环节

- 如果需要的话,事先可以拍些照片。

具体步骤

1) 分享准备的照片或图片。

2) 和孩子们讨论,他们都是在哪儿看到这些数字的,比如房门号、超市、生日贺卡、骰子,这些数字都是用来做什么的。

3) 讨论下这些数字都是用怎样不同的方式呈现的(骰子是用的点数,纸币的数字中间是用小数点来表示英镑和便士的,路标上的数字非常得大,这样人们才能看清限速多少)。

4) 让孩子们自己举一些例子,说说他们是在哪儿看到这些数字的(比如: 报纸上,父母车牌照上所拓的数字)。

5) 展示他们的数字,以及你自己的。

小贴士　　　　进行此活动的关键是让孩子们谈论他们自己有关数字的经历,他们是在哪儿看到这些数字的,他们又是如何使用这些数字的。

拓展

- 在学习形状以及字母表中的字母时,我们也可以用相同的方式进行研究。

该活动体现的数学思维

　　该活动能让孩子们认识到数字是如何发挥各种作用的，是如何排序、如何构成的，数字让我们的生活变得更便捷、更安全。

第十八章

天 气

引言

　　本章中的很多活动都需要在户外进行，如果室外的
空间有限，相应地，我们可以适当修改活动形式。通过
观察一整年中天气和季节的关系，孩子们能看到大量的
自然模型。你们可以用歌唱或交流的方式，呈现短时间
内的季节变化，也可以用照相机将一整年中不同季节里
孩子们和树木的变化记录下来，然后准备一个小型展示
区，将这些照片陈列一整年，从而向大家展示他们是如
何适应不同天气的。

我们的气象站

让我们来探索下当地的天气吧!

教学目标

- 学会运用不同的度量单位进行测量。

所需材料

1) 剪刀数把;
2) 胶带和蓝丁胶或类似物品;
3) 尺子数把;
4) 纸张;
5) 铅笔数支;
6) 一个研究用的塑料或木头盒子,人可以站在它上面;
7) 白漆;
8) 温度计;
9) 一个笔头;
10) 三个塑料汽水瓶子;
11) 卡片;
12) 编织针;
13) 一些火柴棍;
14) 一个软木塞;
15) 沙子。

准备环节

- 对孩子们的家长宣布,他们即将开始自己建造一个气象站。
- 让他们自愿捐出上面指定的材料。
- 通过专业检索,查询建造气象站的方法:

具体步骤

一起修建一个气象站:

1) 搜集雨水(需使用雨量计);
2) 测量温度(需使用温度计);
3) 显示风向(需使用风向标)。

小贴士

• 每日进行测量，然后将测量结果记录在一张图表中，可以是每天、每周或每月的气象表。

• 除了按照气象局网站上那样制作风向标外，还可以制作一种非常简易的风向袋，只用将薄而轻的丝带系在果蔗的一端就可以了。

拓展

• 活动中也可涉及家庭制作的气压计哟！

该活动体现的数学思维

建造气象站的过程中，孩子们会进行长度测量。当他们开始搜集并整理得来的数据时，他们还会用别的计量单位进行度量，比如用摄氏度衡量温度，根据罗盘的方向判断风向。

风

制作旗子，观察风。

教学目标

- 锻炼逻辑思维。

所需材料

1) 一些果蔗或木棍；
2) 薄的织物；
3) 胶水。

准备环节

- 制作旗子：

a. 从薄的织物上剪下各种形状的面料。

b. 沿着所剪面料的边缘涂上胶水，将织物粘在果蔗上，用手按压，等待一会儿直到胶水完全变干。

具体步骤

1) 看到有风在吹动小草和树叶。
2) 把先前做好的旗子拿到户外。
3) 在室外不同的地方，这些旗子飘的方向是否有所不同？

小贴士 在房屋四周，拿出旗子，将它们放在相同的水平高度上进行实验，这样得出的结果才更准确。

拓展

• 除了做旗子之外，还可以制作风车。

该活动体现的数学思维

该活动中，要弄清为什么旗子在有的地方比另一些地方飘得更高，此时，孩子们需使用逻辑思维才能明白其中的因果关系。

影子

观察一天中的影子是如何变化的。

教学目标

- 学会注意变化。

所需材料

1) 室外整天都有阳光的地方；

2) 户外使用的粉笔；

3) 较大的纸张和签字笔（可选）。

准备环节

- 事先看看天气预报，确保整日都是晴天。

具体步骤

1) 在一天中的不同时间段（比如：上午9点、正午、下午3点），沿着一个小朋友的影子画线。

2) 讨论一天中影子有何变化。

3) 询问变化原因。

小贴士

请记住太阳并没有移动，是地球的自转让影子发生了改变，要避免给孩子们太阳在动的错觉（尽管他们会得出这个错误的概念，因为这就是他们认为自己观察到的结果）。

拓展

- 如果可能的话，将影子画在足够大的纸上面，把纸收好。等到了冬天的时候，再做一次同样的实验。现在影子又有什么不同呢？为什么会有这种差异呢？让孩子们讨论影子的长度、太阳距离地平线的高度，以及在一天之中，太阳是如何在天空中移动的呢？

 该活动体现的数学思维

该活动中，孩子们要讨论影子的长度和方向（角度）是如何变化的。他们需要初步探索地球和太阳之间的关系，在此期间，他们会运用数学知识去解释与许多模式和周期相关的问题。

形成你自己的影子

用一个手电筒或投影仪在墙上形成影子。

教学目标

- 了解运动。
- 了解形状。

所需材料

1) 手电筒或投影仪；
2) 空白墙壁。

准备环节

- 在孩子们来之前，移动投影仪（如果使用一个的话）到固定的位置，确保投影仪的线路是被妥善捆好的。

具体步骤

1) 让孩子们用一个投影仪或手电筒在墙上投射出影子。
2) 问他们：
a. "你们能看见多少根手指/多少个玩具啊？"
b. "你们能让影子快速/缓慢的移动吗？"
c. "你们能把影子弄得更高/更低吗？"
d. "你们能让影子变胖/瘦吗？"
e. "你们能让影子向上跳/向下跳吗？"
f. "你的影子还可以做什么？"

小贴士   在询问他们问题之前，先给他们一定的时间去自行探索。

拓展

- 除此之外，你还可以准备一个浅色的平整被单，然后将一个光源放在后面。

• 孩子们可以用玩儿皮影戏的方式，依照上面的各个问题，让阴影移动。

 该活动体现的数学思维

　　该活动中，孩子们会探索许多数学概念，这些概念主要都与形状和空间有关。在形成各种阴影的过程中，孩子们必须学会在另一个层面上思考，即阴影取决于光源的位置。让阴影变胖或变瘦，会需要孩子们将物体远离或靠近光源，这也要求他们使用不同的平面。

四季

观察全年的天气。

教学目标

• 明白重复的模式。

一整年的变化

马上行动起来吧!

教学目标

• 了解重复的模式。

所需材料

1) 用作头脑风暴的纸;

2) 签字笔;

3) 准备一些照片,照片上面有每个季节里户外活动的人们(可选);

4) 爱玛·汤姆森的《莉莉的愿望》(可选)。

准备环节

• 阅读爱玛·汤姆森的《莉莉的愿望》(可选),这本立体书主要讲了有关布偶娃娃莉莉的故事,莉莉在朋友们的帮助下,将一年之中每个季节里主要发生的事儿都想了一遍,然后知道自己有一岁啦。

具体步骤

1) 和孩子们一起讨论,让他们说一说每个季节,他们都知道些什么。询问他们下面的问题:

a. "树木是怎么变化的?"

b. "你会看见什么花?"

c. "天气是怎么样的?"

d. "你们会穿什么样的衣服呢?"

2) 将他们的回答记录下来,或者让孩子们把自己的想法画在纸上,集思广益。

3) 把四个季节的情况汇总，每个季节的天气有何不同呢？

4) 讨论下季节所致的循环模式。

 小贴士　　　　你们可以每天观察一个不同的季节，或将班级内的学生分成四组，每一组负责一个季节。

拓展

• 在你们思考有关季节的事儿时，可以听一听维瓦尔第的《四季》。

• 还可以看一看生物的月度或季度生命周期。（可登陆下面网址查看： www. ladybird-survey. org/lifecycle. aspx）试着讨论下季节对生物生命周期的影响。

 该活动体现的数学思维

　　数学家们会研究各种各样的模式，有些模式在很短的时间之内就会重复，也有些是要等较长的一段时间才会重复的，比如季节。让孩子们明白有些模式是会循环出现的，这是他们需要懂得的很重要的数学概念之一。

穿越四季的庆祝

看看孩子们一年之中都是怎么过生日的。

教学目标

• 练习逻辑推理能力。

所需材料

孩子们生日聚会的照片（事先让孩子们将照片带来）。

准备环节

- 向家长索要生日聚会的照片。
- 确认下孩子们的生日日期，弄清楚他们的生日是在什么季节。

具体步骤

1) 让孩子们分享自己带来的照片，然后一起讨论他们都是怎么庆生的。让他们不要暴露自己的生日日期。

2) 讨论参加生日聚会的客人们都穿着什么样的衣服，问他们为什么这些孩子们会这样穿。

3) 让别的孩子们说一说这个生日聚会是在什么季节举行的。

4) 和带来照片的小朋友确认他的生日，刚刚别的小朋友说对了吗？

 小贴士 你们也可以说一说聚会所举办的地方（特别是如果它是在夏季的户外举办的话）。要留心不是班上所有的小朋友都有参加生日派对的类似经历的。

拓展

- 你们还可以说一说一年中其他的庆典，或者以其中一个节日的庆典为例（比如： 圣诞节），然后看看澳大利亚或新西兰的人们在不同的季节是如何庆祝它的。

该活动体现的数学思维

当孩子们搜集了所有可用信息（比如： 穿着服饰、派对地点）后，他们要运用逻辑推理来推断派对所举办的时间是一年中的什么季节。在他们今后的数学学习过程中，这种能力会不断得以提升。

第十九章

油　画

引言

　　研究颜色、形状和材质能促进孩子们早期数学的发展，通过油画这种孩子们熟悉的媒介，他们能更好地实现这种发展。这些活动也能帮助他们提升全身运动与精细运动的技能，因为他们需要使用各种各样的绘画材料在不同的表面作画。

你最好的年华里

将三原色按照不同的比例混合，从而形成不同的色调。

教学目标

- 使用比例。

所需材料

1) 颜料——只需要三原色；

2) 搅拌盆数个；

3) 一些茶匙；

4) 糖纸或类似的用来上色的东西。

准备环节

- 你可能需要先做一个范本给孩子们看。

具体步骤

1) 尝试着将不同量的三原色混合在一起，比如：

a. 4 茶匙的黄色和 0 茶匙的红色；

b. 3 茶匙的黄色和 1 茶匙的红色；

c. 2 茶匙的黄色和 2 茶匙的红色；

d. 1 茶匙的黄色和 3 茶匙的红色；

e. 0 茶匙的黄色和 4 茶匙的红色；

2) 讨论不同混合方式所形成的不同色度的橘色（或紫色或绿色，取决于所使用的三原色）。

3) 孩子们可以把如何才能调出他们最爱的颜色的方法写下来，让他们的朋友照着这种混合的方法来做，最后对他们所混合出的颜色进行比较。

小贴士

- 鼓励孩子们，尽量让茶匙的量非常精准，从而得到最佳的色调变化效果。

- 多加使用与比例有关的语言，比如三比一（3:1）。

拓展

- 将一种颜色同白色或黑色混合在一起，从而得出不同的色度。

该活动体现的数学思维

　　将不同的颜料混合在一起，能让孩子们对比率和比例进行探索。该活动中，小朋友要将混合出的颜色作为范本，让他们的朋友照着做，这时，他们会明白精确性在测量的过程中是很重要的。

很大规模的画

要大，要醒目！

教学目标

• 探索形状和空间都很大的地方。

所需材料

1) 足够多的颜料；

2) 一些大刷子、画板和滚筒；

3) 可以在上面作画的大物件（看看"具体步骤"的部分来找灵感）。

准备环节

• 确保有足够大的空间可以完成该活动。

具体步骤

通过绘画探索较大的空间，看看孩子们是否能将下方物品画满：

a. 画架上的画纸

b. 正被变成一个……的大箱子

c. 正被变为一个室外黑板的墙壁（还可以用黑板来继续画画）

d. 角色扮演之时所需的干净桌子

e. 巨大的鹅卵石

小贴士　　　　要放心大胆地思考！鼓励孩子们尽量把物品上的空间都涂满，要富有创意地看待孩子们所画的东西。

拓展

• 可以去别的一些地方作画，比如画廊或当地的中学。

该活动体现的数学思维

体验较大的地方和空间，能让孩子们逐渐对比例系数、放大以及不同的大小有所了解。

微型油画

你们已经思考过有关大和高的情景了，现在来想一想超级小的事物吧。

教学目标

- 探索形状和空间都很小的地方。

所需材料

1) 颜料；

2) 一些小刷子、画板、木棍和滚筒；

3) 一些牙签；

4) 可以在上面作画的小物件（看看"具体步骤"的部分来找灵感）。

准备环节

- 不作要求。

具体步骤

通过绘画探索较小的空间，看看孩子们是否能这样画：

a. 使用一个非常小的画笔

b. 将他们的名字画的尽可能得小

c. 在一张邮票大小的纸上，用一根牙签来画画

小贴士

从小处着眼，使用孩子们能操作的最小的东西，同时还要有创意。

拓展

- 用巧克力在草莓上作画。

该活动体现的数学思维

体验较小的地方和空间，能让孩子们逐渐对比例系数、放大（乘上小于0的系数）以及不同的大小有所了解。

第二十章

农　　场

引言

　　本章中的很多活动需要孩子们使用逻辑思维的技巧，在农场背景下，对事物进行分类和分组。可能的话，你可以带着孩子们去一次农场，这样他们就能看到农民是如何让动物保持健康的，农民会将这些动物分类，让它们待在特定大小的田野里。这些活动虽然只是利用微型世界的模型完成的，但是相应地，它们可以被搬到更大的空间中去，在那里，有的孩子们扮演各种动物，有的孩子们扮演看护这些动物的农民。

建立农场

使用微型世界中的农场模型。

教学目标

- 练习逻辑推理。
- 学习估算。

所需材料

微型世界中的农场模型和动物们。

准备环节

- 不作要求。

具体步骤

1) 让孩子们建立一个农场，留他们自己待一会儿。

2) 然后询问他们："放置动物的最佳场所在哪儿？你们为什么要把谷仓放在那儿？"

3) 让他们讨论所做决定的原因。例如，那些能游泳/需要水的动物是不是要放在池塘边上？那些需要遮蔽物的动物是该在树旁边还是谷仓旁边？让他们讨论动物放置的备选场所，并说明原因。

4) 问他们盒子里大概有多少个特殊的动物。数一数来确认。

5) 问他们，所有的动物待在一个特殊的围栏或农场建筑中，是否合适，并确认。

小贴士　　　　　该活动能让孩子们进一步了解动物和他们的需求。

拓展

- 还可以构建别的微型世界活动场地。

该活动体现的数学思维

　　孩子们建造农场的时候，他们会使用估算的方法。数学中的估算是非常重要的，因为当我们计算的时候，它是一个能检验答案是否合理的绝妙方式。通过试错法，孩子们会使用估算来增进他们对数字和计数的了解。思考备选方案的过程，也会让他们更好地沉淀数学气质。

动物分类

让我们帮农民对动物进行分类吧。

教学目标

- 学习有关整理和分类的知识。

所需材料

1) 微型世界中的农场动物；
2) 做标签的纸（可选）。

准备环节

- 不作要求。

具体步骤

1) 告诉孩子们，这个农民现在决定只饲养一种动物，但是他不清楚应该养什么类型的动物。让孩子们帮他将农场的动物进行分类。

2) 孩子们最开始分类的时候很有可能是按照动物的名字（比如：马）来分的，让孩子们想想还有没有别的分类方式（比如：有四条腿的动物、能飞的动物或能下蛋的动物）。

3) 有没有某种类别，是该农民的所有动物都不属于此类的？（比如：野生热带草原动物和生活在水中的动物）

小贴士　　　　要确保孩子们有足够的空间来整理或重新排列这些动物。你可以给他们提供一些纸，让他们做成不同类别的标签。

拓展

- 孩子们还可以把日常生活中所使用的物品，按照不同的方式进行分类整理哟。分类的时候要有创意，让他们尝试想出一种任何物品都不适合的类别。

该活动体现的数学思维

分类活动能让孩子们学会对数据进行处理，让他们明白数据分类能帮助人们将很大的一个场景变得更容易掌控。有些类别将成为空集（比如：野生热带草原动物），这为孩子们提供了一个机会，让他们能对空集的概念有所了解。

围栏和栅栏

保护动物的安全。

教学目标

- 了解栅栏的长度。
- 了解牧场。

所需材料

微型世界中的动物和修筑栅栏的材料。

准备环节

- 不作要求。

具体步骤

1) 让孩子们在动物的周围修筑栅栏，从而保证动物的安全。

2) 问："你所修建的场地适合多少动物？动物日常所需的东西是不是都放在栅栏里面了？"让他们想一想栅栏里的动物是否会拥挤，栅栏里是否有遮蔽物、食物和水。

小贴士　　　　该活动能让孩子们对动物保护这一话题有所思考。

拓展

- 在教室或幼儿园的不同场所，将一部分场地重新安排用以开展此活动的时候，需要想一想孩子们大概要多大的空间。

该活动体现的数学思维

该活动中，孩子们会对周长（栅栏的长度）和面积（牧场场地）有一个初步的了解，这距他们正式接触相关知识还有一段时日，但他们已经在凭直觉进行运用了。在小学和之后的学习生涯中，这些知识也会进一步得以扩充和丰富。

生命周期

探索动物生命周期中的循环模式。

教学目标

- 识别循环模式。

所需材料

1) 在幼儿园或学校里找一只青蛙或一只蝌蚪，让孩子们对它们的生命周期进行观察；

2) 成套的蝴蝶养殖工具或类似物品。

准备环节

- 如果孩子们要去人们不经常去的自然生态区，那么需要确保他们所去的地方是安全的。

具体步骤

1) 观察一段时间内蝌蚪（或蝴蝶的卵或别的动物）的变化，并讨论他们注意到的变化。

2) 尝试着画出生命周期，将他们所看到的记录下来。

3) 最后，说一说这个生命周期是怎么再次开始的，让它循环出现。

小贴士

- 如果孩子们能接近动物，去观察它们的生命周期，那么该活动就会非常成功。

- 你可以在网上或大型园艺商店买到成套的蝴蝶养殖工具。

拓展

- 如果身边没有饲养的昆虫或动物，你们可以通过网络、书本或图表观察生命周期，用这种方法也可以让孩子们参与进该主题的讨论中来。

该活动体现的数学思维

了解到某些模式是循环的，这是孩子们需要掌握的非常重要的数学概念之一。

第二十一章

聚　　会

引言

　　我们很容易就可以找到一个聚会的理由。比如，幼儿园中有小朋友的祖父母或爸爸妈妈要在一个特别的年龄过生日，或学前班的孩子们都在相近的时间过五岁生日。但是，需要注意的是，有的家庭也许不会像其他人那样，他们对生日或别的事情都不会庆祝，这通常是与宗教信仰有关的。如果你有所疑虑，可以问问小朋友的父母或监护人，看看他们在多大程度上，能让小朋友参与相关活动。

制作包装纸

给你自己的包装纸上色。

教学目标

- 复制并继续绘制重复出现的图案。
- 创造一个重复出现的图案。

所需材料

1) 海绵或绘画用的土豆；

2) 颜料；

3) 数张较大的平整的新闻纸，用作在上面绘图；

4) 小尺寸的纸张（A5 大小），用来设计基本的绘制图案。

准备环节

- 你们可以看一看现存的包装纸，对上面的图案进行讨论，说一说这些图案是如何延续（重复）下去的。问问孩子们，他们是否能发现这些图案是如何循环的？是沿着纸滑动（平移）形成的吗？还是转动（旋转）形成的？又或是翻转（反射）形成的呢？

具体步骤

1) 让孩子们在较小尺寸的纸上，设计出基本的绘制图案。

2) 让他们将这个图案复制在较大的平整新闻纸的一角。

3) 需要的话，帮助他们重复绘制出所设计的图案。

小贴士

- 需要检查孩子们在 A5 纸上所设计的图案是否适合被复制。
- 如果图案最后一次重复绘制的时候，不能在大尺寸的纸上完整呈现的话，也是没关系的。图案是会永远重复下去的，所以，在大尺寸的纸上不应该有空白的"边界区域"。

- 活动进行中，我们要不停地和孩子们强调这些用词，比如：滑动、转动和翻转。

拓展

- 在绘制图案的时候，可以使用这些主题，比如：万圣节，圣诞节或复活节。

 该活动体现的数学思维

该活动中，孩子们要初步学会使用与几何转换有关的语言，探索几何学图案。他们也会开始明白这些图案是永无尽头的，它们会不断重复下去。

包包裹

为了传统的派对游戏，一起准备吧。

教学目标

- 使用与大小相关的词汇。
- 了解表面积。

所需材料

1) 一个已经被包好了的小礼物，这样孩子们就不知道它是什么了；
2) 将数张包装纸堆放起来，最下面的是最大的，最上面的是最小的；
3) 胶带；
4) 数把剪刀。

准备环节

- 确保包裹中的礼物已经被包起来了。

具体步骤

1) 向所有孩子们确认，看看他们是不是都知道如何玩儿传包裹的游戏。
2) 告诉孩子们，现在他们将为之后要玩儿的游戏做准备。
3) 在地上画一个圈，将堆放的包装纸置于地面的圈中。问问孩子们，看到圈中堆放的纸，有什么发现。让他们讨论纸张的大小和堆放的方式，即最大的纸在最下面，最小的纸在最上面，并询问他们是否知道你为什么要这么放。
4) 把包裹传给不同的孩子们，让他们动手将礼物包起来。
5) 说一说包裹的相对大小以及它的变化，可以看到随着包装层数的增加，包裹也在不断变大。

小贴士

- 由于孩子们要自行包装这个包裹，所以要确保礼物足够的小，这样才有较大的空间进行一层一层的包装。
- 有的小朋友可能会比较困惑，因为他们平时主要都是在拆包裹。你也许需要反复强调我们正在为之后的游戏做准备。如果你让他们到你身边来包包裹的话，应该可以消减他们由于传递包裹所带来的困惑。

拓展

• 尽管它看起来不是那么美观，但是用报纸包包裹也可以让孩子们了解相关的概念，同时还能帮助你将之前的废弃用纸回收利用。

该活动体现的数学思维

通过为游戏做准备，孩子们会对逆运算的相关概念有初步了解。最开始很小的东西可以逐渐变大，之后把包裹拆下来的时候它又会逐渐变小。这便是加法和减法、乘法和除法互为逆运算的根本。除此之外，他们还会对表面积的概念进行初步探索，在活动的过程中，他们会注意到随着包裹逐渐变大，所需要的纸也是逐渐变大的。

递包裹

传统游戏的数学变化。

教学目标

- 学会轮流参加活动。
- 练习数数。
- 使用与大小相关的词汇。

所需材料

1) 之前孩子们做好的包裹；
2) 大的塑料垃圾袋。

准备环节

- 如果孩子们之前没有一起合作，将包裹层层包好，你需要将一个小礼物包上很多层纸。
- 如果孩子们准备好了它，在游戏开始之前，你还可以再在包裹外面加几层纸。

具体步骤

1) 选一个小朋友开始游戏。
2) 将包裹在孩子们围坐的圈中传递，不用音乐，而用数到指定数字的方式来传递，比如：数到 9。每个人传递包裹的时候都要数一个数字。
3) 第九个小朋友拿到包裹的时候，需要将包裹褪去一层包装。
4) 然后又从 1 开始数数，继续传递包裹。
5) 当第九个小朋友拿到包裹的时候，又需要从包裹上拿走一层包装。
6) 很多人都褪去一层包装后，可能又轮到最开始传递的那个小朋友了。
7) 如果这时还有一些孩子们没有拆过包裹，继续传递包裹，同时不用再数数了，直接传给下一个还没有拆过包裹的小朋友。
8) 再次从 1 开始数数。
9) 一旦每个人都拆过一轮包裹后，让他们开始第二轮游戏。

小贴士

- 安排一个大人到每个拆包裹的小朋友身边，将他们拆下来的废纸扔进垃圾袋中。

• 想让游戏更有趣的话，我们可以数一数每组小朋友的数量，选择一个指定数字，然后让孩子们说数字，要确保每次说的数字不是这个指定数字的因数。

拓展

• 你也可以像传统的游戏那么玩儿，让孩子们不停地传递包裹，当音乐停下来的时候就马上停止传递。

该活动体现的数学思维

　　该活动中，通过围成一圈还能让他们接触数值的模式，孩子们可以练习数数的技巧。我们还可以用音乐让他们听从指示。

包盒子

一个有关包盒子的游戏。

教学目标

• 将不同的盒子和包装纸匹配。

所需材料

1) 各种大小的盒子；

2) 各种大小的包装纸；

3) 胶带。

准备环节

• 确保每张纸能将其中的一个盒子紧密地包好。哪张纸最适合用于包哪个盒子，需要做笔记记录下哟。

具体步骤

1) 将孩子们分成两队，让他们两队面对面地坐在一张很大的地毯上。

2) 在两队间的地面上，将准备好的纸，按照大小顺序排成一列。

3) 在一端，将各种盒子随意摆放。

4) 从其中一个队伍中选择一个志愿者，让他从众多盒子中选一个出来。

5) 让队伍中的孩子们自己决定哪张纸最适合用来包手中的盒子。

6) 让队伍中的志愿者将盒子放在所选的纸上面（一旦放好后，不能更改想法）。

7) 让队伍中孩子们，检验他们所选择的纸，是否为最合适的。选择正确的话可以得一分。

8) 随后，该另一个队伍进行选择和检验了。

9) 如果其中一个队伍做的匹配不正确，就要将这个盒子拿给另一个队伍去匹配（由于活动之前你曾让人去核对，所以你知道哪张纸是最合适的）。

10) 继续游戏，直到所有的盒子都被匹配过一遍后，所得分数更高的队伍获胜。

小贴士

在游戏开始之前，你可以先给孩子们做个示范，告诉他们什么叫做匹配，以免他们之后会有疑问。

拓展

• 我们所使用的纸可以和某些特定的主题有关，例如，生日派对的包装纸用于聚会，圣诞节的包装纸在十二月使用。

 该活动体现的数学思维

　　该游戏中，孩子们会将包装纸和盒子配对，这能让他们对表面积的概念有初步的了解。

猜礼物

让我们玩些有趣的东西，是时候大胆地猜一猜盒子里是什么了。

教学目标

- 对大小和形状进行想象。
- 了解体积的相关概念。

所需材料

一些大小不同、形状各异的空包装盒。

准备环节

- 盒子在之前的活动中已经被包好了，或者你也可以再准备一套形状各异的盒子（比如：篮球的形状或三角巧克力形的盒子）。

具体步骤

1) 孩子们将一个包装好了的空盒子进行传递。在他们传给下一个人之前，他们必须说出一件盒子里可能有的物品。盒子中"可能"有，意味着这个物品可以是不现实的，比如一只水母。但是若他们说出的物品与盒子不匹配（比如：他们不能说是一个"房子"），他们是不能将盒子传递给下一个人的。

2) 传递不同大小和形状的盒子。

小贴士

- 如果参与活动的小朋友数量较多，你们不必一圈下来都传递同一个盒子。
- 让孩子们尽可能地大胆思考。

拓展

- 除了使用盒子，孩子们还可以传递不同的棍子，这时，他们需要说出一个和这个棍子相同高度的物品。

该活动体现的数学思维

对孩子们来说，他们可以通过这种有趣的方式想象盒子的体积。

生日贺卡和蜡烛

对数字进行计算和匹配。

教学目标

- 练习数数。
- 识别数字。

所需材料

1) 选择一些玩具（如果孩子们对于这些玩具的名字不够熟悉，可以把它们的名字展示出来）；

2) 一些写有不同年龄的生日贺卡，每张上都写着它是要送给哪个玩具的；

3) 一个聚苯乙烯所做的圆柱体，上面涂有颜料，让它看上去像是一个生日蛋糕（还可以准备角色扮演所用的蛋糕，上面有可以插蜡烛的孔，亦可以是一个真的蛋糕，孩子们在活动之后还可以分着吃掉）；

4) 带有烛台的小型生日蜡烛；

5) 打火机（交给成人保管），用来点蜡烛。

准备环节

- 如果你选择聚苯乙烯所作的蛋糕的话，给原料上色要花不少时间。

具体步骤

1) 告诉孩子们今天是这些在幼儿园/班级里的玩具的生日。

2) 将准备好的玩具交给不同的孩子们，让他们拿着，并告诉他们这些玩具的名字。

3) 向他们展示其中一个玩具所收到的信/贺卡，让一个小朋友将它打开。

4) 让孩子们推断这个玩具将要几岁了，数字有写在贺卡上。

5) 暗示孩子们要给玩具唱《祝你生日快乐》，并给它们带有蜡烛的生日蛋糕。

6) 向孩子们展示这个蛋糕，选一个小朋友将正确数目的蜡烛插在蛋糕上，一边数数，一边插上蜡烛。

7) 点亮蜡烛（如果可以的话），然后让孩子们一起唱生日歌给这些玩具们听，同时，你要走到玩具们和小部分要吹蜡烛的孩子们的身边，让他们吹灭蜡烛。

小贴士

- 必要的话，你可以查看下教学中心或学校的政策，看看是否准许点蜡烛让孩子们吹灭。要留心确保所有孩子们的安全，不能让他们有被烧伤的危险。

  • 要提醒孩子们，让他们随时记得待在所围成的圈子的原位上，确保他们知道是谁要去吹蜡烛的，安慰那些还没有吹蜡烛的孩子们，告诉他们我们是要轮流来的。

拓展

• 将为一个玩具所准备的小礼物拆开，孩子们可以互相分享。

该活动体现的数学思维

  该活动中，孩子们会认读贺卡上的数字，同时，也要数清楚对应的蜡烛支数。

你被邀请啦!

设计邀请函，发给朋友、家人、玩具们或其他孩子们，让他们来参加聚会!

教学目标

- 学会使用一系列与时间有关的量度。

所需材料

一些白纸或邀请函模板。

准备环节

- 准备一些邀请函模板，如果要用的话，需包含以下几点：

a. 它是写给谁的。

b. 开展聚会的地点。

c. 聚会的时间（日期和具体时间）。

d. 原因（聚会的目的：是谁的生日聚会以及他们要过几岁的生日）。

具体步骤

让孩子们使用模板或白纸，设计他们自己的生日聚会请柬，邀请一些特别的客人来参加聚会。

小贴士

- 事先准备的模板上，有多少已经填好了的内容，取决于孩子们书写的积极性和自信度，因而在内容的量上是有所变化的。
- 如果画图更合适的话，也可以让他们画一些图。

拓展

- 为整个班级做一个请柬，邀请临近班级中的孩子们来参加聚会。让孩子们一同参与书写，共同完成请柬制作的各个部分。然后，在有指导的分组活动中，让他们对这个请柬进行装饰，并写上名字。

该活动体现的数学思维

在进行数据处理的时候，通常会使用是谁？在哪儿？什么时候？以及为什么？诸如此类的提问来搜集信息和回答问题。时间量度中使用了许多不同的计量单位和基准。该活动中，在聚会的时间（模拟的时间和日期）和孩子们的年龄（以年为单位）中都有用到。

第二十二章

让我们制作音乐吧

引言

　　音乐和数学之间有着密切的联系，这些活动会对这二者之间的关系进行探索。你可以让所有孩子们一起参与这些活动，也可以计划让一个成人领着一个小组来开展活动。另外，在乐器持续供应的期间，要将乐器放在孩子们可以取用的地方，这能加深他们之前一同探索时得出的想法，或者能让孩子们有机会在音乐的模式和节奏上有所发展。鼓励孩子们，对他们所作的曲子进行记录和再现，能增进他们对音乐结构和模式的敏悟。

数节拍

让我们一起数一数音乐的节拍吧。

教学目标

- 练习数数。
- 了解有关音乐的模式。

所需材料

为每个小朋友准备打击乐器。

准备环节

- 不作要求。

具体步骤

1) 将乐器发给小组内的孩子们。

2) 让孩子们跟着节奏进行打击，同时要数节拍（1，2，3，4；1，2，3，4；1，2，3，4；诸如此类）。

3) 将孩子们分成两组，两组轮流进行活动。 A组打四个节拍的同时， B组就休息四个节拍（不要碰自己的乐器）。然后，保持节奏， B组打四个节拍，同时， A组休息四个节拍。

4) 将班上的孩子们分成四组，当你指向某一组的时候，这一组的孩子们就打四个节拍，但是，当别的组被指的时候，这一组就得停下休息（不碰乐器）。

小贴士　　在你指挥了一段时间后，选一个你觉得可以领着班上孩子们数节拍和打节拍的小指挥，然后让他来当指挥。

拓展

• 可以尝试不同的节奏，华尔兹如何呢？ 1，2，3；1，2，3；1，2，3……每一小节的第一拍是重的。

• 让孩子们演奏他们最爱的歌曲的节奏，同时他们要数出节拍（这很有挑战性啊！）。

该活动体现的数学思维

该活动中，孩子们要数节拍，要延续之前的音乐模式，这些都会加深他们对于结构的理解。结构在数学、音乐和诗歌中都是相当重要的，在此我们只举了三个例子。

我找到节奏了!

成为盲目的模仿者。

教学目标

- 让这些模式复制并延续下去。

所需材料

为每个小朋友准备打击乐器(可选,因为孩子们也可以简单地将节奏用手拍出来)。

准备环节

- 不作要求。

具体步骤

1) 拍出或演奏出一段很短的节奏,让孩子们像回音那样去重复它。

2) 重复该节奏,让孩子们能复制。

3) 当你和孩子们都准备好了后,改变节奏。

小贴士　　　最开始跟着节奏打拍子的时候,孩子们会觉得用手拍节奏比用打击乐器打出拍子更容易。

拓展

- 选出一位能领着孩子们进行该活动的小指挥。

该活动体现的数学思维

　　不管音乐是简单还是复杂,它都是遵循一定结构的,这种结构直观上令人愉悦。之后,孩子们还会学习如何用音乐记谱法来记录音乐。乐谱中也融入了许多数学知识,例如,分数就被用来表示音符的长度。

探索声音

你可以发出什么样的声音?

教学目标

- 学习有关音长的知识。
- 了解音高。

所需材料

至少能够发出两种音高的一些乐器,每个小朋友要有一个乐器。

准备环节

- 不作要求。

具体步骤

问孩子们以下这些问题。你可以发出下面这些声音吗:

a. 较长的声音? 较短的声音?

b. 较大的声音? 较小的声音?

c. 较高的声音? 较低的声音?

d. 较快的声音? 较慢的声音?

小贴士 一旦孩子们尝试过一种方式,就让他们试着发出不同类型的声音。

拓展

- 除了可以用乐器将上面指定类别的音乐演奏出来外,还可以让孩子们用他们的身体动作来表示不同的声音。比如,他们可以用大幅度的动作代表大声,用小幅度的动作代表小声。让他们说一说自己为什么要选择用这些方式做动作呢。

该活动体现的数学思维

思考用另一种方式发出一种声音,这能让孩子们更有创造性。在数学的学习过程中,创造性是非常重要的,因为它能帮助人们用不同的方式解决问题。音长涉及到对于时长的识别,可以通过数节拍或凭直觉来判断,认识到时光的流逝也是数学研究的意图之一。

第二十三章

面 包 店

引言

　　尽管当地面包店的数量越来越少了，但你也许能有幸带领孩子们近距离接触一家面包店，走进这家店，能让孩子们对本章节的主题有更多的思考。除此之外，你还能邀请那些会在家烤面包或蛋糕的人，他们可以是小朋友的家长，也可以是你的朋友，让他们给孩子们讲讲有关烘焙的知识。本章中的许多活动相较本书中别的章节来说，需要更多成年人的辅助才能完成，所以烘焙的那天你可以让一些家长来帮忙，或是将孩子们分成几个小组，让他们在一周内轮流进行活动。在角色扮演的地方布置出一个面包店，这能给孩子们提供扮演面包师的机会，他们不需要进行精确的测量，也不需要使用烘烤炉。如果你有足够的空间，你可以把面包店布置在咖啡馆旁边（见第十六章），这样可以提供很多好吃的东西啦。

烘焙

让我们做一个蛋糕吧!

教学目标
- 学习有关尺寸的知识。

所需材料
1) 蛋糕制作的方案;
2) 各种食材;
3) 测量所需的器具,比如,计重器和量杯。

准备环节
- 如果制作方案中需要烹调,要保证烘烤炉能正常工作,是可以随时使用的。

具体步骤
1) 和孩子们一起,把蛋糕制作方案从头到尾看一遍。
2) 按照上面所写的那样:
a. 帮助孩子们称一称所需材料的重量。
b. 数一数鸡蛋的数量。
c. 按照所给定的时长进行搅拌。
d. 判断蛋糕需要在多高的温度下烘烤。
e. 据蛋糕所需烘烤的时长,在烘烤炉上设定时间。

小贴士　　　　当你和孩子们说话的时候,尽量多给他们强调与尺寸有关的数学语言,在烘焙的过程中,让他们使用合适的言辞。

拓展
- 不同的小组可以做不同的东西,这样,晚上的时候,你们可以用这些不同的美食来开一个派对。

该活动体现的数学思维
　　　　在活动中,孩子们会在有意义的场景下使用很多不同的度量单位,例如,克或千克,分钟或小时以及摄氏度。

平均分配

如果我们要共享烘焙出的东西，那么每个人应该拿到多少呢？

教学目标

- 在进行平均分配的时候，理解如何做除法。
- 在分组的时候，理解如何做除法。

所需材料

烘烤出的食物，也可以用图片或算筹①来表示它们。

准备环节

- 不作要求。

具体步骤

1) 让孩子们说出正在烘烤的蛋糕有多少，或已经烘烤出了多少。

2) 让孩子们说出这些食物要在多少人间进行分配。

3) 谈一谈平均分配有什么策略。

小贴士

如果这里有很多蛋糕，但是只有较少一些小朋友，可以让他们每次不止分得一个蛋糕，这样能提高活动进行的效率，这需要按小组来做除法。

拓展

- 要有许多需要被分配的食物。

 该活动体现的数学思维

因需要分享而进行的除法，一般都会演变成按小组来做"除"。这个过程能让孩子们明白除法的意义，随后，也能让他们对除法的形式化方法②有更深的理解②。

---

① 算筹：一根根同样长短和粗细的小棍子，用于记数和计算。

② 形式化方法（formal methods）：在逻辑学中是指分析、研究思维形式结构的方法。

杯形蛋糕的问题

让我们做 12 个杯形蛋糕吧。

教学目标

- 练习加法。
- 练习减法。

所需材料

1) 一个松饼托盘；
2) 12 个杯形蛋糕（可以是真的也可以是用作角色扮演的道具）。

准备环节

- 不作要求。

具体步骤

1) 告诉孩子们，我们需要 12 个杯形蛋糕。

2) 向他们展示装有 6 个杯形蛋糕的松饼托盘。

3) 问他们："我们现在还需要多少个杯形蛋糕？"

4) 让孩子们相互讨论他们的答案，并说一说是怎么得出这个答案的。

5) 重复向他们展示装有不同个数杯形蛋糕的托盘。

6) 你可以在黑板上写出算式。

小贴士

- 第二次的话，可以让孩子们决定托盘上盛放多少个杯形蛋糕，这会让他们对答案进行反向讨论，同时验证它的正确性。

- 活动进行到一定的阶段，注意别忘了向孩子们展示没有装蛋糕的托盘和装有 12 个蛋糕的托盘哟。

拓展

- 可以换成不同的情境，比如蛋盒中的鸡蛋（为了能使用更长的时间，建议将它们煮熟）。

该活动体现的数学思维

　　有些孩子们在活动中，会数托盘上剩余的空间，以此来判断还需要多少个蛋糕。这是在通过计算来用加法求得答案。也有的孩子们在计算的过程中会发现不同的方法，他们会将该问题视为减法运算。也有孩子们是通过视觉记忆或根据与 12 相关数字的熟悉度而得出答案的。

用你的长面包!

观察酵母对面包制作的过程产生了什么影响。

教学目标

- 学会描述扩大。
- 学会度量时间的流逝。

所需材料

1) 简单的面包制作方案,附带制作所需的材料或一包面包粉;

2) 塑料板;

3) 大碗;

4) 保鲜膜;

5) 面包烘烤时,需要涂在表面的黄油;

6) 涂黄油所需的刀。

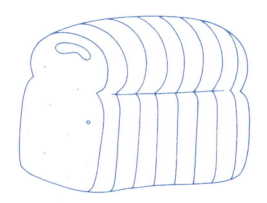

准备环节

- 在你要烘烤面包的时候,检查烘烤炉,看它是否能正常运行。
- 将面板表面擦洗干净。

具体步骤

1) 在活动开始之前,确保孩子们都把手洗干净了。

2) 根据面包制作方案,保证有充足的揉捏和发酵的时间。

3) 在面团发酵之前,让孩子们看一看,发酵期过后也让他们看一看。

4) 讨论面团的前后变化,以及导致这种变化的活跃成分——酵母。告诉孩子们,在面团静置（发酵）期间，酵母会释放出一种名叫二氧化碳的气体，这种气体会让面团变大。

5）根据制作方案进行烘烤。

小贴士　　　　面包粉用起来很方便，因为面包粉中包含了所有需要的成分，你只需要往里加一些水就行了。（但是可以弄一些多余的面粉备着，以防面团太粘。）然而，使用面包粉的话，孩子们就不能利用感觉、嗅觉和测量的方法对单个成分分别进行感知了，特别是发酵过程中最活跃的成分——酵母。也许，我们可以单独准备一些额外的酵母，这样的话，孩子们就可以通过视觉和触觉来感知它了，同时面包粉就专门用来做面包。

拓展

• 我们可以很容易地做出很多种不同类型的面包，以此来庆祝各种各样的节日。根据一年中不同的时间，我们可以选择出一种最合适的面包制作方案。

该活动体现的数学思维

　　酵母对面团的影响是非常大的，观察面团是如何发酵的，这与数学中形状和空间的扩大有关联。在制作面包的过程中，我们会有很多等待的时间，我们可以用计时器记录这些时间，或通过识读钟表来度量。

五个葡萄干面包

唱与烘焙有关的歌曲能让我们更了解数字。

教学目标

- 学会倒着数。
- 每一次减掉一个。

所需材料

1) 背景音乐（可选的）；

2) 从角色扮演的场地拿过来的五个葡萄干面包，或塑封好的、印有葡萄干面包的图片，要将这些图片附着于墙面上，要让它们易于移动。

准备环节

- 如果你对歌曲的调子不确定，用网络将歌曲的第一句歌词搜索出来。
- 将葡萄干面包放在盘子中或将塑封好的图片附着于白板上。

具体步骤

1) 开始唱歌（见下方的歌词）。唱到歌词中的横线部分，就叫一个小朋友的名字，让他在听到对应歌词之时，拿走一个面包。

2) 继续唱歌，直到所有的面包都被拿走。

歌词：

Five currant buns in a baker's shop.

Big and round with a cherry on the top.

Along came _____ with a penny one day,

Bought a currant bun and took it away.

Four currant buns . . .

Three . . .

Two . . .

One . . .

小贴士　　　　你可以把数字 1—5 放在面包上，帮助孩子们学习认读数字。

拓展

• 你可以用任何你所想的数字来开始或终结歌唱，不要每次都是以"five"开头哟。

• 选择孩子们最喜欢的烘焙食物，用它们来替换歌曲中的面包，比如"皮塔饼"、"硬皮面包"或"热腾腾的十字面包"。

该活动体现的数学思维

倒着数数字是对减法运算和每一次减掉一个的早期引入环节。明白到了最后葡萄干面包都没有了，这能让孩子们知道我们可以倒着数到零，但是当我们数数的时候，一般来说都是从"一"开始的哟。

面包店里的角色扮演

孩子们是烘焙师吗?

教学目标

- 学习有关度量的知识。
- 练习除法。

所需材料

1) 角色扮演的场地,用来建立一个面包店;

2) 用以测量的食材,比如葡萄干或面粉;

3) 几只天平;

4) 一些碗;

5) 面粉模型或真的面团;

6) 一些小圆面包、长条面包、馅饼和油酥点心;

7) 一个刷子和一把铲子!

准备环节

- 孩子们需要先去当地的一家面包店,明白那里的具体情况,这样他们才能更好地建立角色扮演的场景。

具体步骤

在面包店角色扮演的场景下,我们可以做的活动有很多,如下:

1) 按照特定的量进行测量和称重

2) 揉捏面粉模型或真的面团

3) 在面粉模型或真的面团上打褶

4) 将蛋糕粉均匀分配

5) 出售与购买面包和别的食物

小贴士

- 提醒孩子们,面粉模型是不可以吃的哟。

- 真正的长条面包和小圆面包的保存方式是在它们表面涂上两三层清漆,每上一层漆后要等它干了后再上第二层(再次提醒孩子们,这些是不可以吃的哟)。

拓展

- 角色扮演的地方可以是一家街角的小店，店里卖有烘焙所需的材料和烘焙好的食物。

该活动体现的数学思维

  在角色扮演的地方，孩子们能模拟出面包师会做的大多数任务。如何度量材料是他们需要掌握的重要技能之一。同时，为了做出大小差不多的杯形蛋糕或长条面包，他们还需要学会分配混合物。另外，给面团打褶的环节还要求他们做事要有条理。

附录

参考文献

书目

Freedman, Claire and Cort, Ben. *Aliens Love Underpants*. London: Simon and Schuster Children's, 2007.

Harris, Peter and Allwright, Deborah. *The Night Pirates*. London: Egmont Books Ltd, 2005.

Helbrough, Emma and Gower, Teri. *1001 Bugs to Spot*. London: Usborne Books, 2009.

King, Valerie. *In Comes the Tide*. Loughborough: Ladybird Books Ltd, 1997.

Manning, Mick and Granstrom, Brita. *High Tide, Low Tide*, London: Franklin Watts, 2003.

Mitton, Tony and Young, Selina. *Once Upon a Tide*, London: Picture Corgi, 2006.

Pfister, Marcus. *The Rainbow Fish*, New York: NorthSouth Books, 2007.

Punter, Russell and Fox, Christyan. *Stories of Pirates*, London: Usborne Books, 2007.

Thomson, Emma, *Lili's Wish*, London: Orchard Books, 2007.

音乐

安东尼奥·维瓦尔第《四季》（1723）（诸多版本）。

活动索引*

领域	子领域	活动名称	页码
个人、社会和情感上的发展	气质与态度	在服装店里	3
		包盒子	235
	自信与自尊	隐藏与计数	54
		鞋子的尺码	96
		我们所用的数字	199
		猜礼物	237
		生日贺卡和蜡烛	238
	建立关系	彩虹鱼	43
		分组游戏	55
		高塔比赛	171
		建造一个高塔	173
	行为与自控	沙堡	12
		数过来数过去	47
		捉迷藏	57
		跳房子游戏	58
		递包裹	233
		平均分配	252
	自理能力	试穿和整理衣服	4
		制作三明治馅料	86
	团队意识	在你的自行车上!	56
		什么时候去野餐?	84
		穿越四季的庆祝	211
交流、语言和读写	用语言沟通	外星人	29
		原来是渔网	41
		洋娃娃的房间	79
		成双的鞋子	103
		金蛋	161
		你被邀请啦!	240
		杯形蛋糕的问题	253

* 此部分按英国早教大纲（EYFS）中的教育目标及领域对本书中的活动进行归类整理，且此处中文译文按中文阅读习惯梳理了汇总表格。

Introduction

Aimee: 'I live at number 4.'
Ashmal: 'I live at number 12.'
Jake: 'Well, I live at number 73.'
Kate: 'I live at 106.'
Aimee: 'Well, I live at number thousand!'
Jake: 'I live at one million!'
(All laugh)

I overheard the above in a nursery recently. The four three-year-old children were standing together on the carpet and Aimee instigated the conversation. What struck me the most was the way that the children joined in spontaneously, understood the numbers were increasing and shared Aimee's and Jake's humour of living at ludicrous addresses.

This is only one little snapshot of the mathematical talk and play that can be seen in early years settings every day. All young children intuitively use number and other mathematical concepts continuously in their play, and take great pleasure in doing so. The key for practitioners and teachers is to plan activities, games and tasks that are mathematical in nature as well as to see the mathematical opportunities in many of the everyday activities that happen in a setting or classroom.

This is a book of practical ideas, games and activities written for children in the early years stages, aged four to five. However, because of its broad nature, much of the content will also be suitable for younger children as well as most six year-olds. You will notice that some of the themes in this book are addressed in other books in the series. This was planned intentionally so that you can take advantage of the themes across several areas of learning. Each activity contains the following sections:

Title

The title provides the theme of the activities (such as 'pirates'), the resources used (such as 'dice') or the mathematical concepts (such as 'number') that the activities, games and ideas relate to in that section.

Aims and objectives

This provides general statements related to the main focuses of the activity.

Resources

A list of the resources you will need is given. Some resources are optional and these are marked clearly.

Preparation

This outlines any preparation that is required over and above gathering the resources.

What to do

This section provides a step-by-step guide to the activity, outlining what you and the children will be doing.

Tip (s)

Tips may be related to the organisation of the activity, resources that can be used, how to engage the children further or what mathematical ideas to focus upon specifically.

Variation (s)

This gives ideas for how the activity can be amended to suit other themes, or developed to extend the original ideas.

How is this maths?

This section explains why the activity is mathematical and how the ideas develop into primary school mathematics and beyond.

Most of the ideas in this book can be adapted for a wide range of themes, so please look through the whole book for inspiration rather than focusing only on a particular theme you may be teaching.

This book includes, but also goes beyond, problem-solving, reasoning and numeracy in curriculum guidance. It creates space for children to explore 'big ideas' in maths, such as infinity and large numbers that excite and amaze. And it introduces ideas of how children's mathematical development can be supported in the early years. Use these games, ideas and activities as a springboard for identifying mathematical opportunities present in all your early years provision. With the aid of this book, it is hoped that you will then be able to move beyond the ideas presented here.

About the author

Dr Alice Hansen taught in England and abroad until moving into Early Years and Primary Initial Teacher Education at St Martin's College, University of Cumbria. She left higher education to become an educational consultant. During that time she worked with a number of educational settings and national bodies, focusing on continuing professional development for teachers in mathematics education. She is now the director of Children Count Ltd, a company that provides a range of consultancy, research and publications for early years and primary educational settings.

Chapter 1

Dressing up

Introduction

Dressing up is an activity enjoyed by all children. This chapter contains activities that can be undertaken in the dress shop role-play area. Alternatively, you may place the clothes in a suitcase for the children to talk about and try on. Remember to include a wide range of types of clothes and jewellery from different cultures.

In the clothes shop

Use the role-play area as a clothes shop to facilitate mathematical discussion.

Can we match it?

Practise 1-to-1 correspondence by finding colours that are the same

Aims and objectives
- To identify colours accurately.
- To group objects according to their colour.

Preparation
- Gather selections of girls' and boys' clothing and accessories that have the same colour. These may be clothes, shoes, hats or bags that the children can wear, available in the role-play clothing shop.

What to do
- Open the role-play clothes shop, inviting a small number of children to browse in your new shop.
- Explain to the children that you had a visitor yesterday who bought only green items and you noticed how smart they looked when everything they wore matched.
- Ask the children if they can select items that are all the same colour.
- Discuss why they have chosen the items they have. Focus discussion on the similar properties of the items (they are all the same colour). Also discuss how they are different.

Tip
You may want to produce cards with colours that match the sets you have created for the children to choose, to help them match the colours and to avoid children selecting the same colour.

Variation
If it is not possible to use the role-play area for this activity, a smaller-scale activity could be to have items for the dolls and teddies to wear, or to use drawings copied onto various colours of

paper for children to stick on their sheets.

How is this maths?

Being able to identify characteristics （attributes） of objects （and later numbers） is important for children to be able to group them. This lays a foundation for them being able to handle data later on. Matching colour also helps children to practise 1-to-1 correspondence.

Putting on and putting away our clothes

Thinking about the use of positional language while wearing and tidying away the clothes in the role play shop.

Aims and objectives

- To use positional language.
- To use ordinal language.
- To compare size.

What to do

- While the children are trying clothes on, talk to them about what they are doing. Reinforce positional language such as 'on', 'in', 'over', 'under', 'through'. E. g. 'Place the hat *on* your head, put your arm *through* the sleeve, the jacket is *over* the shirt'.
- While the children are putting away clothes, talk to them about the position or place of the clothes. E. g. 'The clothes are *in* the drawer, the dress is *on* the hanger, the shoes are *in* the box'.
- While the children are putting clothes on, talk to them about the size of the clothing. 'Is this top *too big, too small,* or *just right*? '
- Talk to the children about the order they put their clothes on. E. g. socks on *first*, shoes on *second*.

Tip   Once you have modelled this language, step back and observe the children taking on the role of shopkeeper and using this language themselves!

How is this maths?

Using positional language and talking about size helps children to make sense of shape and space and supports their geometrical thinking. Using ordinal language helps children to think about order and is another way of thinking about numbers. Comparing size helps children to make sense of shape and measurement.

How much?

An opportunity for children to buy and sell clothes in the clothes shop.

Aims and objectives

- To use language associated with money.
- To handle coins and notes.

Preparation

- Install a till in the role play clothing shop.
- Place price labels on the clothes. You may work with some children to create the labels from scratch.

What to do

- Open the shop, with two children as the proprietors. Encourage the children to read the cost of the item and to charge the customer the amount for the item.
- The children can take money and give change, or use a credit card for the transaction!
- The children may make discount vouchers to encourage customers to return.

Tip   You will need to think about the amounts that you put on the items in the shop. Some people believe that the amounts should be small and in pence, for children to read and handle coins accurately.

Others believe that the amounts on the items should be more realistic because it would not be possible to find a pair of gloves for 5p. Talk with your colleagues about which approach you will take.

Variation

The children may use a calculator or the till to add up the cost of several items.

How is this maths?

It is important that children handle money and learn to recognise the value of coins. Children find understanding the value of coins difficult. Coins of different values are different sizes (for example a 5p is worth more than a 2p, but a 2p is larger). A one-pound coin is the equivalent of one hundred pence, but is represented by only one coin.

Making necklaces

Making necklaces is a fun way to talk about patterns and order together.

Aims and objectives

- To copy or create a repeating pattern.
- To use ordinal language（first, second, third and so on）.

Resources

- Beads, buttons, pasta or similar for threading
- String or wool
- Selection of necklaces or bracelets（bought or made from beads）from role play

Preparation

- Set out the materials in containers. You may wish to separate colours for younger children.

What to do

- Begin to make a necklace using two alternating colours（A, B, A, B: e.g. red, blue, red, blue, red, blue ...）. Ask the children what they notice.
- Can the children tell you what comes next? What would the next two beads be? What about the next three? Can they make it?
- Begin another, using two colours in a pattern（AAB, AAB: e.g. red, red, blue, red, red, blue ...）. Ask the children what they notice.
- Can the children tell you what comes next? What would the next two beads be? What about the next three? Can they make it?
- Ask the children to create their own necklace. Can they make a repeating pattern on their necklace?

Tips

- Start with two colours only. Young children find using more than two or three very difficult.
- Necklaces can be tedious to complete as they are long. Use large beads, or make smaller necklaces for the teddies, or bracelets instead.

Variation

Print patterns on paper using different-coloured shapes. Cut the paper out to dress the paper doll.

How is this maths?

Mathematics is full of pattern. Seeing pattern helps children to solve problems. Being able to say what comes next helps children to visualise shape or colour and pattern. Using ordinal language (first, second, etc.) helps them to talk mathematically.

Designing clothes

Many children like to dress up their dolls or themselves.

Aims and objectives

- To construct using materials.
- To estimate length.

Resources

- Lengths of material – use as wide a range of fabrics as possible
- Ribbon
- Scissors
- Sticky tape
- Photographs of children in clothes（optional）

Preparation

- Set out the materials available to the children.

What to do

- Encourage the children to think about creating their own clothes.
- Talk to them about which clothes they are going to make, and discuss the suitability of the material for the purpose of that clothing.
- Talk with the children about how much fabric they will need to create their clothes. Do they have enough? Is it wide enough? Too long? How do they know? How are they going to find out? What will they do to resolve any problems about the size of the fabric?
- What order will they need to follow to create their clothes?
- Whom will they work with?

Tips
- Children may find it easier to create an item of clothing for their friend.
- You may wish to photograph the children in their creations and display them to provide inspiration for other children.

Variation

Make a costume for a new superhero. How will the costume help them use their super powers?

How is this maths?

Children who use estimation are able to check the accuracy of their work more effectively. The children will develop their understanding of length by using arbitrary units of length（e. g. about a child's height）and standard measures（e. g. a metre stick）to become more accurate in their measuring.

Chapter 2

Oh, we do like to be
beside the seaside!

Introduction

Playing with the resources in this theme offers children opportunities to experiment with different textures. You can transform all the available space into a seaside setting if you want to explore these on a grand scale, or alternatively utilise these activities in the sand and water area.

Sand and water

Use these materials to explore early notions of capacity.

Aims and objectives

• To fill, empty and compare buckets.

Resources

• Large tarpaulin or paddling pool

• Dry sand

• Water tray

• Buckets of different sizes

• Spades and other items to scoop sand and water

• Funnels, sieves, etc. to let sand and water through

Preparation

• Lay the tarpaulin or the pool on the floor or outside and fill with the sand.

• Fill the water tray.

What to do

• Talk with the children about which bucket holds more/less. Discuss ways they could test this. Try pouring from one bucket to another. Does this help?

• What about three containers? Can they order them from which one holds most to least? How can they see if they are right?

• Use words describing how much water or dry sand is in the bucket, such as full, empty, half full, nearly full, as well as talking about what the children are doing. E. g. 'I see you are filling it up, are you going to add some more to fill it up? How many scoops do you think will fill this bucket? What about this bucket? '

Tips

• Colouring water with food colouring helps children to see the level of the water in the containers more easily.

• Conservation of capacity is a very difficult idea for young children. Select buckets of all shapes and sizes. Some may look like they hold more because they are taller but actually they hold less because they are thinner! Researchers say children need lots of experience using different-shaped containers to help them understand conservation of capacity.

How is this maths?

This activity supports children's early development of capacity. It also encourages them to think about how space is filled and how containers of different shapes may have the same, or different, capacities.

Sandcastles

Use an array of containers to construct sandcastles.

Aims and objectives
- To construct sandcastles.
- To decorate sandcastles.

Resources
- Large tarpaulin or paddling pool
- Damp sand
- Buckets of different sizes
- Spades and other items to scoop sand
- Shells, driftwood and other items found at the beach
- Pictures of sandcastles (optional)

Preparation
- Lay the tarpaulin or the pool on the floor and fill with the damp sand.
- Make a sandcastle to leave on the sand for the children to find.

What to do
- Ask the children if any of them have made a sandcastle before. If they have, ask them to demonstrate how they made it. Encourage them to talk about what they are doing during each step in the process. Reinforce any mathematical vocabulary they are using (e. g. put sand *in* the bucket, pat the sand *down*, tip the bucket *upside down*).

- Talk about how they can make sandcastles with more than one storey. Discuss the size of the different storeys. Which bucket might they use first? Why?
- Decorate sandcastles with shells, driftwood, flags, etc. Can they make a pattern that repeats around the outside of the sandcastle?

Tip

The amount of water that is added to the sand is important to get right. Sand that is too dry or too wet will not keep its shape. Try making sandcastles yourself before the children arrive so you know it works.

How is this maths?

Making sandcastles requires a lot of problem solving, especially when the sandcastles fail to stand up the first time! Children need to think about the reason why their sandcastle did not stand up, and think logically about how they could improve their attempt the next time. Using trial and error is an effective problem-solving approach in the early years and beyond.

Beach towels

Let's use our beach towels on the beach!

Aims and objectives

- To sort according to common criteria.
- To compare sizes.

Resources

- A variety of beach towels in different sizes, including one as large as possible

Preparation

- Pile the towels in the middle of the floor, all mixed up.

What to do

- Ask the children to sit in a circle around the towels.
- Explain that you found this pile of towels on the beach and you want to find out more about them. Ask the children what they might want to find out about them.
- Children's responses will vary, and be positive about each one. However, for the purposes of this activity focus on the responses that are more mathematical, such as colour, pattern and size.
- Choose one of the ideas (such as colour) and ask the children to come up in turn and choose a towel, sorting it according to the criterion (characteristic). Discuss the number of towels in each group.
- Identify the biggest towel (this may have been spotted as the children were dismantling the pile). See how many children can fit on the towel, either standing on it or lying on it.
- Ask who thinks they sorted the smallest towel. You are likely to get a number of children thinking their towel was the smallest. Discuss how they can check which is the smallest. Count the number of children who can stand or lie on this towel. Compare, using language such as *more* and *less*.
- Repeat with other towels, ordering them in size. Discuss how this is different from ordering them in order of length only.

Variations

- Children can compare the area of different paper shapes by covering the shapes in counters, cubes or other items.
- Can the children cover the floor with the towels, without overlapping and without leaving gaps?

How is this maths?

This supports children's early understanding of area. By seeing the towels in different orientations, and talking about the size of the shapes, early understanding of the notion of quadrilaterals is also developing.

The tide

This activity explores a pattern as old as the Earth.

Aims and objectives
- To understand how the tide moves in and out of the beach twice a day.

Resources
- Children's picture book about the tide （e. g. *Once Upon a Tide* by Tony Mitton and Selina Young; *High Tide, Low Tide* by Mick Manning and Brita Granstrom; *In Comes the Tide* by Valerie King）
- Long length of blue or white chiffon or similar fabric

Preparation
- Read the picture book

What to do
- Discuss how the tide moves in and out, and the impact that this has on the creatures etc. in the book or on their own experiences of visiting the beach （if appropriate）.
- Talk about the timing of the tide and that it rises and falls around twice a day.
- Ask the children to choose to be one of the creatures （or other appropriate item） from the book. Two adults hold the fabric and pretend that the fabric is the tide rising and falling while the children act out being the creature.
- Discuss what they did when they were the creature. What impact does the tide have on their life? What do they do when it is high tide? Or low tide? Why?
- What would happen if the tide remained low, or high?

How is this maths?
The tide is one example of a naturally occurring pattern. （High tide tends to occur approximately twice a day, but is actually on a 24-hour 50-minute cycle, so it takes place 50 minutes later each day. ） Understanding the repetitive nature of patterns is a fundamental mathematical understanding.

The rock pool

Exploring the creatures in the rock pool always excites children and adults like!

Aims and objectives

- To discuss the features belonging to rock pool inhabitants.
- To sort creatures according to their attributes.

Resources

- Water tray
- Rocks
- Sand
- Plastic creatures such as sea slugs, shrimps, crabs, sea eggs, fish, small octopus, snails
- Plastic seaweed such as neptune's necklace, sea lettuce

Preparation

- Set up the water tray to re-create a rock pool.
- Hide various plastic rock pool creatures and plants in a typical resting place.

What to do

- Encourage the children to explore the rock pool.
- As a find is made, encourage the children to describe the features of the creature.
- Can they sort the creatures in any way? Consider thinking about the patterns on their bodies, the number of legs or methods of movement under the water or overland.

Tip Use ice-cream containers with labels the children have designed themselves to sort the creatures. These will contain the water and allow the children to look at the sets more easily.

Variations

- As an extension the children may sort using two criteria: where would the children's creatures belong in the Carroll diagram below?

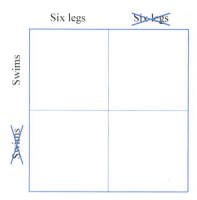

Six legs   ~~Six legs~~

Swims

- You may visit a real rock pool. Remember that rock pools are very fragile environments for a number of creatures and it is essential that the children take great care when exploring them.

How is this maths?

Identifying the features of the creatures may involve counting, or observing pattern. Being able to sort items into categories is within the early stages of handling data.

Chapter 3

Space

Introduction

In addition to the activities in this chapter, you might want to set up a small, darkened area in the room that has been constructed using thick black polythene sheeting. In this area the children can use torches to explore objectives that reflect, and look at the stars in the 'sky' at the top. To make a star-filled sky effect you can glue glitter onto the top of the area or use twinkling low-energy Christmas lights.

Blast off!

Enjoy blasting off with the rockets!

Aims and objectives

- To count backwards in steps of one.
- To follow simple instructions.

Resources

- Mission control centre （this could be anything from the role-play area to a decorated box on the tabletop）
- Rocket（s）made by the children, or toy rockets

Preparation

- Identify who will be ground control and who will be the astronaut taking the rocket into space.

What to do

- Count down from 3, 5 or 10 for the rocket to 'blast off'.
- Take turns being at ground control and being the astronaut.

Variations

- Vary the starting number. Ask the children what number they would like to start with!
- There are many different contexts in which the children can count down – they may count down to dinner, to start a race or to pop up like a jack-in-the-box.

How is this maths?

Children need to be able to count forwards and backwards. Later on they will do this in steps other than ones. Waiting until a given time （in this case 'blast off'）helps children to follow instructions and gain an appreciation of time as duration.

Rocket construction

....

Choose three-dimensional figures to make a rocket.

Aims and objectives

- To construct a rocket that will stand and fly.
- To consider the features of three-dimensional shapes.

Resources

- Construction materials
- Pictures or video material of rockets or toy rockets

What to do

- Show the children a range of rockets. Discuss the purpose of the rockets and the features that help them to achieve their purpose.
- Ask the children what shapes they are going to use/are using to construct their rocket. Talk to them about why that shape is a good shape to use (e. g. the cone has a point that helps it to travel through space).

Tip

Model the correct three-dimensional language, such as cone, cylinder, cuboid, cube.

How is this maths?

Children learn about shape and space by manipulating construction materials. Helping them to think about the features of the shapes enables them to develop an early understanding of geometric definition.

To infinity and beyond!

Aims and objectives

- To consider how distance affects the size of things we can see.
- To use language related to size and distance/length.

Resources

- Two balls of differing sizes, e. g. one football and one golf ball
- Large field or long room

Preparation

- Ask another adult to stand as far away as possible holding a large ball. (The actual size of the ball will depend on how far the adult can move away from the children.)

What to do

- Talk about rockets, and where they travel. Where would the children like their rocket to travel to? Talk about the distances being a very long way (or not, as the case may be!) from the Earth.
- Ask the children to find the adult who is holding the ball at a distance. What ball do they think they are holding? Exclaim to the children that they can't be right (if they have guessed the ball correctly), because you are holding this (small) ball here and it seems larger than the ball the adult is holding. Discuss why this might be happening.
- Ask the adult to return. Encourage the children to observe what happens to the mystery ball as the adult comes closer. Compare the two balls side by side.
- Talk about the Earth being spherical, a giant ball-shaped planet floating in space, and how the sun is many, many times bigger than the Earth but it appears very small in the sky because it is a very long way from us.

How is this maths?

By observing the sizes of the balls at a distance and closely, children have an opportunity to talk about how distance has an effect on our perception of objects. Distance is another way to describe length. For example, 'What is the distance between points A and B?' is the same as asking, 'What is the length between points A and B?'. Talking about large distances in space can also lead children to thinking about the notion of *infinity*.

Stars

Twinkle, twinkle all our stars!

Aims and objectives

- To count a set of points.

Resources

- Cardboard
- Glitter, paint or coloured paper pieces for decoration

Preparation

- Cut out a variety of stars, with different numbers of points:

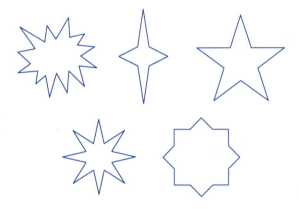

What to do

- Encourage the children to choose and decorate some stars. While doing so, urge them to count the number of points that the stars have.
- Talk with each other about the number of points.
- Display the stars by hanging them from the ceiling.

Tip

You may need to help the children to remember what point they have started counting from and therefore which point to stop counting at. Often young children will keep counting around, or stop at a number that is familiar to them (often 10). Using a finger to identify where the counting has begun is one way.

Variation

Encourage the children to draw and/or cut out their own shapes with the number of points that they want.

How is this maths?

Knowing that the last number stated in a counting sequence gives the cardinal (total) number of items in the set is part of young children's development of counting.

Star symmetry

Exploring symmetry through order of rotation and reflection.

Aims and objectives

- To recognise symmetry.

Resources

- Variety of stars cut out of cardboard, some with no symmetry and others with some rotational or reflective symmetry
- Split pins
- Sheets of paper larger than the stars
- Mirrors
- Paper and scissors for children to create their own stars

Preparation

- Fold some of the stars that have one line of symmetry in half.
- Fold some of the stars that have two lines of symmetry in half and then half again.
- Place some of the stars that have rotational symmetry onto the sheets of paper and attach them with a split pin through the centre of the star. Draw around the star so the outline can be seen on the paper.

What to do

- Let the children explore the stars you have prepared. What do they notice about the stars that have been folded? What happens when they rotate (turn) the stars around the split pin?

- Let the children explore the stars that were left unfolded and unpinned. Can they find the stars that are *symmetrical*? How many times can they fold them? How many times can they turn them before they get back to where the star started from? Can they find any stars that are *not symmetrical*?
- Can they make their own stars? Are they symmetrical? How are they symmetrical? Do they have *mirror symmetry* (they match when they are folded) or *rotational symmetry* (they sit in the shape when they are rotated about the centre)?

Tip   Young children have a natural propensity towards symmetry, particularly reflective symmetry in one vertical line. They also love using the word symmetrical!

Variations

- Children may also explore symmetry through making snowflakes by folding a circle of paper many times and cutting pieces out of it.
- You may go for a walk or look at photographs to see symmetry occurring naturally in many places, such as leaves, flowers and reflections in water.

How is this maths?

It is important for children to learn about symmetry because this will help them later to define shapes.

Day and night

Children can describe many differences between day and night.

Aims and objectives

• To talk about differences.

• To think about time （day/night）.

Preparation

• Take the children outside.

What to do

• Talk about the sky they can see. What can they see today? Is it the same as yesterday? What might it be like tomorrow?

• What does the sky look like at night?

• Are there clouds at night? Talk about how clouds can't be seen because it is dark, but that the clouds are in front of the stars, or closer to us than the stars, so they hide the stars.

• Talk about the moon. What shapes can the moon be? Sometimes it is circular and other times it is a crescent shape.

• What do the children do during the day and during the night?

Tip   The moon can often be seen during the day – it is a misconception to think that the moon is only visible at night.

How is this maths?

The cycle of day and night is a repeating pattern observed in every 24 hours. It has a significant impact on the way humans lead their lives. Children find it easier to start thinking about one day as a unit of time than longer periods such as a week, month, year, etc. Thinking about how the shape of the moon changes over approximately on month also supports children in thinking about the passing of time and about pattern and shape.

Spacemen

Use the song to help children to think about taking away and counting backwards.

Aims and objectives

- To count backwards.
- To take away one.

Resources

- Cardboard flying saucer with five spacemen attached with a product such as Velcro or Blu-Tack®
- Or, rocket with five spacemen inside that can be removed

What to do

- Sing 'Five little men in a flying saucer'.
- As you reach the line in the song '... and one man flew away', stop singing and ask one child to remove one spaceman. Count together the remaining spacemen. Talk to the children about how 'there were five spacemen, one man flew away, so now there are four left' and so on. You also use the term *take away* as the spaceman is being removed from the spaceship.
- Sing the song again. Before counting the remaining spacemen, count backwards from five until you reach the number of spacemen who are in the spaceship. Check you are right by counting them forwards as well.
- Encourage the children to use their fingers to represent the spacemen. Start with five fingers, then put one finger down as the spaceman flies away or as you count backwards. 'How many fingers are left? Let's count the spacemen left.'

Tip   If you are not familiar with the tune, search for 'five little men in a flying saucer nationalelfservice' for a high-quality version of the song to use with the children.

Variation

Other songs provide opportunity for counting backwards and taking away. See pages 99 – 102 in the Songs and Chants chapter for more ideas.

How is this maths?

Children need to learn that *taking away* one is related to *counting backwards in ones*. They can also begin to develop their understanding of *subtraction as* 'taking away' using this type of activity. Using fingers to represent objects helps children to begin to abstract mathematical ideas – their fingers are an abstract representation of the spacemen. Later on they will understand that numbers themselves are abstract and can be used to represent counting (five spacemen, five blocks, five lots of ten, 5x and so on) and measurement (five o'clock, five years old, five metres, five degrees and so on).

Aliens

Let's count aliens!

Aims and objectives

- To count.
- To talk about pattern.

Resources

- Book: *Aliens Love Underpants* by Claire Freedman

Preparation

- Read *Aliens Love Underpants*.

What to do

- Discuss the patterns on the underpants inside the front cover. Which is their favourite pair of underpants? Why? What would they like to have on their own pair of underpants?
- Discuss the features of the aliens. How many legs do they have? Arms? Eyes? Antennae? Hair? And so on.
- How many aliens do they think are inside the underpants leg? How do they know? What do other children think? Discuss answers and praise any answers that have a logical reason given.

Tip   Encourage children to use their fingers to count the features on the aliens. This helps them with understanding that counting involves 1-to-1 correspondence (i. e. one number name to one item being counted).

How is this maths?

Children need to understand that anything can be counted. It is more difficult for children to count items that are not lined up. Being able to identify pattern is a fundamental aspect of mathematics. Working out the number of aliens in the underpants leg helps children to visualise quantity.

Design an alien

This activity provides lots of opportunity for you and the children to talk about number and to count.

Aims and objectives

- To count.
- To identify attributes.

Resources

- Book: *Aliens Love Underpants* by Claire Freedman
- Paper
- Paint, crayons, pencils or the media you wish the children to use

Preparation

- Read *Aliens Love Underpants* or another book that has pictures of aliens for the children to observe.

What to do

- Ask the children to imagine an alien themselves. Can they tell you how many legs it has? How many arms? Eyes? Teeth? Hairs? What is special about their alien?
- Encourage the children to paint, draw or construct their alien. Throughout this time, talk to the children about the number of features they are putting on the alien. Encourage them to count the features.
- Ask questions such as 'How many more arms do you need to draw?', or make observations such as 'I see you have drawn four eyes on the left and four eyes on the right. There are the same number of eyes on each side'.

Variation

Dress up like aliens! Discuss how many legs, arms, eyes etc the aliens have. How do they move? Where do they sleep? Act out being an alien. Talk about how having more arms might assist in certain jobs, or having more eyes might help them to see more things at the same time.

How is this maths?

This activity encourages children to talk about number and to practise counting and adding (by counting on).

Chapter 4

Fishing

Introduction

If you are planning to turn your classroom into an underwater environment try attaching light-blue cellophane and fish the children have made to the windows and hanging other underwater sea creatures from the ceiling. Strips of blue, green and clear cellophane interspersed between the creatures adds a watery feel also.

I've caught a big one!

Children practise their physical skills to catch the 'big one'!

Aims and objectives

- To identify numbers.
- To make numbers beyond 9.

Resources

- Laminated numbers 0 – 9 that are coloured to look like fish, with a paper clip attached
- 'Fishing rods': sticks that have a string hanging from the top, with a magnet at the end

Preparation

- Set up a 'pond' with the laminated numbers displayed in it.

What to do

- Children 'fish' for numbers of their choice, or fish for any number.
- Talk about the number that they have caught. What is that number? Can you count up to that number? Do you know a number that is smaller than that number? A number that is bigger?
- When all the fish have been caught, can they order them from lowest to highest number?
- Encourage the children to place two of the numbers (as digits) together to become another number. Can they name the number? What about three digits?

Tips

- When the 'fish' are placed together, they become *digits*, rather than *numbers*. So, for example, '6' is a one-digit number when it is on its own. However, when in '36', '6' becomes a digit in a two-digit number. It is important to distinguish between 'number' and 'digit' to avoid confusion later on.
- You may wish to vary the size of the number, for example make a large '2' but a smaller '7'. This could lead to discussion about the order of numbers and how that differs from their physical size!

Variations

Blindfold one fisherman. The other children offer clues for the fisherman to identify the fish that has been caught. E. g. 'It is an even number. It is a number greater than 6. Half of the number is 4'.

How is this maths?

Understanding the importance of ordering numbers correctly helps children to become confident counters and, later, use this skill to add, subtract, multiply and divide. Understanding how digits are used to represent numbers supports children's understanding of place value. Offering opportunities for children to talk about the properties of numbers in an open-ended way helps them to develop their understanding of number.

Go Fish!

This is a variation on the traditional card game as the children move with the cards.

Aims and objectives

- To familiarise the children with numbers.
- To learn problem solving and logical thinking.

Resources

- White A5 cards with sets of coloured numbers, laminated. The number of cards used will depend on the size of the group playing the game. For 28 children you may wish to use:

BLUE	YELLOW	RED	GREEN
10	10	10	10
11	11	11	11
12	12	12	12
13	13	13	13
14	14	14	14
15	15	15	15
16	16	16	16

Preparation

- Ensure there is a large space to play this game.
- It may be helpful to draw a line in the centre of the space to keep the two groups apart.

What to do

- Hand out the cards, one to each child.
- Choose seven children to stand in one group and then another seven children to stand in a second group facing them.
- The remainder of the class sit along the side, watching and keeping their cards hidden.
- The children in the two groups talk within each group and decide if they have any sets or groups of the same number. Encourage the children to stand together if they have a partner.

- Ask the first group to identify a number that they would like, that will help them make a set of four numbers the same. They ask the other group if they have that number. If the other group does, the child (ren) holding the card (s) move (s) to sit with group one and specifically with the other children holding that number. If the other group does not, all the children in the group shout out 'Go Fish!' and the group must choose one child from the side to join them.
- The groups take turns to ask for numbers. When a group of four numbers has been gathered, those four children sit at the back of their group to watch.
- The winning side is the group with the most children sitting at the back (i.e. the highest number of sets gathered).

- You can substitute the numbers for any where the children require reinforcement or practice.
- Encourage the children to persuade their peers as to which number to ask for, and to explain their thinking to them.

Variations

- You may wish to reduce the number of cards in a set to three, instead of four. This may speed the game up but will reduce the amount of opportunity for discussion.
- Instead of sitting at the back of the group the children can hand in their cards to the teacher and receive a new card, sitting at the side to join in again.
- Instead of being chosen, children can line up at the side and join a group in turn.

How is this maths?

This strategic game helps to develop children's logical thinking. The children need to use mathematical talk to identify the number that they want to ask for.

Fish race

Who will come first, second or third in this race with their fish?

Aims and objectives

- To use ordinal language （first, second, third and so on）.
- To understand speed.
- To understand distance.

Resources

- Simple paper cut-outs of fish （cut from A4 size）, one per child
- Sheets of newspaper, approximately 8 – 10

Preparation

- The children may want to colour their own fish, or write their name on them to help them to identify their own fish during the races.
- Fold each of the double-spread newspaper sheets several times so that it is about the size of an A4 sheet of paper. The number you will require will depend on how many children are competing at the same time.
- This is best carried out in a large space.

What to do

- Line up a small group of children behind the starting line with their fish.
- On 'go', the children move the newspaper up and down quickly to create a draught behind their own fish, so that the fish moves with the wind along the floor.
- The children continue to move their fish along until all the children have crossed the finish line.
- Repeat the steps above with the remaining children until everyone has had a go.
- You may hold semi-finals and finals with those children who crossed the finish line in their heat first, second or third.
- Pass out gold, silver and bronze medals for the three top competitors. You may want to display the winners, with photographs of the children holding their fish.

Tip   Give the children time to practise moving their fish.

Variation

Some children may like to experiment with fish that are different sizes or made from different materials. Which do they think is most effective?

How is this maths?

The children use ordinal language to discuss who came first, second and third. Solving problems such as 'which is the most effective way to move the newspaper?' or 'which is the fastest fish design?' helps children to consider cause and effect.

Five little fish

A variation on a well-known song.

Aims and objectives

- To count backwards.
- To learn about taking away.
- To learn the days of the week.

Resources

- Lyrics（see below）
- Fish costumes or puppets
- Days of the week and numbers 1 – 5 displayed on cards to hold

Preparation

- Children can dress up or put on fish puppets.

What to do

- Sing the song together（lyrics below）.

  Lyrics:

  （Tune: 'Five little ducks'）

  Five little fish went swimming on Monday

  Through the water and far far away

  Mother Fish called, 'It's time to come back'

  But only four little fish swam back

  Four little fish went swimming on Tuesday ...

  Three little fish went swimming on Wednesday ...

  Two little fish went swimming on Thursday ...

  One little fish went swimming on Friday ... but no little fish came swimming back

  （Slowly）

Sad Mother Fish went swimming on Saturday

  Through the water and far far away

  Mother Fish cried, 'Please don't stay away'

  And five little fish came back on Sunday!

  （Cheer）

- Between verses, talk about how many fish stayed away. Model sentences such as, 'There were five fish and then one stayed away, so there were four that came back'. Show how five fish with one moving away leaves four.
- Between verses, discuss what the next day of the week will be.

Variations

- The children can have fish finger puppets, or show the number of fingers representing the number of fish.
- Start with ten fish, and sing the song with less discussion about the next number.

How is this maths?

Counting backwards and thinking about 'taking away' are two early ways to think about subtraction. When showing a representation, such as a fish puppet, the children are linking number to the number of objects represented. When they are using their fingers they are using abstract representation of the numbers. Knowing the name of the days of the week and that they repeat in a particular order is important for children to think about pattern and how we record time and dates.

Nothing but net

Add and take away the fish.

Aims and objectives

- To learn how to count on.
- To take away.

Resources

- Small toy fish or small cardboard fish that have been cut out and laminated for durability
- One 'net' per child (optional and may not be desirable for some children, see tip below)
- Bag with small cards, as listed below

Yellow cards:

Catch 1 fish	Catch 1 fish	Catch 1 fish	Catch 1 fish
Catch 2 fish	Catch 2 fish	Catch 2 fish	Catch 2 fish
Catch 3 fish	Catch 3 fish	Catch 3 fish	Catch 3 fish

Red cards:

Throw back 1 fish	Throw back 1 fish	Throw back 1 fish	Throw back 1 fish
Throw back 2 fish	Throw back 2 fish	Throw back 2 fish	Throw back 2 fish
Throw back 3 fish	Throw back 3 fish	Throw back 3 fish	Throw back 3 fish

Preparation

- Place the fish in a 'fish tank' or in the 'sea' (a central place on floor or table where all the children can reach).
- If you wish to use nets, provide each child with a fishing net.

What to do

- Children take turns to draw a card from the bag. They follow the instructions on the card by gathering fish from the central pot, or returning them. They then return the card to the bag.
- The winner is the first child to get to a nominated number of fish (for example 15 or 20 fish) .
- If a red card is drawn and the child does not have that number of fish to return, they either miss a turn, or draw further cards until they can follow the action.

Tip   Children who require more counting practice may find it easier to have their fish lined up in front of them rather than in a net.

Variations

- Use larger numbers and increase the number of fish that have to be caught.
- You may have only the yellow cards in the bag, for counting on only. Alternatively each child may start with 20 fish and the winner is the child who has the most remaining after one child's net is empty.

How is this maths?

This game of chance gives children the opportunity to count and look at the effect on their total number of fish of 'catching' (adding) or 'throwing back' (subtracting) individual fish.

Rainbow fish

Aims and objectives

- To recognise numerals.
- To learn accurate counting.

Resources

- Book: *The Rainbow Fish* by Marcus Pfister
- Fish templates（see illustration）– one per child
- Counters
- Dice

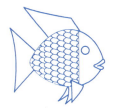

Preparation

- Read *The Rainbow Fish* to the children.
- Provide each child with a 'Rainbow Fish' template.
- Children cover their template with counters on the scales.

What to do

- Children take turns to roll the dice and remove the number of scales（counters）that the dice shows.
- Children must roll the correct number to finish.
- The winner is the child who has managed to give away all their scales first.

Tip   When talking with the children about the 'Rainhow Fish' giving away his scales, discuss what happens to the remaining number of scales on his body（they reduce in number）.

Variation

Children may share one template between one pair of children, for the children to count together and help each other play the game.

How is this maths?

When children use dice they see an abstract representation of a particular number. With experience children will develop knowledge about what each representation means without having to count the number of dots.

Chapter 5

Games

Introduction

You are likely to have an area in your classroom where games are kept. Are they accessible to all the children all of the time? Or do you bring games out for the children to play with at different times? Perhaps you use a combination of these. Of course games can be played as they are traditionally designed. However, you may want to think about the extent to which you could adapt the games to a larger or smaller scale. For example, the children could help their toys to play hopscotch on a table, or a giant snakes and ladders board could be drawn with chalk in the outdoor area. Dice also come in a range of sizes.

Games with dice

Children learn another way to represent number through using dice.

Counting on and back

Use the dice to see how many squares to count on or back.

Aims and objectives
- To take turns.
- To practise counting.

Resources
- Dice
- A 'board', either indoors or out

Preparation
- If necessary create an outdoor game 'board' to reflect the theme.

> **What to do**
> - Children take turns throwing the dice and moving their counter along the requisite number of squares.

Tip Ensure the children learn that they start counting on the *next* square and not the one their counter is already resting on. This helps them when they are 'counting on' in addition.

Variations

If playing on a larger scale, the children could be the 'counters' and move themselves along the board. To practise subtraction use two dice and move along the difference of the two numbers on the dice. Alternatively use one regular dice and another that shows '–' and '+' or the terms 'take' and 'add', or 'forward' and 'back'.

Children practise counting on board games. Using the dice provides an opportunity for the children to see that numbers can be represented in different ways. Counting on or counting back along the board is a useful context for the children to learn about early addition and subtraction.

Snakes and ladders

An alternative three-dimensional construction approach to this traditional board game.

Aims and objectives
- To practise counting.
- To understand greater than/less than.
- To practise problem-solving.

Resources
- Fabric cut into strips to represent the snakes
- Cardboard or paper cut into ladders
- Large number square, say 1 – 50
- One blank dice (prepared as below)
- One regular dice
- Counters, one per child
- One set of smaller number cards with the same numbers as are on the board, say 1 – 50

Preparation
- Lay out the number square.
- On one blank dice draw a ladder and a snake on the same face. Leave the remaining five faces blank.

What to do
- The children start to play the board by rolling the two dice.
- If the 'blank' dice rolls a plain face the child moves their counter along the board as they normally would, according to the number on the regular dice.

- If they roll the face that shows a snake/ladder then they take a number card from the pile.
- If the number is *greater than* the square they are currently on, they place a ladder from their current square to the square on the number card. If it is *less than* their occupied square, they place a snake between the two squares.
- The child moves along the ladder/snake in the same turn.
- The next child takes their turn to roll the two dice and the game continues.

Tip

Have a length of fabric for making the snakes and allow the children to cut the fabric to the desired length. Encourage the children to think about how the snakes' curves have an impact on the *length* of the fabric required. When the board is complete photograph it, print out the photo onto an A4 page and laminate it. This will build up a stock of board games the children can play in class or during rainy lunch times.

Variations

Constructing this game can be applied to a range of contexts, such as 'Jack and the Beanstalk' (where the ladders become beanstalks and the snakes become giants' boots or an axe), 'The Grand old Duke of York' (where different shades of green fabric are used for going up and down hills) or weather (using sunbeams for ladders and streams of raindrops for snakes).

How is this maths?

The children are *counting*, *matching*, *recognising* and *reading* numbers. They are also *problem-solving* and using *reasoning* as they talk about the development of the board.

Floor robot games

Floor robots, such as Bee-bot, Roamer or Pixie, are fun and easy for children to use.

Floor robot competition

Whose robot will win the game?

Aims and objectives

- To learn about addition using counting on.
- To learn about subtraction using counting back.

Resources

- One or two floor robots
- Two sets of number cards that are the same length as the robot moving one step
- Two dice, one red and one blue

Preparation

- Set out the number cards in two lines with a little space between the two lines.

Robot	1	2	3	4	5	6	7	8	9	10

Robot	1	2	3	4	5	6	7	8	9	10

What to do

- Divide the children into two teams.
- Place one floor robot next to, but not on, each of the number 1s on the number track.
- The teams take turns to roll the two dice. The red dice shows how many squares the robot can move *forward* (program the robot to take these steps) and the blue dice shows how many squares the robot should move *backward* (then program the robot to take these steps back).
- The winning team is the team who makes the target first.

Tip
The game may take some time to play. To speed things up, put larger numbers on the red dice. Once the children have become adept at setting the robot to go forward for the red number and back for the blue, encourage them to visualise the moves the robot would take then ask them how the robot could take the shortest route to that number.

Variation

To work with different numbers, use a different start and end number in the number track.

How is this maths?

The children are beginning to use the number track to look at *counting on* and *counting back*. The robot is moving in the same way that they will later use other *number tracks* and then *number lines* to carry out *addition* and *subtraction*.

Floor robot target

Children enjoy estimating and then getting the robot to hit the target.

Aims and objectives

- To estimate length.
- To create instructions.
- To check the reasonableness of estimations.

Resources

- Masking tape or similar
- Two floor robots

Preparation

- Mask out a target zone on the floor with the tape.
- Set the floor robots some distance from the target.

What to do

- Divide the children into two teams. Each will be responsible for one of the robots.

- Encourage the children to discuss in their teams how many robot body lengths the robots are away from the centre of the target.
- One representative from each team will program the robot with the estimated distance.
- The team who comes the closest to the bullseye wins.

Tip   You may put a skittle or similar in the centre for the robot to knock down. Talk about how much further the robot needed to travel, or the distance the robot travelled too far.

Variations

- Different scores could be given for reaching different areas – the closer to the target, the higher the score.
- Face the robots away from the target so the children need to think about rotating the robot and using quarter turns and half turns as well as length.
- Instead of one target only, create a golf course around the floor within which the teams must program their robots to touch each target. The team with the lowest number of moves wins.

How is this maths?

Estimation is a key mathematical skill. By estimating the distance the robot needs to travel, the children are then able to check the reasonableness of their estimations and amend future estimations accordingly.

Beanbags

A resource that is easy to hold and throw.

Aims and objectives

- To visualise numbers.
- To understand addition as 'how many altogether'.
- To understand subtraction as 'how many more' or the 'difference'.

Resources

- Five small beanbags for throwing
- Bag or small container for holding the beanbags
- Bucket or bin or similar for throwing the beanbags into

Preparation

- None required.

What to do

- Show the children you have five beanbags and count them together.
- Throw some of the beanbags into the bucket. Ask the children, 'How many have I got left?' Check together by counting.
- Repeat, encouraging the children to throw the beanbags too.

Tip   Some beanbags may miss. Ask how many got into the bucket and how many missed. This is an opportunity to add together three numbers – the beanbags in the bucket, those on the floor and those yet to be thrown.

Variations

- Ask the children to close their eyes and listen to you or other children dropping the beanbags into the bucket. Repeat with different numbers of beanbags.
- Use other items that may be thrown or dropped into the target.
- Play simply to see how many beanbags can be thrown into the bucket: split the children into two groups where members take turns throwing the beanbags into the bucket. The first team to reach a pre-agreed score is the winning team.

How is this maths?

This is an opportunity for the children to think about the different ways the number 5 can be created, for example 1 and 4, 2 and 2 and 1, and so on. By *visualising* the beanbags in the bucket the children will be able to undertake these simple calculations more effectively.

Hide-and-count

. . . .

This is similar to the traditional Kim's Game.

Aims and objectives

- To practise counting.
- To visualise a number.

Resources

- Any objects that can be handled, for counting
- A tea towel or similar for covering the objects or a bag/box for placing them into

Preparation

- None required,

What to do

- Count out three objects.
- Cover them.
- Show one being taken away.
- Ask, 'How many are still under the cover?'
- Reveal and check.
- Repeat with different numbers.

Tip   Start with smaller numbers and then increase the number of objects being used. When larger numbers are used, start by taking away small numbers or half of the whole set.

Variation

Children can play with each other.

How is this maths?

Children are counting and visualising number. They are thinking about subtraction as *taking away*.

Make a group

· · · · · · · · · · · · · · · · · · ·

A fun way to burn off some energy or to make groups for physical development or PE activities.

Aims and objectives

- To practise counting.
- To understand problem solving.

Resources

- Large amounts of space

Preparation

- None required.

What to do

- Call out a number and ask the children to make groups consisting of that number of children.
- Any children who do not find themselves in a group can join in again for the next round.

Tip

This game helps encourage teamwork. The practitioner/teacher might time each attempt and encourage the children to improve (reduce) the length of time it takes them to get into their groups.

Variation

This can be played in a competitive way where any children who do not find themselves in a group can watch from the side while the next groups form, until there is one child left who is the winner.

How is this maths?

During the activity the children will practise counting. They will also be working out if their group is *too big* or *too small* – both key mathematical concepts.

On your bike!

Children enjoy riding their bikes, scooters or tricycles around a given route.

Aims and objectives

- To follow directions.
- To give directions.

Resources

- Tricycles or scooters or bicycles
- An area pre-painted or taped out with roads for the children to ride on
- Lollipop-type 'stop' and 'go' sign

Preparation

- The children may design and create the route with you.

What to do

- The children move around the route by foot or using the play transport.
- One child may be the lollipop holder, telling the travellers to *go* or *stop* along the route.
- Ask, 'Is there a T-junction? Which way are you going to go now?'

Tip   This activity offers you the opportunity to talk a lot to the children about staying on the *left* of the road and about going *through*, *over*, *under*, *between* and *zig-zagging* around objects on the route.

Variation

Add traffic lights. 'What are the colours? What do the colours tell us to do?'

How is this maths?

There is a lot of mathematical vocabulary that can be used in this activity. Giving and following directions requires the children to use their reasoning skills.

Hide-and-seek

A fun way to give friends directions to a hidden object.

Aims and objectives

- To use positional language.
- To estimate distance.

Resources

- A set of small objects

Preparation

- Place a number of small objects around the room or outside, partially hidden from sight.

What to do

- Ask the children to look around the room or outdoor space to find the hidden objects. Explain they are not to give away the location of any objects they find.
- After a short time, bring the children together. Encourage the children to take turns to describe the location of one object for others to find without pointing!

Tip   The small objects can be related to the current theme or topic. Encourage the children to use positional language such as *on*, *under*, *next to*, *behind*, and so on.

Variations

- One at a time （or in pairs） tell the children if they are warm, hot, cooler, etc. as they move around the space to identify the hidden location of an object.
- The child （ren） could leave the room while the remainder of the children hide an object and then give the directions themselves.

How is this maths?

The children are using positional language to describe the position of an object in their environment. This is very early geometry. If playing the variation above, the children are estimating distance from an object by using 'hot', 'warm', 'freezing', and so on. Using only words and no gestures is very difficult.

Hopscotch

A variation on the traditional game, which children can play independently or in a small group.

Aims and objectives

- To recognise numbers.
- To practise counting.

Resources

- A hopscotch area painted or drawn outdoors, or taped on the floor indoors
- A small object to throw, such as a beanbag or small toy

Preparation

- Tape the hopscotch outline on the carpet or hall floor if no room outdoors.

What to do

- Children throw the beanbag onto the hopscotch area.
- They hop or jump on the numbers of the hopscotch, avoiding the number the beanbag landed on.

Tips

- Talk about what number they have missed out (because the beanbag is on it). Discuss the two numbers it is between. Ask, 'What number is it after? What number is it before?'
- Talk about hopping and jumping and the difference: one leg/two legs.

Variation

Play in the more traditional way, by throwing the beanbag onto the numbers in succession and allowing the next person to have their turn if the bag does not land in the correct square.

How is this maths?

By playing hopscotch the children are recognising numbers and counting.

Chapter 6

All about me

Introduction

Children love to talk about themselves and explore their own bodies. This chapter contains a wide range of activities that explore a variety of mathematical concepts. Take and display photographs of the children undertaking the activities. Displaying these with labels that discuss the mathematical skills that were used (for example, counting: 'I have ten toes,' says Ishmal) will support children beyond the activities themselves.

My body

We can explore our bodies using lots of mathematical ideas.

Aims and objectives

- To practise counting.
- To learn about estimating.

Resources

- None required.

Preparation

- None required.

What to do

- This is an activity based on discussion. Ask the following sorts of questions:
- 'What can you find that there are then of?' (Fingers, toes.)
- 'What can you find that there are two of?' (Legs, arms, eyes, ears, feet, hands, eyebrows, nostrils, knees, ankles, armpits.) 'Why are there two?' (Talk about the *symmetry* of their bodies.)
- 'What can you find that there is one of?' (Nose, belly button.) 'Why is there one?' (Talk about the *midline* or *line of symmetry* of their bodies.)
- Count: 'How many teeth do you have? Do we all have the same number of teeth? Why/why not? How old are you?'
- Estimate: 'How many hairs do you think you might have?'

Tips

- Draw around the children and make a template so they can identify the body parts.
- Although the last point above is an *estimation* activity, for your information there are, on average, 100,000 hairs on a human head, although this varies between individuals as well as according to the colour of a person's hair!

Variations

Don't just stop at counting discrete numbers. Look at other ways to use numbers, e.g.

continuous measures such as children's heights. Children can order themselves according to their height, or compare their height with those of toys or other objects in the room. They can also look at foot length or hand span, waist circumference and so on.

How is this maths?

Young children do not need to count two objects. They can look at a set of two and just know that there are two objects. This is because they develop the notion of 'twoness' very early. Thinking about larger numbers requires them to count. Estimating the number of hairs on their head will elicit a number of weird and wonderful numbers but this will excite them as they talk about all the really large numbers they know. Children are also thinking about symmetry, another intuitive concept. Finally, they are using comparing skills.

Travelling

Explore the different modes of transport that the children use and think about their various purposes.

Aims and objectives
- To represent data in a pictogram.
- To interpret data in a pictogram.

Resources
- Objects or pictures to represent different modes of transport

Preparation
- None required.

What to do
- Discuss, 'How do you normally travel to nursery/school?'
- Give each child an object or picture of their mode of transport
- Ask the children, 'How do we know *how many* people travel by car?' Talk about how having everyone sitting on the carpet all mixed up makes answering this question difficult. Ask for ideas about how it could be made easier. Steer the children into thinking about *grouping* themselves, still holding their objects/pictures.
- Ask the children 'Which is the *most popular* way to travel to nursery/school?' or '*How many more* people travel by car than walk?' Again talk about how this is a difficult problem to solve when the children are standing in groups. Steer the children into standing in rows so they can see which is the longest line.
- Line up the objects, or stick the pictures onto the wall.

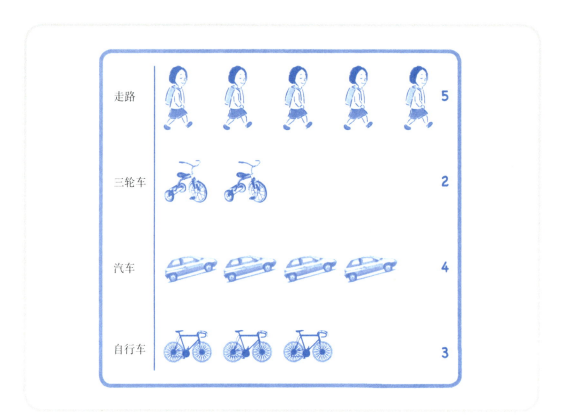

走路		5
三轮车		2
汽车		4
自行车		3

- Have a set of objects/pictures ready that are not going to be used, for example an aeroplane. Talk about why there are no children using this mode of transport.
- With higher-attaining children 'trick' them by spacing out one of the smaller sets of pictures on the wall, and state that more children used that mode of transport. Talk about why your statement is incorrect, and encourage the children to rectify the error. Discuss why it is important to have the same size pictures/objects and to ensure even spaces between them.

Variations

- This can be used with any topic about ourselves, such as types of shoes being worn, shoe size, birthday months, eye colour, number of siblings, favourite books and so on.
- If introducing block graphs, instead of giving the children an object or picture of the mode of transport give them a particular colour of a Unifix® or Multilink® block, for example, so they can make a tower to answer the questions. Similarly provide each child with a coloured square card to stick onto the wall.

How is this maths?

This approach to data handling helps children to make links between graphs and real data items. It helps them to understand that representing data in graphical form can help them to make more sense of it. Having items that are going to be the *null set* (such as aeroplanes in this example) provides an opportunity for children to understand how the *empty set* can also be represented on a graph.

My day

This gives children an opportunity to think about their daily routines in chronological order.

Aims and objectives

- To order events.
- To use time-related vocabulary.

Resources

- Pictures of routines that children would undertake during the day (e. g. getting up, brushing teeth, breakfast, lunch, tea, having a bath, feeding pets, going to bed, travelling to/from nursery/school, going to the mosque, visiting grandparents, playing)
- Blank cards for children to draw their own routines that may not already be represented
- Glue if the children are going to stick the pictures in order

Preparation

- Laminate the pictures if you wish to use them again.

What to do

- Talk with the children about what they do during one day.
- Provide them with the pictures of the events they talk about, in any order.
- Ask the children to order the pictures. Ask questions such as, 'What do you do *first* in the *morning*?', 'What happens *next*?', 'What is the very *last* thing you do at *night*?', and 'Is there anything that happens *between* these two?'
- Encourage the children to tell the story of their day, using as many time-related words as possible. Include times of the day such as morning, afternoon, evening, night, noon, dawn, dusk, day and night.

| Tip | Have more than one card to allow for repeats during the day, and be prepared for surprises as not all children do what you think they would do in the order you might expect! |

Variation

Use *times* and match events with *analogue clocks*. For example, lunch might be at 12 o'clock and bedtime might be at 7 o'clock.

How is this maths?

Understanding the order of events and what time they happen helps children to *sequence*. Sequencing is an important skill to use when attempting to solve problems.

Chapter 7

Houses and homes

Introduction

Many of the activities in this chapter can be undertaken both indoors and out. To support the activities you could set up an estate agents in the role-play area or go for a walk to explore the different types of houses nearby. Making dens and model houses can be carried out on a very large or a smaller scale, and they can be made out of a wide range of materials.

Other people's homes

Children find it fascinating to learn about the way other people's homes are constructed.

Aims and objectives

- To talk about shape.

Resources

- Pictures of non-traditional-British homes （e.g. igloo, tepee, mud homes, homes on stilts, tree houses, houseboats）

Preparation

- None required.

What to do

- Discuss what the houses in the surrounding area look like and how they are built. Talk about the *rectangular* doors, windows and walls. Discuss the construction, such as the *triangular* roof, and what materials have been used in the building, such as *rectangular prism* bricks.
- Explain to the children that you are going to show them some pictures of other types of houses. Do they know any? Encourage them to discuss what they already know about other types of houses.
- Show the children the pictures. Discuss how they are built to keep them stable. Identify the shapes within the dwellings.

Tips

- Adapt the first point （above） as appropriate to your immediate area.
- Model appropriate two- and three-dimensional shape language. For example, a roof may be *triangular*, not a *triangle*. Most children are able very quickly to use appropriate language when it has been modelled by an adult through careful discussion.
- Explore why particular shapes are used in different constructions. For example, igloos are dome-shaped because an arch is a strong shape. The dome also requires no other structure （such as beams or poles） to

keep it up. Additionally, a dome has the smallest possible surface area, which provides the best insulation.

Variation

Ask the children to design and model their own house. Discuss where it is going to be located, what materials are going to be used and what shapes it needs to use in order to make it fit for purpose.

How is this maths?

In this activity the children are exploring how shapes are used in construction in order to make the construction strong and fit for purpose.

A nonsense house

Get creative with this nonsense design activity.

Aims and objectives

- To use shape-related language.
- To think about the properties of shapes.

Resources

- Selection of coloured paper shapes
- A4 paper
- Glue

Preparation

- You may wish to make your own nonsense house to show the children.

What to do

- Talk to the children about their houses and why certain features are the shape they are (e. g. 'Why is a door *rectangular*?') . Include items in the house in the discussion (e. g. 'Why is the table *flat*?') .
- Now encourage the children to imagine a nonsense world where there were houses that could not be used. For example, a *spherical* house that sat wobbling on top of a hill, a *square-based pyramid* for a bed that was very uncomfortable or

a scooter that had *triangular prisms* for wheels.

- Give the children an everyday object, or ask them to think of one of their own. (For example, a car, a house, a bicycle, a table, a television, a sofa).
- Encourage the children to talk with a friend about their object. How could they make it as nonsensical as possible? Then share the answers with the group.
- Arrange the shapes of the object onto an A4 sheet and, when ready, glue them down.
- Share again once finished.

Tips

- Ensure the children continue to talk about the shapes. They may need to talk about the materials being used, but the focus of this activity is the shapes being used.
- You may put the designs together and jointly write a story about a day in the life of Mr and Mrs Shape who live in Nonsenseland.

Variation

Using junk modelling instead of paper shapes to make the nonsense items.

How is this maths?

The children are using their knowledge of the properties of shapes to create objects that are complete nonsense. By producing a design of something that would not be fit for purpose they are thinking in a creative way about the properties of shapes and why we use specific shapes for particular functions.

Making dens

Aims and objectives

- To practise problem solving.
- To learn about measurement.

Resources

- Items for making a den, inside or out
- Cups, fruit or biscuits and water (or role-play tea-making items)

Preparation

- Check there is an appropriate space for this activity, inside or out.

What to do

- Either independently or with support the children can make a den, choosing from a selection of available resources.
- Once constructed, give the children afternoon tea or a snack and eat it with them in the den. Encourage them to pour the water and share the food out evenly.

Tip

During the construction, talk with the children about their design and why they are choosing to construct it that way. Help them to make sense of the space they are using and model appropriate propositional language, such as *under, next to, over* and *between*, as well as early geometrical language such as *cover, big, corner, top* and *side*. When pouring the water talk about *nearly full, full, empty, half-full* and *half-empty*.

Variation

Have afternoon tea in a pre-existing place, such as a Wendy house or outside on the field.

 How is this maths?

While the children are creating their den they are solving problems related to the construction. For example they need to reason about the best materials to use and they are communicating mathematically with each other. Pouring water into cups offers an opportunity to develop concepts related to *capacity*. *Sharing* food leads to *division by grouping* later on.

That's just up our street!

Ordering the houses along a street provides a good opportunity for a lot of mathematical talk about numbers.

Aims and objectives
- To recognise numbers.
- To learn about number patterns.

Resources
- Photographs or drawings of front doors with the house number clearly labelled
- A large street or map drawn out where the houses can be placed (optional)

Preparation
- If using a street to lay the houses upon ensure this is out before the children start the activity. Make sure it is securely fastened because the children will bump it as they position the houses in the correct places.

What to do
- Look at the photos or the pictures of the houses. What can we see on them? (The house numbers.)
- Ask, 'Can you work out who might be neighbours? How do you know that those two houses are neighbouring?'
- Encourage the children to place the houses in the correct order, along both sides of the street.

Tips
- This can be used as part of a theme or topic on the postman and mail. The children could become the post office staff, sorting the mail and then delivering the post to the houses along the street in the most efficient manner.
- Encourage the children to look at the starting number and identify any patterns they see along the road (for example one side will have house numbers that end in 2, 4, 6, 8 and 0 only). Talk about the *odd* and *even* numbers.

Variations

- Some cul-de-sacs contain houses that are in *numerical order*. Younger children or lower-attaining children could be encouraged to place houses around a cul-de-sac that comes off a larger road.

- You may provide a range of properties to challenge further the children's understanding of number. For example, there may be a factory or warehouse that is numbered 24 – 28 because it takes up three plots on one side of the road.

How is this maths?

This activity encourages the children to look at *patterns*. One pattern uses *counting numbers*, where they cross the street each time they get to the next number. Another pattern is to look at the *odd* and *even* numbers on each side of the street. Being able to spot patterns sets the foundation for later mathematical problems using more complex number patterns. This activity also helps them to see how numbers have a purpose (identifying a home) and how they give order and structure, which makes finding a particular home easier for any visitors.

My home

An opportunity for children to think about their own home a little more.

Aims and objectives

- To recognise and order numbers.
- To practise reasoning.

Resources

- None required

Preparation

- Encourage the children's families to talk with them about their own house number and the house numbers of friends, neighbours and family in preparation for this activity.

What to do

- Ask, 'What number house do you live at?', 'Who lives next to you?' and 'What number do they live at?'
- Ask, 'What rooms do you use in your house?', 'What times of the day do you use them?', 'Where would you go if you were hungry?', 'Where would you sit to eat?' and 'Where do you go when you are getting tired?'

Tip

Some children may not know their own house number. You may wish to look up the children's records before this activity to help them complete it. It is likely that many of the children will not know their neighbours' house numbers. They may be surprised to find that it is not a number immediately before or after their own house number!

Variation

Talk further about the numbers that the children live at. What might '23a' mean? What about 1/33 in a row of flats? Does anyone not have a number? Perhaps they have a name, like 'Rose Cottage', to identify their house.

How is this maths?

In this activity children are talking about numbers in an everyday context that is familiar to them. They are also able to talk about the purpose that certain rooms have in their home and reason why this might be the case.

We've got it covered!

A chance to look at repeating patterns on the walls in our homes.

Aims and objectives

- To identify repeating patterns.

Resources

- Wallpaper samples
- Wallpaper border samples

Preparation

- You may wish to make a *unit block* of each wallpaper or border sample by identifying which is the *repeating unit*, cutting it out and mounting it on cardboard （or laminating it） so the children can move it around the larger section of wallpaper.

What to do

- Talk about how people decorate the walls of their homes. Some children will have painted surfaces, others will have tiles （particularly in the bathroom） and some will have wallpaper.
- Show one of the wallpapers or borders you have collected. Ask the children to describe what they can see. Encourage them to identify that the paper is made of repeating patterns.
- Can the children see how the pattern has been made to repeat? Has it been *slid* along the paper （*translated*） , has it been *turned* （*rotated*） and/or has it been *flipped* （*reflected*）？ If you have made a unit block from the sample use it to help the children describe what they can see.
- Divide the children into pairs or small groups, provide them with other samples and encourage them to work out how they are made.

Tip

Wallpaper and border samples can be gathered from decorating stores free of charge. Use wallpapers that the children will find attractive. Papers that use geometric figures enable children to use their mathematical language more than those with figures of popular cartoon characters.

Variation

When looking at celebrations or giving presents as a topic, use selections of gift-wrap instead of wallpaper.

How is this maths?

The children are exploring geometric patterns using early language related to transformational geometry. They will also begin to understand that patterns have no end and that they keep repeating.

Be an interior designer!

This is an enjoyable follow-up activity.

Aims and objectives

- To copy and continue a repeating pattern.
- To create a repeating pattern.

Resources

- Strips of paper approximately 10 cm × 50 cm
- Sponges or potatoes with shapes cut into them for printing
- Paint (limit to three colours)
- Mini white boards and markers, or scrap paper with crayons

Preparation

- Carry out the activity 'We've got it covered!' in preparation for this activity.

What to do

- Show the children a wallpaper border. Discuss the repeating pattern.
- Explain that the children (in pairs if you prefer) are going to design their own pattern.
- Show them the sponges/potatoes and discuss the shapes that are available to use.
- Reveal the paint colours they are able to use.
- Encourage them to talk with a partner about what shapes (limit this to two or three depending on their attainment) and what colour paint they will use.
- Ask the children to record their ideas on their mini whiteboards or scrap paper.

- The children will share with the group how their pattern repeats, both in terms of the shapes used and the colours used. If the children have rotated their shapes, discuss this also.
- Once the pattern designs have been finalised provide the large strips of paper, the sponges and paint for the children to create their own border.
- When finished, ask the children questions such as: 'What shape is the third shape?' 'When does that appear again?' 'And again?' 'What would the 15th shape be?' (ensure you select an ordinal number that is not on the pattern, so the children are required to visualise the continuing pattern) ; 'What shape is after/before the red square?' 'What is the next shape in your pattern?' 'How do you know the next shape is going to be yellow?' 'What is the basic unit you have used in your pattern?'

Tips
- Throughout the printing process talk with the children about the shapes they are using and how the pattern *repeats*.
- Display the borders with typed-up explanations from the children about how they made their repeating pattern.
- You may show the children a television clip from an interior design programme that uses a wallpaper border.
- For younger children simply start a pattern for them and ask them to continue it. Limit the number of shapes to two or three and the number of colours to one or two.

Variation

The children might print their own paper for covering a special book, t-shirt or ribbon, etc.

How is this maths?

The children have designed and made their own repeating geometric patterns. By asking them what comes next they are able to discuss the pattern. When explaining where the triangles appear they are linking the pattern to ordinal numbers (for example second, fourth, sixth and so on). Additionally they are *visualising* the pattern beyond what they can see on their border.

The doll's house

Small-world play always captures children's imaginations.

Aims and objectives

- To use propositional language.
- To learn how to order events.

Resources

- Doll's house with associated items

Preparation

- None required.

What to do

While a group of children are playing with the doll's house encourage them to talk about:

- What the dolls are doing. For example, going *up* the stairs, getting *in* bed.
- The day the dolls are having. 'What have the dolls been doing today?' Can the children place the events in order?
- Why the dolls are in a particular room. Ask, 'Is it lunchtime for the dolls? How are they going to get ready for lunch?' 'Can you help the dolls to get ready for bed?'

Tip　This structured play activity involves you modelling appropriate vocabulary and prompting the children to explore other mathematical ideas as the opportunity arises.

Variation

Using a farm, superhero's lair or other small-world area the same mathematical ideas can be explored in a context that might be more attractive to some children.

How is this maths?

Through small-world play children re-enact events that are real or imagined.

It is possible for you to model and encourage children to use mathematical vocabulary through this natural behaviour. In this activity using positional language develops into geometric concepts, ordering events considers time-related concepts and associating tasks with rooms supports children's problem-solving and reasoning skills.

Chapter 8

The Teddy Bears' Picnic

Introduction

Planning and undertaking a teddy bears' picnic gives children an opportunity to collaborate on a project together. You may want to select one group of older children in the nursery to plan and run the picnic for all the children, or you could have the whole class arranging a day that involves friends and family as well. Running a few stalls or charging a small price for the food could also turn these activities into a fun fundraising event.

Choosing a picnic blanket

····· ······

Which blanket is the best to take?

Aims and objectives

- To practise problem solving.
- To learn about area.

Resources

- A variety of different-sized blankets: some very small and, if possible, one or two that are too large

Preparation

- Jumble up the blankets and put them into a large box.

What to do

- Explain to the children that a picnic blanket is an essential item to take because it provides somewhere to sit and eat the picnic.
- Show the children the box and explain that no one can carry the whole box to the picnic, and that there are probably too many blankets in the box anyway.
- Ask the children if they would like to help prepare for the picnic by selecting the most appropriate blankets.
- Depending on the children either provide further support so they can identify a list of criteria for selecting blankets, or let the children explore the contents of the box and identify their own criteria through blanket selection.
- When complete, ask the children to explain why they chose the blankets they did.

Tips

- Encourage the children to think about the number of children who can sit on each blanket. Talk about how many bottoms can fit on the blanket and how some blankets (for example those that are very long but skinny) might fit fewer bottoms than one that at first looks smaller.
- Be open-minded about the reasons for the children's selections. While you may want to talk about practicality, some children may feel that aesthetic reasons are more important!

Variation

Any theme that requires the children to consider an area of a shape could involve some sorting. For example, the children may need to decide which tables to use for a Red Nose Day table-top sale at lunch time, or which wrapping paper to use to wrap the differently sized boxes.

How is this maths?

Exploring area in this way helps children to think about *conservation of area*. Understanding that the area of a shape may be different to the visual signals the shape gives to the brain is a notion that children will understand with a lot of practical experience.

Time for the picnic?

········   ········

Thinking about what time the picnic will be held helps children to use vocabulary related to telling the time.

Aims and objectives

- To learn to draw o'clock on an analogue clock.

Resources

- Clock face
- Blank paper or invitation templates

Preparation

- Prepare the invitation templates if using.

**Invitation to our
Teddy Bears' Picnic**

To (name of teddy) ——————————

Where? The outdoor area

When? Friday 4th June

What time? ——— o'clock

What to do

- Explain to the children that they will be inviting one of their teddy bears to the picnic.
- Talk about the time the picnic will be held （two o'clock） and show the children two o'clock on the analogue clock.
- Encourage the children to create invitations （or complete the template） and include a diagram of the analogue clock on the invitation so their teddy knows what two o'clock looks like.

Tips

- Vary the amount you have completed the template depending on the children's confidence or motivation in writing. Some children may prefer to draw a picture of their teddy.
- Some children will not have a teddy bear. Encourage the children to bring any toy of their choosing, explaining it does not have to be a teddy bear.

Variations

- Use time-related invitations when the children are inviting people to come to talk to them, or when they are making notices about educational visits they are going on.
- Talk about the duration of the event to help the children to think also about the passing of time.

How is this maths?

Time can be seen in two different ways, passing the time and telling the time. Reading the time on an analogue clock is very complex and confusing. For example, an analogue clock reads ten minutes to twelve but when the minute hand is on the eight it is not eight minutes to the hour! Each hour is given by a number but the minutes are only shown by indentations. Fifteen minutes past can also be said as quarter past, but the hand points at three!

Preparing and making the picnic

The day is arriving! Let's get the picnic prepared.

Sandwich fillings

A data-collection task to ensure the children get their favourite sandwich at the picnic.

Aims and objectives

- To practise counting.
- To learn about data handling.

Resources

- Large pictures of the sandwich fillings on offer
- Sticky notes

Preparation

- Laminate the sandwich fillings pictures if you wish, to reuse when the sandwiches are being prepared.
- Write the children's names on the sticky notes, one per child.

What to do

- Explain to the children that on the day of the picnic they will be making their sandwiches and so to ensure that everyone gets a sandwich they want to eat, we need to organise how many of each filling we need to buy.
- Show the children the filling options and display them clearly while they are being discussed. Ask the children to choose their favourite filling for their sandwich.
- Pass the children the sticky note with their name.
- Ask one child do identify their favourite filling. Give them the picture of that filling and ask them to stand in a designated area in the room. Repeat until all the pictures have been given out.
- Ask the remaining children to sit next to the person holding their favourite filling.
- The person holding the picture will take the sticky note from each child in turn and place it on the picture.

- Ask the groups to return one at a time and collate the information on a board. Talk about which is the *most popular* filling, which is the *least popular* and why that might be the case.
- Remind the children that they will be using the filling they have identified in their own sandwich.

Tip Encourage the groups to check that the number of sticky notes they have corresponds to the number of children in their group.

Variation

The children may write their own name on their sticky note. The activity could be undertaken in the same way as the data-handling activity in 'Travelling' (see pages 77 – 79), using a pictogram or block graph instead.

How is this maths?

The children are sorting the sandwich fillings and identifying how much of each filling is required. This is a type of data handling that helps them achieve a specific purpose and reduces waste.

Making the sandwiches

On the day of the picnic the children can make their own sandwiches.

Aims and objectives
- To follow instructions.
- To estimate quantity.

Resources
- Instructions on a recipe card (numbered, with illustrations)
- Bread
- Butter or spread
- Fillings
- Butter knives

- Cutting boards and plates
- Fillings cards with children's named sticky notes on them （from previous activity）

Preparation

- Set out the utensils, bread, butter and one filling and its instructions on each table.

What to do

- Demonstrate to the children how to make a sandwich by following the instructions on the recipe card:
  1. Lay the bread out.
  2. Butter the bread.
  3. Spread the jam （or whatever filling is on the table）.
  4. Place the slices of bread together.
  5. Put the sandwich onto a plate.
- Remind the children that they are sharing the filling and butter with all the children at their table so they need to think carefully about how much they are taking.
- Identify which children will be working at which table.
- Send one group at a time to wash their hands.
- The children can then make their sandwich.
- Ask the children to place the sandwich on the plate with their named sticky note from the filling picture.

Tips

- The more adults that are present the better support can be given to those children who may need a little extra help.
- As the children are following the numbered instructions encourage them to use *first*, *second*, and so on.

Variations

- Make the toast with various spreads.
- Make porridge with various additions for a visit from Daddy Bear, Mummy Bear and Baby Bear.

 How is this maths?

Following instructions such as those in a recipe helps children to think about *ordinal numbers* (first, second, third ...). The children are also *estimating* the quantities of butter and filling required to make their sandwich.

Shapely sandwiches

Children enjoy eating sandwiches that are made into novel shapes.

Aims and objectives
- To practise conserving area.
- To name different shapes.

Resources
- Sandwiches made in previous activity
- Selection of biscuit cutters

Preparation
- If not following this activity on from the previous one then make some sandwiches or toast some slices of bread for the children to cut.

What to do
- Discuss how children normally have their sandwiches cut. Draw examples on the board, or demonstrate with existing sandwiches. Talk about the shapes that are made (*right-angled triangles, squares, rectangles*).
- Explain that today the children are going to make different shapes using cutters.
- Show the children the selection of cutters that are available to them. Discuss the shapes they make.
- Demonstrate how to use a cutter safely (i. e. check the sharp side is on the bread and push down with a flat palm) and most effectively (i. e. ensure the position of the shape is carefully planned out to reduce waste and check that it has cut through completely before removing).
- Show one piece of bread cut with the cutter in the middle and show how few/no other shapes can now be made.

Tip   Do not discard some shapes because they are 'too hard' for the children. For example, the shape below is a *dodecagon* because it has 12 sides. The children will love learning the names of new shapes!

Variation

This activity can also work when the children are making biscuits. Roll out the biscuit dough and cut the shapes before baking.

 How is this maths?

The children have to use their knowledge of *conservation of area* to choose the best place to use the cutters. By moving the cutters around until best use is made of the bread children will learn that what the cutter simply looks like can be deceptive in terms of how much space it uses!

It's a wrap!

Finally, the sandwiches need to be wrapped to take on the picnic.

Aims and objectives
• To estimate surface area.

Resources
• Sandwiches
• Greaseproof paper or similar for wrapping the sandwiches
• Small bags to place wrapped sandwiches in for carrying to the picnic

Preparation
• Cut the greaseproof paper into various sizes, some of which will not wrap a sandwich because they are too small and others that are too big and a waste of paper/wrapping.

What to do

- Place a selection of cut paper in the centre of each table.
- Encourage the children to take turns to look at the available paper and pick one piece to wrap their sandwich with.
- The other children can judge the child on how accurate their choice of paper was – was the paper too *big*, *too small*, or the *correct size*?
- Keep the named sticky notes with the sandwiches as they are placed in bags, one per child.

Tip   You may encourage the children to cut the paper themselves.

Variation

Match different-sized wrapping paper to boxes, cups to bottles of water or icing to biscuits, and so on!

How is this maths?

Estimating the surface area of an object is tricky. This activity gives children practice at this using visual clues. The more they practise, the more accurate their estimates will become.

Chapter 9

Feet

Introduction

The activities in this chapter could be planned and organised as a component of the 'All about me' activities in Chapter 6, or run alone. In addition to thinking about their own feet, the children could also explore the feet of other animals and think about why those feet are adapted to include certain features. In some cultures exposing feet to others can be insulting so be careful to know the children in your class before carrying out these activities.

My feet

Children love to compare their feet with other children's feet.

Aims and objectives

- To compare length.
- To understand ordering.

Resources

- Blank sheets of paper （or 2 cm-squared paper – optional）
- Crayon or felt tips
- Scissors

Preparation

- Ask the children to remove their footwear if appropriate, or they can keep their shoes on if they wish.

What to do

- Ask each child to stand still on the paper while you （or their friend） draw around their foot.
- The children can cut out their foot or leave it on the sheet.
- Encourage the children to order the feet in some way, for example from *longest* to *shortest*.

Tip   Children are likely to find they are ticklish when their feet are drawn around, so be sympathetic to this. If you use 2 cm-squared paper the children can compare the area of their feet by counting the squares. Smaller squares are more difficult to keep an accurate count of.

Variation

Draw around hands or whole bodies.

How is this maths?

Children are able to *compare* their foot with other feet. *Indirect comparison* occurs when children know that if child A's foot is shorter than child B's, and child B's foot is shorter than child C's, then child A's foot must be shorter than child C's. The term for this was coined by Piaget: *transitivity*. It underpins a lot of logical reasoning in mathematics.

Shoe sizes

Let's take a look at our shoe sizes.

Aims and objectives

• To use numbers in measurement contexts.

Resources

• A shoe sizer known as a Brannock Device®, from a shoe shop（optional）

Preparation

• None required.

What to do

• Ask the children to take off their shoes and identify their shoe size by reading it on the shoe.

• Order the shoes according to size. Ask, 'Who has the biggest shoe? Who has the middle-sized shoe? How would we work that out？'.（Encourage counting from the outsides to find the middle shoe or shoes if there is an even number of shoes.）

• Talk about what size is – does it mean longest or widest or both?

• Ask, 'What is shoe size？'

Tip   The discussion may move into width if, for example, the shoe size is 5F as the alphanumeric system includes a width indicator.

Variation

You might talk about how shoe sizes revert to size 1 after size 13!

How is this maths?

Talking about shoe size gives children an opportunity to talk about numbers in another context. While it is still *standardised*, shoe size is a measurement that the children will use less regularly.

Types of shoes

Sort the shoes for the role-play shoe shop.

Aims and objectives

• To sort and classify.

Resources

• Shoe shop role-play area
• Selection of shoes
• Shoe boxes
• Shelving in the role-play area for shoe display and storage

Preparation

• No preparation required if the role-play area has been set up previously.

What to do

• Explain to the children that the shop has had another delivery of shoes but they have been mixed up.
• Can the children sort them and make labels on the shelves for the different types of shoes?
• During and after the sorting, talk to the children about the decisions they made. Ask questions such as 'What groups have you arranged the shoes into? Are there any shoes that do not fit those groups? What are you going to do with them? How are you planning to arrange the groups in the storage area? What labels are you making?'
• Encourage some customers to come into the shop to comment on the arrangement of the shoes in the shop. Ask, 'What do you like about the categories the shoe salespeople have arranged the shoes into? Would you have done it any differently? Why?'

Tip   Allow the children to come up with their own methods of sorting the shoes. Categories might include colour, practical use, season, materials made from, like/dislike and size.

Variation

Any objects can be sorted, depending on the topic/theme being followed. For example, when looking at 'Jack and the Beanstalk' the children might sort a number of seeds, or when learning about food the children might sort according to types of food.

How is this maths?

Being able to categorise items into manageable groups is an important aspect of handling data. Being able to group numbers later on helps to solve more difficult calculation problems.

Trying shoes on

Select your shoes from the role-play shop and buy them today!

Aims and objectives

- To use language related to size.
- To recognise amounts written down.
- To recognise coins and notes.

Resources

- Selection of children's shoes (ask all the children to bring in a named pair of their own)
- Shoe measurer (Brannock Device®) from a shoe shop (optional)
- Price labels for shoes
- Bags to put the new purchases in
- Play money
- Till

Preparation

- The role-play area will have been set up prior to this activity. Make price labels with the children displaying the price they think the shoes should be charged at.

What to do

- Encourage children to enter the role-play area. Some will be the shop assistants and others will be customers.

- Once in role the children will serve or be served in the shop by trying on a number of shoes, listening to recommendations and feedback about size.
- Once an appropriate shoe has been identified, the children can purchase that pair.

Tip   Encourage the children to use vocabulary such as *size*, *big*, *tight*, *small*, *width*.

Variation

This type of activity can happen in other shop role-play areas, such as trying on clothes, hats or gloves.

How is this maths?

The children are using mathematical language to explain the shape and size of shoes, comparing them to their feet. Although the amounts of money exchanged are unlikely to be realistic at this stage, they are using number in a context that is meaningful to them.

Boxes

Putting shoes in boxes that match the size and colour labels.

Aims and objectives

- To learn about sorting.
- To practise logical thinking.

Resources

- A selection of laminated pictures of shoes that are in a range of colours and styles (suggested criteria below) :

	Pair A	Pair B	Pair C	Pair D	Pair E	Pair F	Pair G	Pair H
Size	Adult	Adult	Adult	Adult	Child	Child	Child	Child
Colour	Blue	Red 	Green	Yellow	Blue	Red	Green	Yellow
Fastening	Velcro	Velcro	Laces	Laces	Velcro	Velcro	Laces	Laces
Season	Summer	Winter	Summer	Winter	Summer	Winter	Summer	Winter

- Shoe boxes that are labelled according to the shoes (these 'boxes' may be labelled envelopes or similar)

Sample labels:

Preparation

- Make up the shoe cards (see suggested table in 'Resources' section above) .

What to do

- Display the boxes with their labels.
- Encourage the children either to a) choose one box and find the shoes that meet the criteria on the box labels, or b) choose any pair of shoes and then identify the box that they belong to.

<table>
<tr><td>**Tips**</td><td>• You do not have to label the boxes with all of the criteria you have designed.

• If you are designing your own criteria, plan the shoes logically if you want to use the same cards again to play the game in the next section （see 'Guess who?' below）.</td></tr>
</table>

Variations

• The children may want to design their own shoes that meet the criteria on the box. If these are laminated they can be used as part of the game by other children.

• Any context can be used. For example, （fictitious） insects can be made according to size, patternation on back, number of eyes, length of legs and so on. Trees can be created according to height, colour, leaf shape and so on. Dinosaurs can be created according to length, height and weight, dietary requirements and so on. The important thing to remember is that there is an identifiable logic to the design.

How is this maths?

The children are applying *logical reasoning* to solve the problem. They are identifying whether the shoe meets or does not meet the criteria.

Guess who?

Identify which shoe is missing from the set.

Aims and objectives

• To practise logical thinking.

Resources

• The shoe cards from the 'Boxes' activity above

• Labels from the boxes （optional）

Preparation

• If the cards have already been made there is no further preparation required.

What to do

• Place all the shoe cards face up on the table. Ensure the attributes of the shoes are known to the group.

• Two children leave the group while the remainder of the children remove one of the cards. Shuffle them around so that it is not immediately obvious where the card has been taken from.

- When the children return, they need to identify the attributes of the missing shoes. (This is where the labels from the boxes may be useful as an *aide-mémoire* for the pair.)
- Once the shoes have been identified, the game starts over with a new pair of children.

Tips

- Play this game only when the children have played 'Boxes' for some time. They need to be familiar with the shoes and their attributes for the game to be successful.
- You may begin by playing with a smaller number of shoes (i. e. using only children's shoes will have the number of shoes in the set and make it easier) .

Variation

See Variations in 'Boxes' .

How is this maths?

In order to solve the puzzle the children must apply *logical thinking* in order to identify which *attribute* is missing. Logical thinking is a prerequisite for problem solving and mathematical investigations later on.

Pairs

Use shoes as a context for counting in twos.

Aims and objectives

- To practise counting in twos.
- To use 'pair' to indicate two.

Resources

- Cards with the numbers 1, 3, 5, 7, 9, 11, 13, 15, 17 and 19 on them in one colour, e. g. black
- Cards with the numbers 2, 4, 6, 8, 10, 12, 14, 16, 18 and 20 on them in a second colour, e. g. red
- Ten pairs of shoes

Preparation

- Line up the shoes in pairs.

What to do

- Ask the children what they notice about the shoes (elicit responses such as 'they are in twos').
- Ask the children to count the shoes (1, 2, 3, 4 and so on).
- Place a number card above each shoe as it is counted.
- Encourage the children to think about another way to count the shoes (i. e. in twos).
- Count in twos, pointing to the even number cards. Ask the children, 'What do you notice?'
- Repeat counting in twos. As the children see the connection with the second shoe of each pair and the even numbers, begin to remove the odd number cards.
- If appropriate after a while remove some of the even-number cards when counting, to encourage the children to think about the number pattern and help them begin to memorise it.

Tips

- Encourage the children to use the term *pair* when talking about two shoes.

- The children will be making the link between the *enactive* (physical) and the *symbolic* (numerals) because you are bringing together the shoes and the number cards.
- What patterns can the children see?

Variations

- To extend this ask, 'I have three pairs of shoes, so how many shoes do I have altogether?'
- You can practise counting in fives by using children holding up their hands, or pictures of hands, showing five fingers. Counting in tens can be achieved by using two hands. Counting in threes can be done using tricycle pictures (counting the wheels) and counting in fours using animals (counting four legs).

How is this maths?

Counting in twos is a prerequisite to learning the two-times table with understanding.

Have you got sole?

Make prints with different shoe soles.

Aims and objectives

• To recognise and discuss symmetry and pattern.

Resources

• Variety of old boots and shoes that have interesting and varied soles
• A variety of paints and large shallow trays to pour them into
• Large sheets of paper of cardboard for printing on
• Art aprons
• Old newspaper
• Washing bowls for dipping shoe soles in when changing colour
• Old towels for drying off washed soles

Preparation

• Ensure the floor is covered with newspaper or plastic that can be cleaned.
• Secure large sheets of paper onto the floor.
• Set out the paints into large shallow trays（large enough for the boot soles to be placed in and covered with paint）.

What to do

• Talk to the children about the patterns they can see and feel on the soles of the shoes. Do they see a difference in the types of soles depending on the type of shoe?（For example a boot may have a thicker sole and deeper grooves compared to a slipper, which may be a lot thinner and smoother.）
• Explain that they are going to use a range of colours and shoes to make a printed picture. Talk about how the different soles will create different textures and how the children can use different soles and colours for different elements of their prints.
• Demonstrate how the children can print using the soles. Identify where soles with the same colour paint on them can go, and show them how to clean a sole of its paint if they want to change the colour.
• The children may design their print first, or they may create it as they go!

Tips

- This activity is best undertaken in pairs or small groups of children around a large sheet of paper.
- Encourage the children to talk about the pattern and the texture of each sole as they work to design and print their art.
- Encourage the children to identify *parallel lines*, *zigzags*, *circles*, *waves* and other geometrical shapes, as well as *thin*, *thick*, *long*, *short* and so on.

Variation

Use other items to provide different textures, depending on any theme or topic.

How is this maths?

The children are using geometrical language to describe the patterns they observe on the soles.

Chapter 10

Songs and chants

Introduction

Children love to sing and chant. The songs in this chapter are all related to mathematical concepts, such as counting forwards and backwards, counting in twos, exploring shape and positional language. It is also possible to explore these ideas through story and rhyme and often you will find story books that retell the songs. Leaving out a CD player with a microphone and/or headsets will encourage children to sing along during continual provision and to perform to others.

1, 2, 3, 4, 5

Use fish for counting and learning left and right.

Aims and objectives

- To practise counting to ten.
- To identify left and right.

Resources

- Backing music（optional）

Preparation

- If you are not sure of the tune，find the song using an internet search of the first line of the lyrics.

What to do

- Sing the song through together，showing the ten fingers as the numbers are counted.
- Show the little finger on the right hand when singing the last line.

Lyrics

One, two, three, four, five,

Once I caught a fish alive.

Six, seven, eight, nine, ten,

Then I put it back again.

'Why did you let it go?'

Because it bit my finger so

'Which finger did it bite?'

This little finger on the right.

Tip Ensure that the children are holding up their right hand to show their 'little finger on the right'.

Variation

Other counting songs include 'This old man' ('he played one, he played knick knack on my drum') and 'The pirate song' ('When I was one I'd just begun the day I went to sea').

How is this maths?

The children are practising counting and identifying their right little finger. Counting develops into *addition*, and knowing right from left is important when giving and following directions later on.

One elephant came out to play

Elephants can help us to remember how to count!

Aims and objectives

- To practise counting.
- To learn how to use 'one more'.

Resources

- Backing music (optional)

Preparation

- If you are not sure of the tune, find the song using an internet search of the first line of the lyrics.

What to do

- Ask the children to sit in a circle.
- Identify one child to be the elephant. That child plays and dances, as if they are on a spider's web, in the space in the middle of the circle.
- Sing the song (see words below).

Lyrics

One elephant went out to play upon a spider's web one day.

S/he thought it such tremendous fun that s/he called for another elephant to come.

- When the song says that the elephant *called for another elephant to come*, the first child chooses another child to come into the middle.
- Continue as long as space allows.

Tip   Pause the singing as each elephant joins, and count how many elephants there are now.

Variations

- Use pictures of elephants that children place on a spider's web made of string as the song progresses. You may also write or show the numerals representing the number of elephants on the spider's web.

- Draw a card out of a pile to show how many more elephants have been invited! The lyrics would be, for example:

Six elephants went out to play upon a spider's web one day.

They thought it such tremendous fun that they called for another three elephants to come.

Work out how many elephants are on the web altogether.

How is this maths?

Inviting one more elephant to play models *adding one more*. Knowing the number that is *one more* helps children understand the *counting numbers* and the concept of *counting on*. This is early addition.

Ten green bottles

Use this old favourite to practise counting backwards.

Aims and objectives

- To practise counting backwards.
- To understand taking away one at a time.

Resources

- Ten green bottles（or pictures of them）numbered 1－10
- Backing music（optional）

Preparation

- If you are not sure of the tune, find the song using an internet search of the first line of the lyrics.
- Set up the bottles in a row.

What to do

- Start singing the song（see lyrics below）. When the song reaches one bottle accidentally falling, remove one bottle or picture.
- Keep singing until all the bottles are gone.

Lyrics

Ten green bottles hanging on the wall,

Ten green bottles hanging on the wall,

And if one green bottle should accidentally fall,

There'll be nine green bottles hanging on the wall.

Nine green bottles hanging on the wall,

Nine green bottles hanging on the wall

And if one green bottle should accidentally fall,

There'll be eight green bottles hanging on the wall.

Eight green bottles hanging on the wall.

Eight green bottles hanging on the wall.

And if one . . .

. . . There'll be one green bottle hanging on the wall.

One green bottle hanging on the wall,

One green bottle hanging on the wall.

And if that green bottle should accidentally fall,

There'll be no green bottles hanging on the wall.

Tip   Remove the bottle with the highest number on it each time. This will show the correct number of remaining bottles. Count them to check.

Variations

- Other items related to the theme or topic being studied can be substituted for the green bottles.
- Other songs that encourage *counting backwards* in ones include, 'Five currant buns' ('in a baker's shop'), 'Five little speckled frogs' ('sat on a speckled log'), 'Five little ducks' ('went swimming one day'), 'Ten in the bed' ('and the little one said "roll over, roll over"') and 'Five little men in a flying saucer' ('flew round the Earth one day').

How is this maths?

Counting backwards is an early entry into *subtraction* and *taking away* one. Knowing that no green bottles exist helps children understand that it is possible to count backwards to zero, but that we begin at one when we start counting.

Ten fat sausages

Count back in twos in this activity.

Aims and objectives

- To take away two.

Resources

- Backing music （optional）

Preparation

- If you are not sure of the tune, find the song using an internet search of the first line of the lyrics.

What to do

- Identify ten children to volunteer to be the sausages sizzling in the pan. Ask them to stand at the front.
- Start singing the song （see lyrics below）. When the song reaches the point that one sausage goes 'pop' the first child sits down where they are and as another sausage goes 'bang' the second child also sits down.

Lyrics

Ten fat sausages sizzling in the pan,

Ten fat sausages sizzling in the pan.

If one went pop and the other went bang,

There'd be eight fat sausages sizzling in the pan,

Eight fat sausages, sizzling in the pan . . .

- Sing until all the sausages （children） are sitting down.

Tips

- Identify the order in which the sausages （children） will go 'pop' and 'bang' （i.e. sit down） before you start, to help maintain the momentum once the song has begun.
- Give some time between verses for the children to work out how many sausages are left in the pan.
- Practise counting in twos.

Variation

The sausages sizzling in the pan can be changed to a current topic. For example, 'ten balloons floating in the sky'.

How is this maths?

Counting backwards is an early entry into *subtraction* and this song encourages *taking away* two. Knowing that no sausages exist helps children understand that it is possible to count backwards to zero, but that we begin at one when we start counting.

I'm a circle

Sing these lyrics to the well-known tune of 'Frère Jacques'.

Aims and objectives
- To explore some properties of circles.

Resources
- Circular or spherical objects to roll (optional)

Preparation
- If you are not sure of the tune, find it using an internet search of the lyrics 'Are you sleeping, are you sleeping, Brother John?'

What to do
- Sing the song together (see lyrics below).
- The children can use their 'magic fingers' to draw circles in the air or roll circular objects to each other around or across the room.

Lyrics
I'm a circle, I'm a circle,

Big and round, big and round.

I can roll to you and I can roll to you,

Along the ground, along the ground.

Tip   If using circular objects, select as varied a range of objects as possible.

Variation
In later verses substitute 'circle' with the name of an object such as 'round wheel' or 'sphere' (for a ball).

How is this maths?
Children need to learn that shapes have a number of properties. By singing that a circle is round, they are learning about its *curved side*. By singing that

the *sphere* is round, they are learning about its *curved* face. Providing the children with a range of objects helps to extend their understanding of the properties of shapes and ensures that their view of them does not become limited to one or two instantiations（examples）.

The farm is shaping up

'Old MacDonald' helps us to learn about shape.

Aims and objectives

- To use properties to identify two-dimensional shapes.

Resources

- A deck of cards with a shape drawn on one side
- A feely bag large enough to hold the cards

Preparation

- Shuffle the cards and place them into the feely bag.
- If you are not sure of the tune, find the song 'Old MacDonald Had a Farm' using an internet search of the song title.

What to do

- Select one child to draw one card out of the bag and say the spoken line in the song when appropriate (see lyrics below).
- Sing the song together.

Lyrics

In this bag I have a shape, I wonder what it is?

Will you help me to find out just what shape it is?

(Spoken) It has ____ corners and ____ sides

(Sung) So, do you know what shape this is? Tell me if you do!

- The child who gives the spoken clues responds to the children's guesses of what shape it is with 'yes' or 'no'.

Tips

- Draw the shapes on the cards in different orientations and colours to challenge children's notion that shapes can only be a particular prototypical shape (e.g. a *triangle* can only be a triangle when it is *equilateral* and has a *horizontal baseline*).
- Write the name of the shape on the card as well as drawing the figure.

Variation

Use photos or pictures of three-dimensional solids for the children to describe, or place a solid in the feely bag for the child to feel and give the properties （number of *corners* or *vertices* and *faces*）.

How is this maths?

Children need to learn that shapes have a number of properties. In this singing game children will use two-dimensional geometric vocabulary such as *corners* and *sides*. If playing a three-dimensional version they will use *vertex*, *vertices* and *faces*.

Positional language

Lots of songs help us to use positional language.

Aims and objectives

• To use accurate positional language.

Resources

• Backing music （optional）

Preparation

• If you are not sure of the tunes, find the songs using an internet search of the lyrics.

What to do

• Sing a range of songs that use positional language. These include:

The grand old Duke of York,

He had ten thousand men.

He marched them *up* to the *top* of the hill

And he marched them *down* again.

And when they were *up* they were *up*,

And when they were *down* they were *down*,

And when they were only *halfway up*

They were neither *up* nor *down*.

Humpty Dumpty sat *on* a wall.

Humpty Dumpty had a great fall.

All the king's horses and all the king's men

Couldn't put Humpty together again.

Jack and Jill went *up* the hill

to fetch a pail of water.

Jack fell *down* and broke his crown

and Jill came tumbling after.

Up Jack got and home did trot

as fast as he could caper.

He went to bed and bound his head

with vinegar and brown paper.

Ring, a ring o'roses,
A pocket full of posies;
Atishoo, atishoo,
We all fall *down*.

- Where appropriate the children can act out the positional language.

Tip   Keep the positional language（italicised in the lyrics above）in your mind
so you are accenting these words when you sing them with the children.

Variation

Watch videos of these traditional nursery rhymes or ask the children to use puppets to act out
the rhymes.

How is this maths?

Using positional language helps children to make sense of shape and space
and supports their geometrical thinking.

Chapter 11

Mathematical walks

Introduction

We learn mathematics to help us to make sense of the world, and so exploring further afield while we think about mathematics is a fun activity to undertake with children. The walks that have been suggested in this chapter are offered as a starting point. As you walk about in your area you may well find other mathematical ideas you can explore with the children. It is also possible to stay inside to carry out several of these activities if you prefer.

As small as small can be

How small can your collection be?

Aims and objectives

• To use language related to size.

Resources

• Very small containers, enough for one per child or pair of children

Preparation

• Go on the designated walk yourself to check that it is safe for the children and that there are enough items that can be collected on the way.

What to do

• Give the children the containers. Ask them, 'What things can you think of that are small enough to go into your box?'. Share ideas.

• On the walk challenge the children to find five things to put into the box.

• On your return compare the contents by asking about who has the same things and which things are different.

Tip   Ensure you have discussed health and safety matters with the children as well as the need for respect for neighbours and living things.

Variation

Use one box per adult-led group to potentially generate more discussion during the walk.

How is this maths?

The children are visualising items that might be smaller than the box. The children are using trial and error as they try objects in the box. The children are finding similarities and differences in the objects found. They are using language such as *too big* and *that fits* as they explore their surroundings.

A head for heights

This walk encourages children to think about objects that are taller or shorter than they are.

Aims and objectives

- To estimate height.
- To compare using non-standard units.

Resources

- Digital camera

Preparation

- Go on the designated walk yourself to check that it is safe for the children and that there are enough items that can be photographed on the way.

What to do

- Explain to the children that you are going on a walk together to find objects that are *taller* and *shorter* than the children.
- Think about some of the objects that you might see on the way. List those on the board or a sheet of paper.
- Undertake the walk, photographing objects that are seen on the way with a child next to each to show if the object is *taller* or *shorter* than the child.
- On your return show the digital photos on the interactive whiteboard and discuss which objects are taller and which are shorter than the children.

Tip Ensure you have discussed health and safety matters with the children as well as respect for neighbours and living things.

Variation

Print out some of the photos from the walk. In another session encourage the children to group the objects into taller and shorter. Encourage them to discuss if the object will remain the same height or change, and why.

How is this maths?

The children are using their *estimation* skills and then *direct comparison* by placing themselves next to an object and photographing it.

Shape hunt

A hunt with a difference.

Aims and objectives

- To observe different shapes within the environment.

Resources

- A set of cards in a small pouch the children can each carry around their neck, or in an envelope they can carry – one set each or per pair

Preparation

- Go on the designated walk yourself to check that it is safe for the children and that there are enough items on the way that will meet the criteria.

What to do

- Before setting off, talk to the children about the shapes in their pack. Ensure the children can say the names (e.g. *sphere*, *rectangular prism*, *cylinder*).
- Photograph the objects that the children see.
- On the group's return view the photos on the interactive whiteboard to discuss.

Tip   Ensure you have discussed health and safety matters with the children, as well as having respect for neighbours and living things.

Variations

- Print off the photos and display them on the wall. Include on the display the mathematical terms alongside the names of the everyday objects.
- The packs may also include drawings of two-dimensional shapes, such as *triangle*, *circle*, *rectangle* but if this is the case ensure that it is the *face* of the object that is being photographed and discussed so that the brick that is a rectangular prism doesn't become known as a rectangle.

How is this maths?

The children are using their visualisation skills to imagine and observe three-dimensional shapes in their environment. They discuss their findings with their friends using accurate terminology in order to develop their mathematical communication skills.

A focus on one shape

Explore a shape of the day.

Aims and objectives
- To observe shape being used in the environment.

Resources
- None required

Preparation
- Go on the designated walk yourself to check that it is safe for the children and that there are enough items on the way that will meet the criteria.

What to do
- Before setting off talk to the children about the 'shape of the day', e. g. circle.
- During the walk ask, 'What circles can you see?'
- Identify whether the circles are the face of another shape (a wheel, a kind of circular prism) or a sphere (a ball).
- The children could draw what they have seen on their return, to create a display about their 'shape of the day'.

Tips
- Ensure you have discussed health and safety matters with the children, as well as respect for neighbours and living things.
- The shape could be the 'shape of the week' or even the 'shape of the month'!
- Ensure you show the children a number of different ways the shape can be used, to broaden their understanding of what the shape looks like and how it can be used in the environment.

Variation

Encourage the children to bring into nursery/school examples of objects or toys that have the 'shape of the day' in them.

How is this maths?

The children are using their *visualisation* skills to imagine and observe three-dimensional shapes in their environment. They discuss their findings with their friends using accurate vocabulary in order to develop their mathematical *communication* skills.

Colour

Observe natural beauty through coloured-card viewfinders.

Aims and objectives

- To identify colours.
- To categorise colours.

Resources

- Coloured cards with a circular hole cut out of the centre, enough for three per child

Preparation

- Laminate the coloured cards after the hole has been made in the card to make the cards sturdy and reuseable.
- Go on the designated walk yourself to check that it is safe for the children and that there are enough items on the way that will meet the criteria.

What to do

- Ask the children to find items on the walk that are the same colour as the cards they have.
- Discuss the colour and photograph the object.

Tips

- Looking through the hole will help identify the object's colour.
- Ensure you have discussed health and safety matters with the children, as well as respect for neighbours and living things.

Variation

If items are photographed they can be printed out and displayed on the wall; perhaps make a rainbow, or group the objects according to their colour.

How is this maths?

Although colour might be thought of as art or design more than mathematics, mathematics (ratio) is used to mix colours. Assigning an object a certain colour categorises that object. Colour is used in science (horticulture) to order some flowers. There is also a science and mathematics link to draw when looking at how prisms refract (bend) light at different angles causing different colours.

Texture

Aims and objectives

- To sort objects according to texture.

Resources

- Texture cards or a list of textures（optional）

Preparation

- Go on the designated walk yourself to check that it is safe for the children and that there are enough items on the way that will meet the criteria.

What to do

- Find items that are smooth, rough, cold, soft, spongy, dry and so on.
- Collect or photograph them.
- On return to the nursery/classroom, sort the objects into texture groups.
- Display.

Tip   Ensure you have discussed health and safety matters with the children, as well as respect for neighbours and living things.

Variation

Ask the children to bring in objects that have the particular textures you are looking for.

How is this maths?

The children *classify* and *group* the objects according to their properties（texture）.

Chapter 12

Pirates

Introduction

'Pirates' is always a favourite topic with young children. The activities in this chapter help you to think about how to exploit the mathematical ideas within the types of activities you might normally carry out when undertaking this theme. Activities such as map making and map reading can be undertaken indoors or out, on a smaller scale or larger, depending on the space you have available to you. You could turn the whole classroom into a treasure island, or use the role-play area, or create a temporary island on a carpet area.

A living treasure island

Who can find the treasure?

Aims and objectives

• To give and follow directions.

Resources

• Items to transform an area into a treasure island（e. g. hoops, coloured paper, 'treasure'）

• Labels for north, south, east and west

Preparation

• Develop the treasure island with the children.

What to do

• The children are sitting around or on the treasure island.

• One child is selected to leave the area.

• The remainder of children hide treasure（such as gold coins）under objects on the island.

• The child returns to be given directions about where to find the buried treasure.

Tip　　Use however many paces north, south, east or west to provide directions.

Variation

Instead of using *compass directions*, use paces towards particular items on the treasure island.

How is this maths?

This type of activity encourages children to make sense of the space around them. Later on they begin to use *coordinates*.

Treasure maps

X marks the spot!

Aims and objectives
- To give directions.

Resources
- Blank map template （optional）
- Paper
- Pencils and colours

Preparation
- The previous activity, 'A living treasure island', is a good preparatory task for this activity.
- Look at a range of treasure maps from pirate books such as *The Night Pirates* by Peter Harris and Deborah Allwright or *Stories of Pirates* by Russell Punter and Christyan Fox.

What to do
- Encourage the children to draw their own treasure maps, either of an island they are familiar with or their own imaginary island.
- X marks the spot – where is the treasure?
- Ask, 'What else is on the map?' and 'How can you get from the cove to the treasure?'
- Encourage the children to talk about their maps and put a key on them to explain the symbols used.

Tip You could make the maps look old by dipping them into cold tea and screwing them up!

Variation
Other themes or topics also lend themselves to making maps. For example, the children may want to draw maps showing their journey from home to nursery/school, the park, a relative's house or the local shop.

How is this maths?

The children are beginning to translate the three-dimensional world into a two-dimensional representation using symbols and a key to explain them. Later they will learn other symbols to develop the concept of maps further. The children are also able to explain and follow directions to and from particular points on the map. This demonstrates clear logical thinking.

Message in a bottle

Send the treasure map away.

Aims and objectives

- To practise estimation.
- To check results.

Resources

- A number of dry plastic bottles of all different shapes and sizes, more than one per child

Preparation

- Ensure that there are enough bottles for each child.

What to do

- Discuss how treasure maps were traditionally placed in bottles for safe keeping from water and the sea.
- Ask the children how they think the maps were put into the bottles (i.e. rolled up).
- Allow the children, in small groups at a time, to select a bottle they think their map will fit into.
- Check by rolling and inserting the map.
- Allow the children to change the bottle if necessary.

Tip   Before they have checked the bottle's suitability talk to the children about why they have selected that particular bottle.

Variation

Encourage the children to work in pairs so they are able to talk about their estimations more effectively.

How is this maths?

The children are visualising their map in the bottle. They are required to visualise it rolled up and to take into consideration the *length* of the bottle and map, as well as how tightly the map can be rolled in relation to the size of the bottle's neck. This involves a lot of *conservation of surface area*.

Treasure chest

Aha, me hearties! Finding treasure is golden!

Aims and objectives

- To learn about problem solving.
- To learn about sharing.

Resources

- A treasure chest (can be a box covered in gold-coloured paper with a lid)
- Treasure (chocolate gold coins or costume jewellery)
- Balance scales (for helping the children to share out using weight)

Preparation

- Ensure that the treasure in the box can be shared evenly between the number of children in the group.

What to do

- Explore what is in the box.
- Ask, 'How much treasure is there?'.
- Ask, 'How can we *share* the treasure *equally* between us? Is there another way? And another way?' Discuss ways to share until there is general agreement between the 'pirates'.
- Talk to the children about how they know they are sharing equally as they carry out the sharing process.

Tip The children might count or weigh some items of treasure (e.g. the chocolate coins). They may need to exchange some of their items (e.g. one necklace is worth two bracelets).

Variation

Use other objects related to a current theme or topic.

How is this maths?

The children are developing their understanding of *division as equal sharing*. This may be a difficult task due to the variation in treasure items and so the children will have a lot of *problem solving*, *negotiation* and *logical thinking* to undertake.

A pirate investigation

This puzzling investigation will get your pirates thinking!

Aims and objectives

- To practise logical thinking and reasoning.
- To learn about communication.
- To practise problem solving and investigating.

Resources

- Three sets of: pirate hat, eye patch, cutlass (each set is a different colour from the other two).
- Crayons, coloured pencils or felt tips the same colours as the three sets
- Recording sheet (optional, see Preparation below)

Preparation

- If encouraging the children to use the recording sheet, photocopy sets of hat, eye patch and cutlass so that there are eight sets on one side of A4 paper.

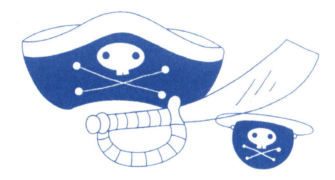

What to do

- Ask for one volunteer who is going to be a confused pirate.
- Show the pirate the box and ask them to pick out one hat, one eye patch and one cutlass and put them on.
- Reveal what else is in the box and ask them to change one, two or three of the items they are wearing. Repeat as many times as you think is necessary for the children to understand that there are many options for the confused pirate.
- Ask the children, 'How many different outfits can the confused pirate wear? '

- Working in pairs the children can investigate this question.
- Using the recording sheet （by colouring in the items using the three colours） helps the children to keep track of what they are discussing.
- Discuss conclusions at the end, asking the confused pirate to dress up again if necessary.

Tips

- Once the children think they have identified all the possibilities, encourage them to check in a logical （*systematic*） way. One possible way to do that is to start with all the same-colour items, then change only one object at a time, then two and finally three.
- With younger children you may want to start with just two sets （colours）.

Variation

This activity can be applied to a range of topics or themes. For example, in a topic about winter the children can use three different sets comprising a hat, scarf and gloves.

How is this maths?

This investigation encourages the children to think through a problem in a *systematic* way to ensure they have all *possibilities* covered. This skill is an essential investigative approach to foster in children.

Ahoy there!

· · · · · · · · · · · · · · · · · ·   · · · · · · · · · · · · · · · · · ·

Build your own pirate ship.

Aims and objectives

- To understand estimation.
- To check estimations with direct comparison.

Resources

- Role play area or construction area
- Resources for making a pirate ship
- Pictures of and books with pirate ships

Preparation

- If necessary, prepare the areas where the children will be building their pirate ship（s）.

What to do

- If appropriate, give the children the option of building a pirate ship together in the role play area or independently/in pairs in the construction area.
- Discuss what a pirate ship needs（e. g. flagpole, plank, bird's nest）by gaining inspiration from books and pictures.
- During the construction phase, ask questions such as 'How many planks（strips of paper to attach to the wall）do we need？' and 'What shape are you using there？'

Tip   Provide a variety of pictures of pirate ships so the children can identify common features to include in their ship design without being（too）stereotypical of pirates.

Variation

The role-play and construction areas can be used to build any construction related to the current topic or theme.

The Jolly Roger

Create and then fly the pirate flag.

Aims and objectives

• To recognise reflective symmetry.

Resources

• A4 paper – black and white
• White-coloured pencils
• Scissors
• Glue

Preparation

• Produce a template of half a Jolly Roger, if required

What to do

• Hand out the black paper to the children and ask them to fold it in half.
• Encourage the children to draw half a Jolly Roger with a white-coloured pencil, using the template if required.
• Cut out the skull and crossbones, keeping the eyes and nose as they fall out.

- Open out the black paper.
- Stick the black paper onto the white paper.
- Fly the flags on the pirate ships or display them in the room.

Tips
- Discuss why the two sides of the flag look the same and how that relates to folding the paper in half.
- This is a difficult task for children so ensure that there are lots of adults about to lend a hand.

Variation

Different themes encourage different types of symmetrical patterns to be cut out and glued onto a contrasting background. One popular task is the snowflake, where blue paper can be cut and glued onto white, or vice versa.

How is this maths?

It is important for children to learn about symmetry because this will help them later to define shapes.

A pirate's life for me

Design a pirate's top.

Aims and objectives

• To make and continue a repeating pattern.

Resources

• Template of a blank T-shirt （see below）

• Coloured pencils, crayons, paints or strips of coloured paper to cut out and glue on

Preparation

• Select a range of pirate pictures that show their tops.

What to do

• Look through the pictures and discuss the pirates' tops. Ask, 'What do you notice?' Help the children to identify that they are often striped, with two alternating colours.

• Ask the children if they would like to design their own pirate's shirt.

• On an affirmative response provide the children with a blank T-shirt template and media to use.

• While the children are drawing and colouring talk to them about the *repeating pattern* in the T-shirt. For example, 'What colour are you going to use next? Why that colour? What colour will be on the fifth row? How do you know that?' .

Tip   Once the children have selected the （normally two） colours they are going

438

to use, put the others out of reach so they are not tempted to include other colours not originally intended to be in the repeating pattern.

Variations

- Some children may like to design T-shirts that are still patterned but are not made only with stripes!
- The children may be encouraged to bring in an old T-shirt to paint with fabric paints after they have designed their T-shirts. They may wear them if they have a dress-up pirate day or when they are in the role-play pirate ship.

How is this maths?

Mathematics is full of pattern. Seeing pattern helps children to solve problems. Being able to say what comes next helps children to visualise shape or colour and pattern. Using ordinal language (first, second, etc.) helps them to talk mathematically.

Chapter 13

Big and small

Introduction

Thinking about size is a precursor to learning about all aspects of measurement. Children are often very excited to find and make very large items or very small items. Shining an overhead projector onto a big sheet of paper on the wall will provide large images that the children can create their own picture.

Order! Order!

Ordering from smallest to biggest using a range of objects.

Aims and objectives

- To order according to size.

Resources

- A range of objects, either arbitrary objects from the setting/school or items related to a specific topic

Preparation

- None required.

What to do

- Have the items set out on a table and encourage the children to look at them.
- Encourage discussion about what the children see, the attributes of the objects and what they know about them.
- Ask, 'Which object is the *biggest*? How do you know that? Which is the *smallest*? Why do you think that?'
- Take the two objects identified as biggest and smallest and place them at either end of the table. Challenge the children to complete the line, *ordering* the objects from smallest to biggest.
- While the children are doing that, talk to them about the decisions they have made. Ask, 'How do you know this one is bigger than that?'

Tip Carefully select the resources you use to represent 'big' items. A toy elephant that is smaller than a toy mouse may be confusing!

Variation

What exactly is meant by big and small? Order objects in other ways such as *height*, *width*, *weight* and *capacity*. Provide resources for the children to enable them to check their *estimations*.

How is this maths?

This gives children the opportunity to compare different objects. Indirect comparison occurs when children know that if object A is smaller than object B, and object B is smaller than object C, then object A must be smaller than object C. The term for this was coined by Piaget: *transitivity*. It underpins a lot of *logical reasoning* in mathematics.

Making things bigger

Using a magnifying glass or microscope creates lots of possibilities.

Aims and objectives

- To use magnification.
- To find patterns.

Resources

- Small objects that have been collected arbitrarily or that relate to the current toipc or theme
- Magnifying glasses
- Microscope （optional）

Preparation

- Create a display of the objects that have been collected.

What to do

- Talk together about the objects. Ask, 'Which object do you like? Why is that?'
- Use a magnifying glass to look at the objects. Talk about what effect the magnifying glass has on the object when they look through it.
- Ask, 'What can you see?' Encourage the children to describe the patterns they can see through the magnifying glass.

Tip   Use the magnifying glasses to look at the objects that have been found in the 'Texture' walk （see page 156）. Look at how the surface of the objects creates the different textures that were found.

Variation

Use a photocopier or scanner to make things bigger.

How is this maths?

This activity encourages children to think about pattern that occurs naturally. Naturally occurring patterns were a source of interest for mathematicians a long time ago and still fascinate mathematicians and scientists today.

Investigating small creatures

Learn a little more about the outdoor environment.

Aims and objectives

- To practise problem solving.
- To look for pattern.

Resources

- An outdoor area that is rich in insects or other wildlife
- Insect observation packs（with clear container and magnifying glass）
- Books on wildlife or pictures of the wildlife in your outdoor area
- Digital camera that takes pictures using the macro setting（optional）
- Paper and pencils for making sketches of the insects

Preparation

- Visit the outdoor area to investigate the possible creatures that you will find. If necessary encourage some creatures, such as woodlice that can be encouraged by laying damp wood flat onto the ground where it is shadier.

What to do

- Explain to the children that they are going to be explorers.
- Share out the equipment the children will be taking exploring with them and discuss what the items are for.
- Talk about being respectful of living things.
- When outside, place the insects or other bugs into the magnifying container one at a time.
- Encourage the children to observe the insect carefully, counting its legs and identifying the three sections to its body（head, thorax and abdomen）.
- Ask an adult to take a photograph or the children to sketch the insect.
- Make a note of where it was found and what its habitat is like.

Tips

- A useful book is Usborne's *1001 Bugs to Spot* by Emma Helbrough and

Teri Gower.

- Ensure the living creatures are replaced carefully in their own habitat when observations are complete.

Variation
You could go further afield to visit a bird sanctuary or butterfly house.

How is this maths?
There are many patterns on insects that are mathematical in nature. For example, butterflies and ladybirds have symmetrical patternation. Insects always have six legs: three on the left and three on the right. Similarly spiders have four and four, making eight.

Making a home for wildlife

Encourage more wildlife into the outdoor area.

Aims and objectives
- To practise measuring.
- To learn about categorising.

Resources
- Materials for making the wildlife shelter or home

Preparation
- Research the possible wildlife homes or shelters that are appropriate for your outdoor environment. Gather together the resources required to make the home or shelter. If possible, involve the children in the decision-making.

What to do
- Build the home or shelter together with the children. They will be involved in measuring, cutting, gluing, hammering and so on.
- Once the item has been established, observe the wildlife that uses it (e. g. birds on a feeding station).
- If possible, photograph the visitors and keep a record.
- Display the findings.

Tip   Although it is American, the National Wildlife Federation provides a useful checklist for how to create a wildlife habitat that is applicable to all nurseries and schools.

Variation

It may be possible to set up a remote camera inside the home or shelter and observe the wildlife that uses it on the nursery or school computer.

How is this maths?

Making the home or shelter involves *measuring*, which will become more accurate as the children learn more about length. Once the home or shelter is *in situ*, observing the wildlife provides an opportunity for the children to undertake *data handling* or observe *patterns* in the animals' behaviour.

Create something big!

Aims and objectives

- To talk about the big, bigger and biggest.

Resources

- Junk modelling materials, including items that are large to the children

Preparation

- Ensure you have gathered enough materials for the children to carry out this activity.

What to do

- Ask the children, 'What is the *biggest* thing you know?' as a way in to discussing very large objects.
- Ask the children if they would like to make the biggest thing they can possibly make.
- Clear a space, indoors or out, that enables the children to start construction.
- Ask, 'Is it *big* enough yet? How can you make it *bigger*? What is the *biggest* you can make?'
- Continue until the children cannot safely make it bigger.

Tips

- *Bigger* relates to a number of physical features of objects, so ensure you provide experiences that include considering *height*, *width* and *weight*.
- Remember to photograph the construction once finished as it will probably have to be dismantled soon after, unless you have a huge area going spare! The children will enjoy dismantling the construction and this will give you an opportunity to talk about *small*, *smaller* and *smallest*.

Variation

Instead of using junk materials, can the children make the tallest tower out of construction materials? The children could use papier mâché to make the construction more permanent.

How is this maths?

Exploring size in this way helps children further to understand shape and space. They may also develop their understanding of *infinity*, where space is limitless.

Chapter 14

Jack and the Beanstalk

Introduction

An old favourite, the story of Jack and the Beanstalk offers a number of mathematical activities for young children. Some of the activities in this chapter need a longer time, such as growing seeds, but others can be carried out more quickly. Some of the activities encourage children to visualise height and distance; creating and manipulating pictures in the mind helps children's mathematical thinking as they move through primary school and beyond.

Planting seeds

Observe Jack's beans grow.

Aims and objectives

- To learn about measuring.
- To practise ordering.

Resources

- Bean seeds （any climbing variety）
- Clear containers for planting （some yoghurt pots are clear enough and can be recycled for this purpose）
- Cotton wool or compost
- Digital camera （optional）

Preparation

- Ensure there is a space in the nursery or classroom for the bean pots to be observed easily.

What to do

- Plant the climbing bean seeds in the clear containers. Ensure that the bean seed is pressed against the side of the container if you want the children to observe the root growth.
- Keep the seeds watered well.
- Observe the plant growth every day. If possible, photograph the bean daily to keep a record of the growth.
- Display the photos to show the development.
- Photos should be ordered appropriately.

Tip   Other plants that grow quickly are peas and sunflowers.

Variations

- The children may also measure the *length* of the bean plant as it grows, writing the length in *centimetres* in a table or chart.
- Photographs can also be used to record other changes, such as shadows over a day.

How is this maths?

Change over time can be recorded, either by photograph or by other data
（such as measures）. Understanding this starts children on the road of
recording scientific evidence and understanding data handling.

Let's harp on about it

Make a harp to serenade the golden goose and encourage her to lay some golden eggs.

Aims and objectives

- To learn about length and pitch.

Resources

- Elastic bands
- Wood
- Nails
- Hammer

Preparation

- None required.

What to do

- Hammer into the wood a series of nails along the base. Hammer in above corresponding nails so that the distance between the base nail and the nail above it increases each time (see illustration).
- Stretch the elastic bands between each base nail and the nail above it.
- Play the 'harp', listening to how the sound changes depending on the length of each elastic band.
- Talk about why the sounds change.

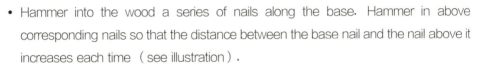

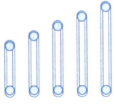

Tip   The pitch becomes higher as the elastic band is stretched further.

Variation

Instead of using wood and nails, stretch the elastic bands over a variety of different-sized plastic containers.

How is this maths?

Pitch and harmonics are closely related to *fractions*. This is an early way to explore this concept.

Golden eggs

Help the giant and Jack keep account of the golden eggs.

Aims and objectives

- To practise addition.
- To practise subtraction.

Resources

- Golden eggs (these could be boiled eggs that have been spray-painted, golden-wrapped Easter eggs or plastic toy eggs)
- A basket

Preparation

- If possible, reread the story of 'Jack and the Beanstalk' and focus discussion around the goose laying the golden eggs and Jack stealing them.

What to do

- Count three eggs into the basket, saying that the goose has laid these eggs for the giant.
- Tell the children that Jack *takes* two of the eggs and count two eggs as they are taken out.
- Ask the children, 'How many eggs are in the giant's basket now?' Encourage the children to explain why they think there is that number of eggs left. Check.
- Continue the activity by placing eggs into the basket and removing some.

Tips

- Ask the children to suggest the number of eggs that the goose lays or Jack steals. This would help you to asses their understanding of number in this context.
- Vary the number of eggs used depending on the children's attainment.

Variation

You could use an egg carton to hold the eggs instead of a basket. This would help the children to visualise the numbers in a context that may be more familiar to them.

How is this maths?

The children are *counting*, *adding* and *taking away* the eggs. They are *visualising* the number of eggs in the basket and checking their *mental* calculations.

Retelling Jack and the Beanstalk

Sequencing and ordering events.

Aims and objectives

- To learn about sequencing.
- To learn about ordering.

Resources

- The 'Jack and the Beanstalk' story
- Either a template with spaces for the children to draw pictures or write about the key events in the story, or pictures from the book of key events that the children can put into order
- Prompt cards of ordinal and time-related words for display as a memory aid (optional)

Preparation

- None required.

What to do

- Read (or reread) the 'Jack and the Beanstalk' story.
- Talk together about what happened *first* in the story. Ask, 'What happened *next*?' and so on until the story has been retold.
- Ask the children to work in pairs to retell the story to each other. Encourage them to use language such as *first, second, third, next, then* and *last*. If available and appropriate, display these words as an *aide-mémoire* for the children.
- After retelling to each other, give out the templates or the story pictures and ask the children to record their story to show the correct order.

Tip For younger children use the pictures in the book to support the retelling of the story.

Variations

- The children can act out the story in small groups instead of recording it as above.
- Any stories can be recalled and ordinal and time-related language encouraged.

How is this maths?

Some mathematical tasks require children to find the solution by carrying out a series of steps in a particular *order*. This activity helps children to think about sequence. The activity also helps children to use *ordinal language* such as *first*, *second* and *third* as well as *time*-related vocabulary such as *next*, *then* and *last*.

Climb the beanstalk

A chance to visualise a long distance.

Aims and objectives

• To visualise length and distance.

Resources

• None required

Preparation

• If possible, reread the story of 'Jack and the Beanstalk' and focus discussion around Jack climbing up an down the beanstalk.

What to do

• Ask the children to pretend to be Jack climbing the beanstalk.

• Wave goodbye to Mum and start climbing the imaginary stalk. As you start, look at the house behind Mum. Ask, 'What size is it?' (big).

• After a short time ask who is getting tired. Show the children that you are tired. Perhaps wipe your brow with one arm but then hold onto the beanstalk again quickly for fear of falling. Explain your arms are aching and your legs are tired.

• Talk with the children about how you have all climbed a long, long way up the beanstalk and that you are nearly at the giant's house.

• Ask, 'What was that noise?' Explain you heard the giant and you all need to get home. Look down. 'Can you see your house? How big is it from all the way up here?' (It is very very small, almost so small it cannot be seen!)

• Climb down the beanstalk. Look down again. 'What can you see now?' 'How big is your house now?' (Encourage the children to think of an item that is about the same size, for example a mouse.)

• As you climb further down the imaginary beanstalk continue to ask the children to look down and explain how big their house looks now. Depending on the children's answers you will be able to comment on how close to the ground they now are. Compare different children's responses with each other by commenting that one child must have climbed down faster than another.

Tip   If you have another adult they may shout 'Fee-fi-fo-fum' at the appropriate time to initiate the descent.

Variation

You could also look up as you climb or descent to visualise or imagine the giant's castle.

How is this maths?

The children will be exploring *perspective* through imagining climbing and descending the beanstalk. They will visualise *distance* and the impact that this has on objects that are a long way away. Artists often use mathematics to develop perspective in their pictures. Perspective mathematics is also used to design the spray-painted advertisements on sports pitches that look as if they are standing up, creating a clever illusion.

One small step for Jack, one giant step outside!

Think about the giant by investigating his footprint.

Aims and objectives

- To practise visualisation of size.
- To practise measuring.

Resources

- Mud, sand or similar for creating the giant's footprint
- Letter from the giant (see wording below)
- Template of footprint if needed

Preparation

- Before the children arrive, set up the giant's footprint outside using appropriate resources. Try to make the footprint as large as it can possibly be.
- Prepare another adult for their role.

What to do

- At a prearranged time send another adult outside for some reason while you are doing something else with the children.
- On their return the other adult will be excited because they think that the giant may have been around the nursery/school looking for Jack because he has left a muddy footprint outside!
- Take the children outside to look at the evidence. Talk about the footprint: 'How *long* is the footprint?' *Measure* it if appropriate. 'How *wide* is the footprint? So how big do you think the giant's foot actually is? Show me how long a toe might be!'
- Ask the children to wonder how *tall* the giant might be if this is his footprint. Encourage them to visualise the giant's *height* by comparing it to the nursery/school buildings.

Tips
- If you are not confident in producing the footprint from scratch yourself,

use an overhead projector to shine a shoe print onto a large sheet of card. Use this as your template.

- If you think any children will become distressed at the thought of a giant coming into the premises then avoid this activity. Alternatively you or another adult could find a letter from the giant that reads:

Dear children,

I have been looking for Jack because I know he has been stealing my golden eggs. I'm afraid that I left a rather muddy footprint in your playground and because your broom was too small for me to use I had to leave it there!

I know that Jack is not with you and so I will not visit any of you again. I am sorry to disturb you. I'd also like you to know that I really am a friendly giant and very polite, not like the story tells you!

Kind regards,

The Giant

Variations

- Use chalk on the carpet inside – keep the proportion of the footprint so that the giant could fit in the room!
- The children may write back to the giant telling him what they have investigated and know about his height, toe-size and foot-length, etc.

How is this maths?

The children are exploring very early ideas of *ratio* and *proportion* by using the foot to visualise the height of the giant.

Chapter 15

Towers

Introduction

This chapter is very much related to length and height.
If you are near a building that contains a number of
stairs you may want to take the children on a walk to
climb them, counting how many steps they have
climbed. Thinking about different towers within the
children's environment and beyond helps them to
understand construction further, which later develops
into geometric understanding.

Tall tower competition

Whose tower is the tallest?

Aims and objectives

- To learn about indirect comparison of length.

Resources

- Construction equipment
- Masking tape
- Unmarked stick

Preparation

- Use the masking tape to identify the areas within which the children must construct their towers, ensuring that the spaces are as far away from each other as possible.

What to do

- Announce that there is a competition to build the tallest tower using the materials in the construction area.
- Show the children the area that their group will be constructing the tower within.
- Announce the time they have and set them off on the task.
- During construction speak to the children about how they are constructing their towers and how they plan to make them *tall*, or the *tallest*.
- At the end of construction talk about which tower is the *tallest*. How can the children check without moving their towers?
- Using the unmarked stick, place it next to each tower in turn and mark the height of each. Use this to check the tallest tower.
- You may wish to award a small prize to the winning team!

Tip   Provide a lot of equipment. You may need to borrow equipment from other classrooms. If so, identify it in some way so it can be returned safely.

Variations

- Have only one group at a time building a tower and use the stick to record the heights. Challenge the next group to build their tower higher. Keep going until all groups have had a turn.

- Alternatively build one tower that each group contributes to.

How is this maths?

The children are exploring length and what terms such as *longer* mean. By using the stick they are using *indirect comparison* to identify the tallest tower. Indirect comparison occurs when children know that if tower A is taller than tower B, and tower B is taller than tower C, then tower A must be taller than tower C. The term for this was coined by Piaget: *transitivity*. It underpins a lot of logical reasoning in mathematics.

Construct a tall tower

A less competitive version of the previous activity.

Aims and objectives

• To practise direct comparison of length.

Resources

• Wooden blocks of various shapes
• Pictures of world-famous towers such as Eiffel Tower （Paris）, Freedom Tower （Miami）, Qutub Minar Tower （Delhi） and Emirates Tower （Dubai）.

Preparation

• Study the pictures of the famous towers from around the world.

What to do

• Challenge a small group to build a tower that is taller than one of the children in the group.
• As they are building it, speak to them about their design and how they are ensuring that it will not fall down. Explore what shapes they are using to ensure the tower is as secure as possible, drawing on what they saw in the pictures of other towers.

 Tip   A tower may be more secure if it is wider at the bottom and narrower at the top.

Variations

• Use different construction materials.
• Build other objects rather than towers.

 How is this maths?

The children are developing and using their knowledge of shape and space to build a tower that is *taller* than them. They will use *trial and error* throughout. Learning from mistakes is an important skill when developing a mathematical disposition.

Drawing a tower

How tall can you go?

Aims and objectives

• To explore the relationship between length and height.

Resources

• Long thin paper

• Pencils

Preparation

• Show the children the pictures of the towers you have gathered together for 'Construct a tall tower' to encourage them to think about what towers look like.

What to do

• Have a selection of paper of different lengths for the children to choose from.

• Encourage the children to draw their tower on the paper. Discuss with them how *long* and *wide* it is.

• When the towers are finished display them on a wall. Discuss the *heights* of the towers and *order* them. Did the towers look different when they were flat on the table? Have they really changed, or do they look the same?

Tip

Allow the children to change the dimension that they are working in. For example, do they want to work on the floor or on the paper stapled to the wall? Encourage them to hold the paper up in different directions.

Variation

This is not limited to drawing towers. The children can draw people or giraffes, flowers or trees, or shapes, or write numbers on a long strip of paper.

How is this maths?

Young children find it difficult to understand that an object does not change when it has moved from the horizontal plane to the vertical plane and vice versa. Enabling them to manipulate their own drawings and paper allows them to explore *conservation of length*.

Thinking about towers

Why do we need towers?

Aims and objectives

- To understand the use and application of tall structures.

Resources

- A set of photographs of towers in the local area or from further afield

Preparation

- Take photos of towers in the local vicinity to add to the other tower pictures the children have been using.

What to do

- Talk to the children about the towers that they are familiar with in their environment. Find the tower（s） they are talking about from the picture bank to help the other children engage in discussion.
- Show other towers. Ask, 'What are the towers used for? '
- Once individual towers have been discussed, encourage the children to identify common features of some of the towers. For example, accommodation and office blocks enable a lot of people to live and work in an area that is very limited on the ground. Some towers （pylons） are designed to keep items （cables） safely off the ground and away from people, and other towers （mobile phone masts or aircraft control towers） have to lift something permanently （signals or controllers） high into the sky.

Tip　　This activity helps children to think about towers being used for a number of different purposes and challenges their stereotypical notions of what towers are for （e. g. Rapunzel）.

Variation

Include talk about historical towers such as lighthouses and television signal transmitters.

How is this maths?

As well as knowing mathematical facts, children also need to know how mathematical concepts are used and applied in real life. This helps make mathematics meaningful to them and shows how mathematics has a purpose.

Being tall

How tall can you be?

Aims and objectives

- To make ourselves tall, taller and tallest.

Resources

- None required

Preparation

- None required.

What to do

- Ask the children, 'Can you stretch like a tower? Show me.'
- Ask the children to move around the room like tall animals they know, such as a giraffe, llama or elephant.
- Ask, 'Why do these animals need to be tall?'.

Tip   These animals are taller than us, but they all move differently. Some creatures have developed wings so they can fly to reach food sources and also to be protected.

Variation

The children can also move like animals to explore other notions such as speed or agility.

How is this maths?

The children are exploring the notion of height. Understanding concepts related to *measures*, *shape* and *space* will help develop more sophisticated geometric thinking later.

Lock her in the tower!

Use animated film to explore and visualise spirals and height.

Aims and objectives
- To link shape and height.

Resources
- A clip of an animated film where a fair maiden, princess or similar has been kept captive in a tower

Preparation
- None required.

What to do
- Play the video clip.
- Discuss, 'Why do you think the girl was locked in a tower?' (For inaccessibility reasons.)
- 'How is it possible to get into the room at top of the tower?' (Via a spiral staircase.)
- 'Why a spiral staircase?' (Because the stairs would be too steep if it was not curved.)
- 'What other ways could the girl escape?'

Tip   Show other video clips to help contrast with the first one played.

Variation
Be as creative as possible in developing escape routes. Which one would be most effective? Why?

How is this maths?
The children are visualising a *spiral* inside a *cone*-shaped tower. Mathematically speaking, if the tower is not tapered towards the top and it is

cylindrical the staircase is technically a *helix*, but don't be too picky about that! Understanding concepts related to *measures*, *shape* and *space* will help develop more sophisticated geometric thinking later.

Chapter 16

The Café

Introduction

The activities in this chapter could be carried out in a larger space, such as a school hall, or outside area, or in a café set up in the role-play area. They could also be carried out by all the children together, taking on different roles such as the waiting staff, the kitchen staff or the customers. Alternatively children might prefer to take turns. You may have a local café that the children can tour before they are involved in setting up their café in the nursery or school. Parents or children from another class might be invited to the café also.

The tables

Transform the room into a café.

Aims and objectives

- To practise 1-to-1 correspondence.
- To count in twos or fives.

Resources

- Classroom tables
- Table numbers for display
- Chairs

Preparation

- Arrange the tables into a café style, perhaps with a small group of children helping. Discuss with the children how they would like the tables be set out.

What to do

- Arrange the tables so the children are sitting in twos or fives – practise counting in twos or fives together so see how many people are in the café.
- Place a table number on each table, to help with ordering and taking orders (see later activities).
- What will be at each setting? Spoons, place mats, serviettes? Once decisions have been made, encourage the children to set their own place at the table.

Tip Take a trip to a local café to look at how the tables are arranged, as well as the other activities that go on there.

Variation

Setting the table can also happen in the doll's house, at a restaurant, at home in the role-play area or at lunchtime in the dining room/dining area.

How is this maths?

It is important that children understand 1-to-1 correspondence, identifying a relationship between two or more items. For example, in this activity the children will know that for each child there should be on knife, one fork, one spoon and one tumbler. Later on in mathematics relationships beyond 1-to-1 develop. These are used to solve problems, undertake statistical analyses, algebra and many other tasks.

Garçon, I'd like to order please

Choose what you would like to eat in the café.

Aims and objectives

• To recognise and read numbers in a money context.

Resources

• café menus

• Coins (toy or real)

Preparation

• The menus may have been created by the children earlier.

• Give the children coins to spend in the café.

What to do

• In pairs children look at the menus and the *price* of the items available. They talk about what they would like. They discuss the price of the food and how much *money* they have to spend.

Tip

Discuss the menus with the children first, if they have not been involved in making them. Use pictures of the food items to support their comprehension. Also show the number of *coins* required alongside the value in numbers.

Variations

Ordering food and paying for it can happen in a wide range of contexts and the role-play area provides the ideal opportunity for this. For example, it could turn into a fish and chip shop, a Chinese takeaway, an Indian restaurant, a baker's shop, a pâtisserie, a pie shop or a butcher's shop.

How is this maths?

Children need to recognise and name coins. As we move towards living in a cashless society where everything is paid by card or other means, it is essential that young children understand the value of money as soon as possible.

May I take your order now?

A follow-on activity in the café.

Aims and objectives
- To write numbers.

Resources
- Notepads and pencils
- Dressing-up clothes for each *garçon* (waiter) and *serveuse* (waitress)

Preparation
- None required, if previous two activities have been undertaken.

What to do
- Explain to the waiters and waitresses their role, which includes:
  a. Writing the table number down
  b. Taking the order
  c. Leaving the bill
  d. Collecting the money
- With adult assistance, send the waiters and waitresses to their customers!

 Tip   If you number each item on the menu the waiters and waitresses can write the relevant number rather than needing to write the item's name.

Variations
- Orders can be taken in any of the places listed earlier, i. e. the role-play fish and chip shop, Chinese takeaway, Indian restaurant, baker's shop, pâtisserie, pie shop or butcher's shop.
- Orders could be taken on the telephone in these places and the customer could find their

items waiting to be collected when they arrive at the role play area.

How is this maths?

The children are using mathematics to record information. For example, they are writing table numbers and menu items or their corresponding numbers. Using and applying their mathematical knowledge is an important skill to encourage and develop.

Mixing drinks

Make yummy fruit squash to drink in the café.

Aims and objectives

- To practise counting.
- To use ratio.
- To learn about capacity.

Resources

- Fruit squash concentrate
- Jugs
- Cups or tumblers
- Drinking water

Preparation

- Check children's health records regarding allergies to ensure all children are able to partake.

What to do

- The drinks need to be made up to pass on to the customers.
- Read the label of the squash together. What does it mean 'to every part concentrate add six parts water'?
- Discuss, 'How much does this jug hold?'. Encourage the children to count the number of cups that go into the jug. Start with one 'part' concentrate. Count it into the jug together. Add six 'parts' water. Discuss whether or not the children think there is room for another seven cups to be added. Add more if so. Keep going until the jug is full.
- When ready pour the squash into cups. Ask, 'How many drinks have we made? Is that enough? How many more do we need? How do we know where to fill the jug to?'

Tip Think carefully about what will measure the 'part'. It doesn't have to be a cup, it could be any clean item. Try to select something small enough to require the children to undertake the activity more than once.

Variation

Follow recipes for fruit cocktails. For example, an 'orange and lemon zest' could contain five parts orange juice, one part lemon juice and three parts lemonade.

How is this maths?

The children are using *ratio* to make the squash. In the example above the ratio is one part concentrate to six parts water. That is a ratio of 1 : 6. Engaging in activities that require children to use ratios in meaningful situations early on helps children to be able to calculate using ratios, and learn the relationship between ratio and proportion, fractions, percentages and decimals, later in their primary school career.

I choose that glass

Glass sizes can be deceptive!

Aims and objectives

- To understand conservation of capacity.
- To check the accuracy of results.

Resources

- A range of tumblers (approximately six) that hold a varying amount of liquid

Preparation

- Ensure two or three of the tumblers hold less than they look like they might, compared with the other tumblers.

What to do

- Tell the children that they can choose any tumbler they wish to have their favourite drink in.
- Discuss which one (s) they would choose and why.
- Focus on the decision made by some children to select the tumbler that holds the most. Ask, 'How do you know that tumbler holds the *most*? How would we *check*?' (Do not check at this stage.)

- Ask the children to see if they can *order* the tumblers from the one that holds the *most* to the one that holds the *least*.
- During their discussions if necessary challenge their thinking. For example, if they are focusing only on height point out to them that the tall tumbler is very thin but another (shorter) tumbler is wider.
- Once they have made their decision ask them how they may check to see if they have got the order correct.
- The children check using their own method. If there were some mistakes encourage the children to discuss why they were wrong.

Tip Some children may choose a tumbler because it is attractive to them, rather than because it is the largest. This is fine. However, focus on the response of a child who chooses the largest tumbler.

Variation

Bottles can also be used to explore *conservation of capacity*. Parcels that are different sizes and weights (i. e. some small heavy parcels and one or two larger light ones) can also be used to explore *conservation of weight*.

How is this maths?

Conservation of capacity is a difficult concept for children to understand because the visual impact that the object has means that we often focus on the height only, rather than its capacity. By having many opportunities to explore conservation of capacity, experience will help children to develop their understanding.

Decorating biscuits

What patterns will you put on your biscuit?

Aims and objectives

• To make and continue a pattern.

Resources

• Biscuits
• White icing
• Icing pens
• Sweets
• Sprinkles

Preparation

• The biscuits may have been made earlier by the children or could be shop-bought.

What to do

• Spread the biscuits with the white icing.
• Use sweets, sprinkles or icing pens to create a design.

Tip   Provide a range of biscuit shapes. Circular biscuits encourage symmetrical patterns with more lines of symmetry than rectangular biscuits.

Variation

Ice the biscuits according to a theme, or make your own biscuits so the children have a wider range of shapes to decorate, such as stars.

How is this maths?

Mathematics is full of *pattern* in number and shape. Seeing pattern helps children to solve problems. Being able to say what comes next helps children to visualise shape or colour and pattern. Using *ordinal language* (first, second, etc.) helps children to talk mathematically.

Displaying the biscuits

How are we going to 'show off' the biscuits for premium sales?

Aims and objectives
- To understand pattern.

Resources
- Cake platters – a selection
- Digital camera (optional)

Preparation
- None required.

What to do
- Ask the children how the biscuits can be displayed for the most sales.
- The children might arrange them on a tiered cake stand. If so, is there logic to their presentation? (Either in the numbers placed on each tier, or placing like biscuits together, or alternating the biscuits, etc.)
- The children might take photos of the biscuits and display those.

Tip   Allow the children to decide themselves and their creativity may surprise you!

Variation

Hang the biscuits from the Christmas tree.

How is this maths?

The children are creating their own *patterns* using the biscuits. They are using their *logical thinking* to do this. Pattern and logic are both essential skills for children to develop in mathematics as they support children in carrying out mathematical tasks later on.

Chapter 17

Fun with numbers

Introduction

The activities in this chapter are focused on children learning about numbers. They will explore numbers in a wide range of contexts and see numbers displayed in many different ways. Encourage the children to think about large numbers also – they get very excited by looking at and reading numbers such as 100 or 1000!

Air finger-numbers

Create numbers using only your index finger.

Aims and objectives

• To read and write numbers.

Resources

• None required

Preparation

• None required.

What to do

• The children trace numbers in the air with their index finger, using big movements.

Tip   Children love to write numbers that are related to them, such as their age, how old they will be next birthday, their house number and so on.

Variation

The children hold a short stick that has a ribbon attached to it and make numbers in the air with the tip of the stick.

How is this maths?

The children are learning to write numerals.

Other numbers at your fingertips

Make numbers with your finger using a range of materials.

Aims and objectives

• To read and write numbers.

Resources

• Paint

- Shaving foam
- Sand
- Trays

Preparation

- Pour each of the resources into their own tray. The paint needs to be a very thin layer.

What to do

- Write numbers in the shaving foam, paint or sand.
- Encourage the children to follow your lead.
- Ask them to write certain numbers or ask them what numbers they want to write.
- Use a flat hand to rebuild the shaving foam or shake the trays of paint or sand to start again.

Tips

- The shaving foam offers a slightly different texture for the children to explore.
- As well as creating the numbers ask the children what they know about the number – for example, is it their age? Mummy's age? What number does it come after? What is the number after that?

Variations

- Glue and glitter or PVA and string/wool offer another texture to write in.
- Try breathing on a mirrored surface and writing with a finger in the condensation.

How is this maths?

The children are learning to write numerals.

Play dough numbers

Make lots of snakes and turn them into numbers.

Aims and objectives
- To read and write numbers.

Resources
- Play dough

Preparation
- If necessary, make the play dough. Here is a recipe if you do not have one already:

  250g plain flour, 50g salt, 140ml water, 1 – 2 tablespoons of cooking oil and, if using, a few drops of food colouring.

  Mix the flour and salt in a large bowl. Add the water and oil. Knead well (add slightly more flour or water as necessary) until the dough is smooth and not sticky. Add food colouring and continue to knead until the colour is fully blended. Place into a plastic bag and refrigerate until chilled.

What to do
- With the children roll the play dough into 'snakes' (long and skinny sausage shapes).
- Use the 'snakes' to form numbers they are familiar with.
- Can the group make all the numbers from one to ten?
- Can the digits be used to make other numbers the children know?
- What is the biggest number they know?

Tip   Identify a number that the children are still learning and ask them to make small and big play dough versions of the same number. This will help to consolidate what the number looks like because they are repeating it several times.

Variation
The children could make their names out of play dough letters.

How is this maths?

The children are learning to read and construct numerals.

String-thing numbers

Let's get sticking!

Aims and objectives

• To read and write numbers.

Resources

• Glue stick or craft glue

• Wool or string

• Card or thick paper

Preparation

• None required.

What to do

• Encourage the children to 'draw' a number using the glue.

• Cover the glue with wool or string.

• Display.

Tip   During the task talk with the children about what they know about their numbers. 'How is the number made? Where do you see the number? What numbers is it *between* when you count? Name a number *greater than* that number. Name a number *less than* that number.'

Variation

Use glue and then sprinkle glitter over to make the numbers.

How is this maths?

The children are learning to read and construct numerals. They are also sharing with their peers and adults what they know about numbers.

Making big numbers

....

Use whole bodies to make numbers.

Aims and objectives

• To read and write numbers.

Resources

• Large floor space such as a hall

• A4 sheets with the numbers 1 – 10 on them

Preparation

• None required.

What to do

• Ask a small group of children to lie on the floor while their peers shape them into a number.

• Repeat for many numbers. Talk about which numbers are similar in shape and why.

Tip   Take a photo looking down on the children so the participants can see the outcome also.

Variation

Use larger numbers or ask children to create their own numbers within their group so more children have an opportunity to join in each time.

How is this maths?

This activity helps children to identify where numbers are similar and different, which can help them talk about common errors made such as reversing their 5s, or confusing 2 and 5 with each other.

'I can' with a calculator

Let the children play and explore.

Aims and objectives

• To read and write numbers.

Resources

• Calculators

Preparation

• None required.

What to do

• Provide the children with calculators to explore what numbers they can make.

• Read the numbers they create for them if they are unable to.

• Ask them to challenge each other to make numbers.

Tip   The children will enjoy listening to you read off the calculator numbers they have never heard before, such as twenty-three million, four hundred and sixty-four thousand, one hundred and seventy-six!

Variation

Give no direction and let the children have free access to the calculators over a period of time. After a designated period ask them to share with each other what they have found out.

How is this maths?

The children will explore numbers that are far larger than those that regular nursery or setting activities might offer. It also introduces *decimal* and *negative* numbers to the children. This activity excites young children who want to find out more about these new numbers!

Numbers we use

We use numbers all the time – let's explore!

Aims and objectives

- To read numbers.
- To use and apply number.

Resources

- A number of photographs or pictures of numbers in everyday use （for examples see 'What to do' section）

Preparation

- Take photos if necessary.

What to do

- Share the photographs/pictures.
- Talk with the children about where they have seen the numbers （e. g. house doors, the supermarket, on birthday cards, on dice） and how they are used.
- Talk about the different representations （dice use dots, money has a decimal point in the middle of the number to show the pounds and pence, the road sign is big for people to see how fast they are allowed to travel）.
- Encourage the children to bring in their own examples of where they have seen numbers （e. g. the newspaper, a rubbing of their parents' car registration plate）.
- Display their numbers alongside yours.

Tip   The key to this activity is to get the children talking about their own experiences of number, where they see them and how they use number.

Variation

You could do the same with shapes or with letters of the alphabet.

How is this maths?

This activity helps children to see how numbers support many purposes and how they give *order* and *structure*, which makes life easier and safer for us.

Chapter 18

Weather

Introduction

A number of the activities in this chapter make use of any outdoor area available. If your outdoor space is limited then the activities can be adapted accordingly. Looking at weather and seasons across a year helps children to see a large-scale natural pattern. You could talk and sing about the seasons over a short period, or dedicate a small display space for a whole year to photographs of the children and the trees through the seasons to illustrate how they adapt in different types of weather.

Our weather station

Let's explore our local weather ourselves!

Aims and objectives

- To measure using different units.

Resources

- Scissors
- Sticky tape and Blu-Tack® or similar
- Rulers
- Paper
- Pencils
- A sturdy plastic or wooden box that can stand on its side
- White paint
- A thermometer
- A pen top
- Plastic fizzy drink bottles （3）
- Card
- A knitting needle
- Matchsticks
- A cork
- Sand

Preparation

- Announce to the children's parents that the children will be making a weather station.
- Ask for donations of the resources identified above.
- Visit www. metoffice. gov. uk/education/kids/weather_ station. html for instructions on making the weather station.

What to do

- Construct a weather station together that:
  - a. Collects rainfall （rain gauge）
  - b. Measures the temperature （thermometer）
  - c. Shows wind direction （wind vane）

- Take daily measurements and record these together on a daily, weekly or monthly weather chart.
- Instead of making the wind vane that is on the Met Office website it is possible to make a very simple wind 'sock' by attaching thin, light ribbon to the end of a garden cane.

Variation

You may even want to include a home-made barometer!

How is this maths?

To construct the weather station the children will be *measuring* using *length*. When they start gathering and collecting *data* from the weather station they will also be measuring in other units, such as *temperature* in degrees Celsius and wind direction according to the *compass directions*.

Wind

Make flags and observe the wind.

Aims and objectives

• To practise logical thinking.

Resources

• Garden canes or sticks

• Thin fabric

• Glue

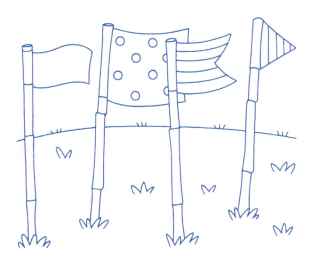

Preparation

• Make the flags:

   a. Cut different shapes out of the fabric.

   b. Glue along the end of the fabric that is to be attached to the cane. Press the glued edge to the cane and leave until completely dry.

What to do

• Watch the wind blow the grass and the leaves on the trees.

• Take the flags made previously outside.

• Do they fly differently in different parts of the outdoor area?

Tip   Hold the flags at the same height to get a fairer test around the premises.

Variation

Make windmills instead of flags.

 How is this maths?

Understanding *cause and effect* makes use of logical thinking. Understanding why the flags fly better in some locations than others utilises this skill.

Shadows

Observe how shadows change during the day.

Aims and objectives

- To notice change.

Resources

- Outdoor area that has the sun all day
- Outdoor chalk
- Large paper and felt-tip pen (optional)

Preparation

- Check the weather forecast to ensure the sun is going to stay out all day.

What to do

- Draw around a child's shadow at different times of the day (e.g. 9am, noon, 3pm).
- Discuss what happens over the day.
- Ask why it happens.

Tip

Remember that the sun is not moving. Rather, it is the earth spinning on its axis that makes the shadows change. Try to avoid suggesting to the children that the sun moves (although they will come up with this misconception themselves because this is what they think they observe).

Variation

If possible draw on large paper and keep. Then redo in winter. How are the shadows different now? Why? Discuss *length* of shadows, the *height* of the sun against the horizon and how the sun appears to travel across the sky during the day.

How is this maths?

The children are talking about how the shadows change in relation to length and also direction (angle). They are beginning to explore Earth and our sun, for which there are many patterns and cycles that have been explained using mathematics.

Create your own shadows

Use a torch or overhead projector to make shadows on the wall.

Aims and objectives
- To learn about movement.
- To learn about shape.

Resources
- Torch or overhead projector
- Blank wall

Preparation
- Move the projector（if using one）into position before the children arrive. Ensure the lead is safely taped down.

What to do
- Encourage the children to make shadows against the wall using an overhead projector or a torch.

  Ask:

  a. 'How many fingers/toys can you see? '

  b. 'Can you move the shadow fast/slowly? '

  c. 'Can you move the shadow high/low? '

  d. 'Can you make a wide shadow or a narrow shadow? '

  e. 'Can the shadow jump up and down? '

  f. 'What else can your shadow do? '

Tip   Let the children play and explore for some time before asking your questions.

Variations

- You may set up a plain, light-coloured sheet with a light source behind it instead.

- The children could use shadow puppets to make them move as per the questions above.

How is this maths?

There are a number of mathematical concepts being explored in this activity, mainly related to shape and space. By forming the shadows the children may have to think on another plane, depending on the position of the light source. Making a wide or narrow shadow may require the child to move in and out from the light source, which also requires them to use a different plane.

The four seasons

Aims and objectives

- To understand repeating patterns.

Change throughout the year

Let's spring into action!

Aims and objectives

- To understand repeating patterns.

Resources

- Brainstorming paper
- Felt-tip pens
- Pictures showing people out and about in each of the seasons （optional）
- *Lili's Wish* by Emma Thomson （optional）

Preparation

- Read *Lili's Wish* by Emma Thomson （optional）. This pop-up book follows the story of rag doll Lili who, with her friends' help, works out she is one year old by thinking about key events she remembers happening in each of the seasons.

What to do

- Talk with the children about what they know about each of the four seasons. Ask questions such as:
    a. 'How do the trees change? '
    b. 'What flowers do you see? '
    c. 'What is the weather like? '
    d. 'What clothes do you wear? '
- Record their answers, or ask the children to draw their ideas on the brainstorming sheet.
- Bring the four seasons together. How is the weather in each season different?
- Talk about the cyclical pattern that the seasons make.

512

Tip   You may look at a different season each day, or split the class into four groups with each group focusing on one season.

Variations

- Listen to Vivaldi's 'Four Seasons' while you are thinking about the seasons.

- Look at a life cycle presented by month or season (see www. ladybird-survey. org/ lifecycle. aspx for one example). Discuss the impact the seasons have on the life cycle.

How is this maths?

Mathematicians look at all sorts of patterns. Some of them repeat after a very short time, others such as the seasons repeat after a much longer time. Understanding that some patterns are cyclical is an important mathematical notion to begin to develop.

Celebrating through the seasons

Taking a look at how the children celebrate their birthdays around the year.

Aims and objectives

- To practise logical reasoning.

Resources

- Photos of children's birthday parties (ask the children to bring these in beforehand)

Preparation

- Request party photographs from parents.

- Check children's birthday dates to confirm in which season they fall.

What to do

- Talk with the children about how they celebrate their birthdays by sharing the photos they have brought in. Ask them not to reveal the date of the birthday!
- Discuss the clothes that the guests are wearing. Ask why the children would be dressed like that.
- Ask the other children to identify which season the party may have been held in.
- Check when the child's birthday is. Were the class correct?

Tip   You may also talk about the location of the party (particularly if it is outdoors in the summer). Be mindful that not all the children will have had similar experiences of birthday parties.

Variation

You can talk about other celebrations through the year, or take one celebration (e.g. Christmas) and look at how others in Australia or New Zealand celebrate it in a different season.

How is this maths?

The children are using logical reasoning when they are gathering all the available data (i. e. clothing worn, location of party) and deducing the time of year the party was held. This skill continues to be developed throughout their journey in mathematics.

Chapter 19

Painting

Introduction

Exploring colour, shape and texture encourages early mathematical development, and paint is a medium children are familiar with to carry this out. These activities also help children to develop their gross and fine motor skills by using various painting resources to paint on different surfaces.

In your prime

Mix primary colours using ratios to make different hues.

Aims and objectives

- To use ratio.

Resources

- Paints – primary colours only
- Mixing pots
- Teaspoons
- Sugar paper or similar to paint on

Preparation

- You may wish to make your own copy first to show the children.

What to do

- Try mixing different amounts of primary colours. For example:
  - a. 4 yellow spoons and 0 red spoons, then
  - b. 3 yellow spoons and 1 red spoon, then
  - c. 2 yellow spoons and 2 red spoons, then
  - d. 1 yellow spoon and 3 red spoons, then
  - e. 0 yellow spoons and 4 red spoons.
- Discuss the different shades of orange (or purple or green, depending on the primary colours used) the different recipes make.
- The children can write a recipe for their favourite colour and encourage their friend to copy it and compare the product.

Tips
- Encourage the children to be as accurate as they can with their teaspoonfuls to gain the best result of the changing hues.
- Reinforce language related to ratio, such as three to one (3 : 1).

Variation

Use one colour and white or black to create different shades.

How is this maths?

Mixing paints enables young children to begin to explore *ratio* and *proportion*. By creating colours for their friend to copy they begin to learn that *accuracy* is important when *measuring*.

Painting on a large scale

···   ···

> Be big and bold!

Aims and objectives

- To explore large areas in shape and space.

Resources

- Paint – lots of it!
- Big brushes, pads and rollers
- Large items to paint on (see 'What to do' section for ideas)

Preparation

- Ensure there is a space large enough for the activity.

What to do

- Explore large space through painting. Can the children paint the *whole* of the:
  a. sheet of paper on the painting easel?
  b. large box that is being turned into a . . . ?
  c. wall that is being turned into a blackboard area outside (using blackboard paint)?
  d. role-play area's new table?
  e. boulders?

 Tip   Think big! Try to encourage the children to leave no space unpainted! Be creative in identifying what the children can paint.

Variation

Go elsewhere to paint, such as a gallery or a local secondary school.

 How is this maths?

By experiencing large areas and spaces the children are beginning to learn about *scale factors*, *enlargement* and *different sizes*.

Super-small painting

You've thought big and tall, now think super-small.

Aims and objectives

• To explore small areas in shape and space.

Resources

• Paint

• Small brushes, pads, sticks and rollers

• Toothpicks

• Small items to paint (see 'What to do' section for ideas)

Preparation

• None required.

What to do

• Explore small space through painting. Can the children paint:

a. using a very small paintbrush?

b. their name as small as they can?

c. using a toothpick on a piece of paper the size of a postage stamp?

Tip   Think small! Use the smallest objects the children can manipulate. Be creative.

Variation

Paint strawberries with chocolate!

How is this maths?

By experiencing small areas and spaces the children are beginning to learn about *scale factors*, *enlargement* (by less than 0) and different *sizes*.

Chapter 20

The farm

Introduction

Many of the activities in this chapter help children to use their logical thinking skills to group and categorise in a farm context. If possible, a trip to the farm will help the children to see how the farmer keeps the animals healthy by grouping them and keeping them in particular-sized fields. The activities here are related to small-world play but equally could be adapted to a larger space where some of the children become the various animals, looked after by others who are the farmers.

Setting up the farm

Using the small-world farm.

Aims and objectives

- To practise logical reasoning.
- To learn about estimation.

Resources

- Small-world farm and animals

Preparation

- None required.

What to do

- Ask the children to set up the farm and then leave them alone for a short time.
- Then ask, 'Where is the best place to put the animals? Why did you put the barn there? '
- Discuss the reasons for the decisions made. For example, are the animals that can swim/need water near the pond? Are those that need shelter near trees or a barn? Discuss alternative places the animal could have been placed and why.
- Ask how many particular animals the children estimate there are in the box. Check by counting.
- Ask if the children think that the animals will all fit in a particular pen, or a farm building. Check.

Tip   This develops children's understanding of animals and their needs.

Variation

Set up other small-world play areas.

How is this maths?

The children are using *estimation* when they are setting up the farm. It is essential that estimation is used in mathematics because it is an excellent way to check the reasonableness of answers when calculations are carried out. Through trial and error the children are also using estimation to develop their understanding of *number* and *counting*. Thinking about alternatives helps to develop a mathematical disposition.

Sorting the animals

··········

Let's help the farmer to sort the animals.

Aims and objectives

- To learn about sorting and categorisation.

Resources

- Farm animals from the small-world area
- Paper to make labels (optional)

Preparation

- None required.

What to do

- Explain to the children that the farmer has decided to farm only one type of animal now, but is not sure what type he should keep. Ask the children to help the farmer by sorting them into types of animals.
- It is likely that the children first sort according to what they are called (e.g. horse). Encourage the children to think about other ways to categorise the animals (e.g. animals with four legs, animals that can fly or animals that lay eggs)
- Are there any categorisations that would mean this farmer had no animals (e.g. wild savannah animals or animals that live in the water)?

Tip   Ensure the children have enough space to arrange and rearrange the animals. You may provide paper for them to use so they can create labels for the groups.

Variation

The children can categorise and group everyday objects in a range of ways. Encourage them to be creative and also to identify a category that no objects fit into.

How is this maths?

Sorting leads children into *data handling*. It helps them to understand that *grouping data* can help them to make a big set more manageable. Having items that are going to be the *null set* (such as wild savannah animals in this example) provides an opportunity for children to understand the notion of the *empty set*.

Pens and fences

Aims and objectives

- To learn about fence length.
- To learn about field area.

Resources

- Fencing and animals from the small-world farm

Preparation

- None required.

What to do

- Ask the children to build fences around the animals to keep them safe.
- Ask, 'How many animals can you fit in the space you have created? Do the animals have everything they need in the space?' Encourage the children to think about overcrowding, shelter, food and water.

Tip   This activity helps the children to think about animal welfare.

Variation

Think about how much space is needed in different areas of the nursery/classroom when the children are rearranging a part of it for an activity.

How is this maths?

The children are exploring early *perimeter* (fence length) and *area* (field) in this activity. It will be some time before they are introduced to these formally but here they are intuitively using the ideas. These will develop further as they move through primary school and beyond.

Life cycles

Explore cyclical patterns through animal life cycles.

Aims and objectives

- To identify cyclical patterns.

Resources

- A frog or tadpoles in the nursery/school grounds where the children can observe the life-cycle process
- Butterfly kit or similar

Preparation

- Ensure the area is safe for the children to visit if going to a nature area that is not regularly visited.

What to do

- Observe the tadpoles （or butterfly eggs or other animal） over time. Discuss the changes that the children notice.
- Start to map the cycle to keep a record of what they have seen.
- Eventually talk about how the cycle begins again, making it cyclical.

Tips

- This activity works well when the children have access to the animal in order to see the life cycle happening themselves.
- You can find butterfly kits for sale on the internet or in large garden centres.

Variation

If no access is possible to live animals or insects, looking at life cycles online, in books or on charts is another way to engage children in the topic.

How is this maths?

Knowing that some patterns are cyclical is an important mathematical notion to understand.

Chapter 21

Parties

Introduction

It is easy to find an excuse to have a party! Perhaps a child's grandparent or an adult in the nursery is reaching a special age, or some of the children in Reception are all turning five at around the same time. However, be aware that some families may not celebrate birthdays or other events as other people do. This is normally related to religious beliefs. If you are in doubt, it would be worth asking the parents or carers about the extent to which they want their child (ren) joining in.

Make wrapping paper

Print your own wrapping paper.

Aims and objectives

- To copy and continue a repeating pattern.
- To create a repeating pattern.

Resources

- Sponges or potatoes for printing
- Paint
- Large sheets of plain newsprint paper for printing on
- Small sheets of paper （about A5） for designing the basic print pattern

Preparation

- You may wish to look at existing wrapping paper and discuss the patterns on the paper and how they continue （repeat）. Can the children see how the pattern has been made to repeat? Has it been *slid* along the paper （*translated*）, has it been *turned* （*rotated*） and/or has it been *flipped* （*reflected*）?

What to do

- Encourage the children to design a basic print pattern on the small sheets of paper.
- Ask the children to replicate it in one corner of the large plain newsprint paper.
- If necessary, help the children to repeat their pattern.

Tips

- Check the first design on the A5 paper for the children – are they going to be able to replicate it?

- Remember that it doesn't matter if the pattern cannot fit completely onto the large sheet on its last repeat. Patterns continue forever so there should be no white 'border space' around the large sheet either!
- Reinfore the language *slide*, *turn* and *flip* as you continue to talk with the children during the activity.

Variation

Print using a theme such as Hallowe'en, Christmas or Easter.

How is this maths?

The children are exploring geometric patterns using early language related to transformational geometry. They will also begin to understand that patterns have no end and that they keep repeating.

Wrap the parcel

Prepare together for the traditional party game.

Aims and objectives

- To use vocabulary related to large and small.
- To understand surface area.

Resources

- A small gift already wrapped so the children do not know what it is
- A number of sheets of wrapping paper piled so that the largest sheet is on the bottom and the smallest is on the top
- Sticky tape
- Scissors

Preparation

- Ensure the gift for the middle of the parcel is already wrapped once.

What to do

- Check all the children know how to play pass the parcel.
- Explain that they will all be preparing for the game now, and then they will play it at a later date.
- Place the pile of paper on the floor in the middle of the circle. Ask the children what they notice about the pile of paper in the centre. Discuss the different sizes and how the paper is piled with the *largest* at the bottom and the *smallest* at the top. Ask the children if they know why you might have done that.
- Pass the parcel to different children and ask them to wrap the gift.
- Talk about the relative size of the parcel and how it is changing, becoming *bigger* and *bigger* as it is wrapped.

Tips

- Because the children are wrapping the parcel themselves, ensure the gift is particularly small and that there is a lot of room for growth in the pre-prepared papers.
- Some children may become confused because they normally *unwrap* the

parcel. You may need to explain several times that the children are preparing for the game. Asking children to come to you to wrap the parcel may avoid the confusion that passing the parcel around the circle could bring.

Variation

Although it may not look as attractive, newspaper works just as well in developing children's understanding of the concepts and it helps you to recycle previously used paper!

How is this maths?

By preparing for the game the children are exploring very early notions of *inverse operations* – what started small becomes *bigger* and will then become *smaller* again as it is unwrapped. This is fundamentally what happens with addition and subtraction, and multiplication and division being inverse operations. Early notions of *surface area* are also explored by noticing that the paper needs to become bigger as the parcel also becomes bigger.

Pass the parcel

A mathematical variation on the traditional game.

Aims and objectives

- To learn about taking turns.
- To practise counting.
- To use vocabulary related to large and small.

Resources

- The parcel made earlier by the children
- Large bin liner

Preparation

- If the children have not collaboratively wrapped the parcel you will need to create one by wrapping a small gift in several separate layers of paper.
- If the children did prepare it, you may need to add more layers before the game is played.

What to do

- Identify a child to start.
- Pass the parcel around the circle but instead of using music count to a given number, say 9, and pass on each count.
- When the ninth person receives the parcel they unwrap one layer.
- Counting starts again from 1 and the parcel is passed around again.
- When the ninth person receives the parcel they unwrap one layer.
- When several people have unwrapped a layer it may be that a child gets the parcel again.
- If there are some children who have not unwrapped the parcel yet continue to move the parcel, without counting, to the next child who is yet to unwrap.
- Start counting from 1 again.
- Once everyone has had a go unwrapping then give children the opportunity for a second turn.

Tips

- Ask another adult to go to each child unwrapping the parcel and collect the used paper in a bin liner.

- To make the game flow, count the number of children in the group and select a number to count to each time that is *not* a factor of that number.

Variation

You could play the traditional game where the children pass the parcel around the circle until you pause the music.

How is this maths?

The children are practising their counting skills. They are also being involved in a numerical pattern that develops around the circle. Using music helps children to follow directions.

Wrap that box

A game that involves wrapping boxes.

Aims and objectives

• To match boxes with wrapping paper.

Resources

• A number of boxes, all of varying sizes
• A number of sheets of paper, all different sizes
• Sticky tape

Preparation

• Check that the sheets of paper will each wrap one of the boxes snugly. Make a note for yourself as to which paper matches each box most appropriately.

What to do

• Divide the group into two teams and sit them facing each other on a large carpet area.
• Line the sheets of paper in size order on the floor between the two teams.
• Display the boxes in an arbitrary way at one end.
• Ask for a volunteer from one team to select one box.
• Encourage the team to offer suggestions as to the paper that would wrap it best.
• The volunteer places it on one sheet of paper. (Once the paper has been touched the child is unable to change their mind!)
• They check that it is the best fit. If they are correct their team scores one point.
• It is now the other team's turn.
• If a team is incorrect (as the adult who has checked beforehand you will know which one is the best fit) the box is passed to the other team to try.
• The game continues until all the boxes have been covered. The winning team is the team with the highest score.

Tip   You may want to demonstrate before the game starts what an appropriate fit is, to avoid confusion later on.

Variation

Use paper that matches a particular theme, for example birthday party wrapping paper for parties and Christmas paper in December.

How is this maths?

Early notions of surface area are explored in this game, by matching paper to boxes.

Guess the present

Time to be creative and have some fun guessing what could be in the box!

Aims and objectives

- To visualise size and shape.
- To understand volume.

Resources

- A number of empty wrapped boxes, all different sizes and shapes

Preparation

- The boxes may have been wrapped in the previous activity, or you may need/want to set up a different set of boxes of varying shapes (including, say, a basketball shape or a triangular Toblerone box).

What to do

- The children pass one wrapped empty box around. Before they pass it to the next child they must state one item that could be in the box. The item that 'could' be in the box may be nonsense (e.g. a jellyfish) but they cannot pass the box until they have identified something that could actually fit in the box (i.e. they could not say 'house').
- Pass around different-sized and -shaped boxes.

Tips

- You do not have to pass the same box right around the circle if there is a large group of children.
- Encourage the children to be as creative as they can.

Variation

Instead of boxes, pass around different sticks and the children have to state an object that is about the same height as the stick.

How is this maths?

This is a fun way for children to visualise the *volume* of boxes.

Birthday cards and candles

Counting and matching numerals.

Aims and objectives

- To practise counting.
- To recognise numbers.

Resources

- Selection of toys（with names displayed if the children are not familiar with their names）
- A number of birthday cards with different ages on them, each written out to a different toy
- A polystyrene cylinder painted to look like a birthday cake（or a role-play cake that has holes for candles, or a real cake the children can share later！）
- Small birthday candles with holders
- Lighter（for an adult only）to light the candles

Preparation

- Painting the cake takes some time if you go for that option!

What to do

- Explain to the children that today is the birthday of several of the toys in the nursery/ class.
- Pass the toys out for different children to hold and remind the children of their names.
- Show the children the envelope/card for one of the toys and ask one child to open it.
- Deduce that the toy is turning the number that is on the card.
- Suggest that the children sing the toy 'Happy Birthday' and give them a cake with candles.
- Show the children the cake and select one child to push the correct number of candles into the cake, counting as they go.
- Light the candles（if appropriate to do so）and ask the children to join in singing 'Happy Birthday' to the toy while you are moving towards the toy and small group of children who will blow the candles out.

Tips

- If necessary, check on your centre/school policy about lighting candles and children blowing them out. Take appropriate precautions to ensure all the children remain safe and are not in danger of being burnt.
- Remind the children of the need to stay where they are in the circle and ensure the children know who is going to blow the candles out. Reassure the children that they will all get a turn.

Variation

Unwrap a little present for the toy that the children can share.

How is this maths?

The children are reading the number on the card and counting out the corresponding number of candles.

You're invited!

Design invitations for friends and family, toys or other children to come to the party!

Aims and objectives

• To use a range of time-related measurements.

Resources

• Blank paper or invitation templates

Preparation

• Prepare invitation templates, if using, to include:

a. Whom it is addressed to.

b. Where the party is.

c. When (date and time).

d. Why (purpose of party: whose birthday is it and how old are they going to be?)

What to do

• Using the template or blank paper the children design their own birthday party invitations for a special guest.

Tips

• Vary the amount you have completed the template depending on the children's confidence or motivation in writing.

• Encourage the children to draw pictures if this is more appropriate.

Variation

Make a whole-class invitation to invite a neighbouring class of children to a party. Construct parts of the invitation in shared writing time and then, during guided group work, encourage children to decorate the invitation and write the name on it.

How is this maths?

The who, where, when and why questions are often used in data-handling cycles to gather data and answer questions. Measurement of time uses many different *units* and *bases*. Here the time of the party (analogue time and date) and the age of the child (in years) are used.

Chapter 22

Let's make music

Introduction

Music and mathematics are very closely related. These activities explore the relationship between the two subjects. You can involve all the children together in these activities, or they can be planned as an adult-led activity for a small group of children. Leaving instruments available for children to use during continuous provision can emphasise ideas explored together previously, or offer children the opportunity to develop their own rhythms and patterns. Encouraging them to record and play back their compositions helps to reinforce intuitive structure and pattern in music.

Count the beat

Count the beat of the music together.

Aims and objectives

- To practise counting.
- To learn about pattern.

Resources

- Percussion instruments – one per child

Preparation

- None required.

What to do

- Hand out the instruments to the children in the group.
- Encourage the children to count as they play the instrument to match the beat（1, 2, 3, 4, 1, 2, 3, 4, 1, 2, 3, 4 and so on）.
- Divide the children into two groups. Alternate the groups so, while group A is playing four beats group B is resting（not playing their instruments）for four beats. Then, keeping the beat, group B plays for four beats while group A rests.
- Divide the class into four groups. The children will play four beats when you are pointing to their group but will rest（not play）when another group is being pointed to.

Tip   Ask a child to be the conductor after you have modelled the role for a while and you have identified a child that might be able to lead the class in the counting and playing.

Variations

- Try a different beat – what about a waltz? 1, 2, 3, 1, 2, 3, 1, 2, 3 and so on. Put an emphasis on the first beat of each bar.
- Encourage the children to play the rhythm of a favourite song while they count out the beats （this is challenging！）.

How is this maths?

Counting the beat and continuing the pattern develops an understanding of structure. Structure is important in mathematics, music and poetry, to name just three examples.

I got rhythm!

Be a copycat.

Aims and objectives

• To copy and continue patterns.

Resources

• Percussion instruments – one per child （optional as the children can simply clap the rhythm）

Preparation

• None required.

What to do

- Clap or play a short rhythm for the children to repeat like an echo.
- Repeat the rhythm for the children to copy.
- When you and the children are ready, change the rhythm.

Tip When first following rhythms the children may find it easier to clap rather than play instruments.

Variation

Identify a child who can lead the children in this activity.

How is this maths?

Music, no matter how simple or complex, follows structures that are intuitively pleasing. Later on the children will learn to use musical notation to record the music. Musical notation uses a lot of mathematics – for example, fractions are used to identify the length of notes.

Exploring sounds

What sorts of sounds can be made?

Aims and objectives

- To learn about duration.

- To understand pitch.

Resources

- A selection of musical instruments that can play at least two pitches – one per child

Preparation

- None required.

What to do

- Ask the children the following questions.   'Can you make:

    a. *Long* sounds?   *Short* sounds?

    b. *Loud* sounds?   *Quiet* sounds?

    c. *High* sounds?   *Low* sounds?

    d. *Fast* sounds?   *Slow* sounds? '

Tip   Encourage the children to make a different type of sound once they have tried one way.

Variation

Instead of using instruments play music that represents the aspects identified above. Encourage the children to use body movement to reflect the sounds. For example, the children might use big movements to represent loud and very small movements to represent quiet. Talk about why they are moving in their chosen ways.

How is this maths?

Thinking about producing a type of sound in another way encourages children to be creative. Being creative in mathematics is important because it helps people to solve problems using different approaches. Duration involves identifying length of time, perhaps intuitively or by counting beats. The passing of time is also a mathematical notion.

Chapter 23

The bakery

Introduction

Although local bakeries are becoming fewer in number, you may be fortunate to be close enough for the children to visit one to spark off the ideas in this chapter's theme. Alternatively, you could invite a parent or friend who bakes bread or cakes at home to talk to the children about baking. Many of the activities will need to be undertaken with more adult support than others in this book, so you may want to enlist the help of parents for a baking day, or arrange for small groups of children to take turns over a week. Setting up a bakery in the role-play area offers children an opportunity to assume the role of a baker without the need to be precise in measurements or to work with a hot oven. If you have space you may set up the bakery next to the café (see Chapter 16) so that goodies can be supplied.

Baking

Let's all make a cake!

Aims and objectives

• To learn about measurement.

Resources

• Cake recipe
• Ingredients
• Measuring equipment such as weighing scales and measuring cups

Preparation

• Ensure the oven is working and available if the recipe requires cooking.

What to do

• Read through the recipe with the children.
• Follow the recipe by:

    a. Helping the children to *weigh* the ingredients.

    b. *Counting* the number of eggs.

    c. Mixing for a given length of *time*.

    d. Identifying what *temperature* the cake needs to be cooked at.

    e. Setting a *timer* according to how long the cake needs to be in the oven.

Tip

Reinforce the mathematical language related to measurement when you speak with the children. Encourage them to use appropriate vocabulary throughout the baking process.

Variation

You may make a different item with different groups so you can have a party at the end of the day with the different goodies.

How is this maths?

The children are using a number of different units of measurement in a meaningful context, for example grams or kilograms, minutes or hours and degrees Celsius.

Sharing evenly

················   ················

If we are sharing our baking, how many will we get each?

Aims and objectives

- To understand division as sharing evenly.
- To understand division as grouping.

Resources

- The cooked items, or pictures/counters to represent them

Preparation

- None required.

What to do

- Ask the children to identify how many items are being made, or have been made.
- Ask the children to identify how many people the items are going to be shared between.
- Talk about strategies for sharing the items evenly.

Tip

If there are several items and few children then encourage them to share out the items more than one at a time because it speeds up the process. This is division by grouping.

Variation

Have a range of items that need to be shared.

How is this maths?

Division by sharing often develops into division by grouping. This progression helps children to understand what division (as a concept) means and helps them to understand more formal methods of division later on.

The cup-cake problem

Let's make 12 cup-cakes.

Aims and objectives
- To practise addition.
- To practise subtraction.

Resources
- One muffin tray
- 12 （real or role-play） cup-cakes

Preparation
- None required.

What to do
- Explain to the children that we need 12 cup-cakes.
- Show the tray with six cup-cakes in it.
- Ask, 'How many more cup-cakes do we need?'.
- Encourage the children to talk to each other to share their answers and ways of working it out with each other.
- Repeat for other numbers of cupcakes on the tray.
- You may wish to model the number sentence on the board.

Tips
- Encourage the children to decide how many cup-cakes will be in the tray to start the next time. They will be responsible for leading the discussion afterwards about the answer and checking if it is correct.
- Remember to include starting with no （0） cup-cakes and 12 cup-cakes at some stage.

Variation
Use different contexts, such as eggs in an egg carton （boil them for longevity!）.

How is this maths?
Some of the children will simply count the remaining spaces. This is finding

the answer through using *addition by counting on*. Others will see the problem as a *subtraction* where they find the *difference by counting on*. Some children may just know the answer through visualisation or familiarisation with *number bonds* to 12.

Use your loaf!

· · · · · · · · · · · · · · · ·   · · · · · · · · · · · · · · ·

Observe the effect yeast has during the bread-making process.

Aims and objectives

- To describe enlargement.
- To measure the passing of time.

Resources

- Simple bread-making recipe with ingredients or a packet of bread mix
- Plastic sheeting
- Large bowl
- Cling film
- Butter for spreading on the bread when it is baked
- Knife for spreading the butter

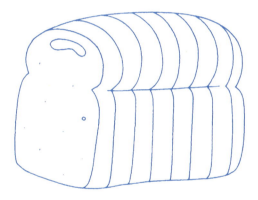

Preparation

- Check the oven is available and working at the time you will be baking your bread.
- Scrub down the kneading surface so that it is spotless.

What to do

- Ensure the children wash their hands well prior to starting.
- Follow the bread recipe, ensuring plenty of kneading and raising time is allowed for.
- Give the children the opportunity to see the dough before it is left to rise and after the allotted time.

- Discuss the change and the active ingredient that caused it – yeast. Share with the children that the yeast lets off a gas called carbon dioxide during the resting period （fermentation） and the gas causes the dough to *increase* in size.
- Bake according to the recipe.

Tip   Bread mixes are very easy to use because they include all the ingredients you require and you simply add water （but have a little more flour on standby in case the dough becomes too sticky）. However, you miss out on the opportunity for the children to feel, smell and measure the individual ingredients separately, particularly the active ingredient, yeast. Perhaps have some more yeast available separately so this can be seen and touched by the children, while the bread mix is used to make the bread.

Variation

There are many types of bread that you can make quite simply to celebrate different festivals. Select an appropriate recipe for the time of year.

How is this maths?

The yeast has a profound effect on the dough. Looking at how the dough has risen is related to shape and space and specifically *enlargement*. There is a lot of waiting during the bread-making process. This *passing of time* is measured using times or by reading the time on the clock.

Five currant buns

Singing songs related to baking helps us to understand number.

Aims and objectives

- To count backwards.
- To take away one at a time.

Resources

- Backing music （optional）
- Five currant buns from the role-play area or five laminated pictures of currant buns that can be attached to the wall and easily removed.

Preparation

- If you are not sure of the tune, find the song using an internet search of the first line of the lyrics.
- Set up the currant buns on a plate or stick the pictures to the board.

What to do

- Start singing the song （see lyrics below）. Where there is a gap in the lyrics, name one child from the group to take a bun at the appropriate moment in the song.
- Keep singing until all the buns are gone.

Lyrics

Five currant buns in a baker's shop.

Big and round with a cherry on the top,

Along came _____ with a penny one day,

Bought a currant bun and took it away.

Four currant buns . . .

Three . . .

Two . . .

One . . .

Tip   You may want to place the numerals 1 – 5 on the buns to help the children learn to read the numbers.

Variations

- Start and end the song at any number you wish! Do not be constrained by starting with 'five' each time.
- Choose the children's favourite baked items and substitute them in the song, for example 'pitta bread', 'crusty loaves' or 'hot cross buns'.

How is this maths?

Counting backwards is an early entry into *subtraction* and *taking away* one. Knowing that no currant buns exist helps children understand that it is possible to count backwards to zero, but that we begin at one when we start counting.

The role-play bakery

Aims and objectives

- To learn about measurement.
- To practise division.

Resources

- The role-play area set up as a bakery
- Ingredients for measuring such as raisins or flour
- Scales
- Bowls
- Play dough（see recipe on page 229）or real flour dough
- Buns, loaves, pies and pastries
- A brush and shovel!

Preparation

- The children may have visited a local bakery to learn what goes on there so they can develop the role play area further themselves.

What to do

There are many activities that can be undertaken in the bakery role play. These include:

- Measuring and weighing specific quantities.
- Kneading the play dough or real bread dough.
- Plaiting the play dough or real bread dough.
- Dividing the cake mixture evenly.
- Selling and buying bread and other goods.

Tips
- Remind the children they cannot eat the play dough!
- Real loaves and buns can be preserved by varnishing them two or three times, leaving a drying period between each coat.（Again, remind they are not to be eaten.）

Variation

The role-play area can be a corner shop selling baking ingredients and baked items.

How is this maths?

In the role play area the children can enact most of the tasks that bakers carry out. *Measuring* ingredients is a necessary skill to master. *Dividing* mixture in order to make evenly sized cup-cakes or loaves is another. Plaiting the dough requires the children to be *systematic*.

Appendices

References

Books

Freedman, Claire and Cort, Ben, *Aliens Love Underpants*, London: Simon and Schuster Children's, 2007.

Harris, Peter and Allwright, Deborah, *The Night Pirates*, London: Egmont Books Ltd, 2005.

Helbrough, Emma and Gower, Teri, *1001 Bugs to Spot*, London: Usborne Books, 2009.

King, Valerie, *In Comes the Tide*, Loughborough: Ladybird Books Ltd, 1997.

Manning, Mick and Granstrom, Brita, *High Tide, Low Tide*, London: Franklin Watts, 2003.

Mitton, Tony and Young, Selina, *Once Upon a Tide*, London: Picture Corgi, 2006.

Pfister, Marcus, *The Rainbow Fish*, New York: NorthSouth Books, 2007.

Punter, Russell and Fox, Christyan, *Stories of Pirates*, London: Usborne Books, 2007.

Thomson, Emma, *Lili's Wish*, London: Orchard Books, 2007.

Music

Vivaldi, Antonio, *The Four Seasons*, 1723 （numerous editions）.

Index of activities